Understanding consciousness has long been hampered by use of over-simplistic working hypotheses, such as: there is only one consciousness, or that all awareness is consciously accessible. This Single Mind Fallacy is here replaced with more accurate neuroscience-informed Paradigm Shift in order to include the existence and action of powerful behavioral sources found in the preconscious, subconscious, and unconscious. Thus, a modular consciousness model is both required and illuminating.

As the first step, McLean's Triune Brain Model was expanded to the Quadrimental Brain Model, due to the discovery of extensive non-motor properties of the cerebellum. However, because of the bilaterality of the vertebrate brain, this model was insufficient and thus led to the development of the Dual Quadbrain Model with its semi-independent modular consciousness elements (Morton, 2011, 2015). The Dual Quadbrain Model accommodates multiple elements of consciousness, including those originally proposed by Freud and others. By rapid access by the temporarily dominant consciousness module to the central seat of power, the Dual Quadbrain Model can account for essentially all of human behavior from diabolic to divine.

In the Dual Quadbrain Model, the cerebral hemispheres contribute to nor- mal waking consciousness. That is #1, The left hemisphere "Reporter" specializes in top-down analysis of important details, including language. #2, The right hemisphere "Imaginer" specializes in bottom-up analysis of the global view, including spatial imagery.

Five evolutionarily earlier brain elements powerfully operate outside of hemispheric consciousness. #3 The ancient limbic cingulate cortex appears to be the site producing a unilateral executive "Ego." Critically, the Ego acts at least one second to several seconds in advance of our conscious awareness of the intention to act. This is

- strong support for the Dual Quadbrain Model.

The Ego determines whether to use, #4. the unilateral brain core reptilian "Id" to pursue a win-lose, violent solution. Or to use, #5. the unilateral cerebellar social brain "Superego" to pursue a win-win nonviolent solution to the issue at hand.

#6. A mutated-defective developmental arrest repair program ("xDARP") is also housed on the cerebellar opposite to the Superego. Its unconscious activation leads to inappropriate struggles, often between mates, which are the source of common escalating conflicts leading to crimes of passion. The xDARP is similar to Freud's "Thanatos", Hubbard's "Reactive Mind", and Tolle's "Pain Body".

Last, besides the "Id", the other unilateral element of the brain core, #7, the "Servant", is a final effector of behavioral output. It selflessly obeys higher brain directional imperatives, be they from a currently dominant internal brain element, or even from an external hypnotic dominator.

The #5, social brain neocerebellar Superego appears to be the source of the seemingly mysterious, hidden, non-supernatural "Higher Intelligence" or "Holy Spirit", which comes to the fore in life-altering, near-death experiences. These include some initiations, religious conversions, deep meditation, or hallucinogen-induced "Ego death and transcendence" experiences. Such incidents appear to have been at the origin of the world religions. They also can best be directly explained by the Dual Quadbrain Model.

Thus, we are a "Society of Seven", a committee of self-aware elements, most of which are outside of normal consciousness. The Dual Quadbrain provides a logical and testable framework accounting for all of human consciousness and behavior.

REVIEWER'S COMMENTS

"Dr. Morton should be nominated for the Nobel Peace Prize for his brilliant and thought-provoking work: "Modular Consciousness." Not since Darwin has such a world-changing wealth of new ideas come to challenge our knowledge of the workings of the human mind!"

E. A. HANKINS III, MD, Dermatologist, UCLA School of Medicine, Curator of Vertebrate Zoology and Founder of The World Museum of Natural History, Riverside, California

"This book provides a look into the dark pit of reality that lies outside of our usual awareness. Taking a journey into the realm of paradoxical behavior should prove to be a trip worth taking. Bruce Morton has provided a new paradigm to untie this Gordian knot. You may find some of the premises unsettling, but no advance in the understanding of consciousness has happened without things being shaken up."

ROBERT C. MARVIT, M.D., Neuropsychiatrist, President Hawaii Medical Association

"A major contribution by a pioneering neuroscientist to grounds for thinking that a killing-free world is possible."

GLENN D. PAIGE, Ph.D., Author of NONKILLING GLOBAL POLITICAL SCIENCE, Founder of the Center for Global Nonviolence.

"It is surprising that despite explosive advances of knowledge about our outer world, we know remarkably little about who we are and how to become happy. Written by an enlightened person, Professor Bruce Morton, this book is a revolution in our knowledge about the human Self."

EUGENE NALIVAIKO, Ph.D., Associate Professor, Neurocardiology Laboratory, School of Biomedical Sciences and Pharmacy, University of Newcastle, Newcastle, NSW 2308, Australia

"This landmark work expresses Dr. Morton's illuminated vision of a nonkilling world of moral, environmental, and social responsibility. As I read the book, I found myself coming ever closer to Morton's Social Brain Source with its elevated view of optimal Human Survival."

JOSEPH SINGER, Chemical Engineer, Print Artist, Photographer, and Co Author, Honolulu, HI.

"Morton has constructed a coherent and provocative model to explain the human experience. This work is a must read for anyone interested in the scientific basis of spirituality."

MARK NOKES, Ph.D., Physicist, Former Vice President of a Silicon Valley company.

"The importance of this book cannot be overstated. Dr. Morton has provide us a monumental paradigm-shift regarding who we are as humans. I predict its effect will be enormous."

DENNIS G. McLAUGHLIN, Ph.D., Neuropsychologist, Co-Founder of Care Hawaii.

"Even if only half of Dr. Morton's ideas turn out to be empirically supported, he will still have made an unparalleled contribution to the understanding of human behavior at many levels".

MICHAEL P. KELLEY, Ph.D., Clinical Psychologist, Washington, D.C. USA.

"Dr. Morton's book shines new thinking on the human brain and its modularity. His assertion s are strongly documented and rigorously argued. This book is a must read!"

KATHRYN KO, M.D., MFA, Chief, MetroNeurosurgery, New York, NY.

Also by Bruce Morton:

NEUROREALITY: A SCIENTIFIC RELIGION
TO RESTORE MEANING
Megalith Books, 2011
(amazon.com)

TWO HUMAN SPECIES EXIST: THEIR HY-
BRIDS ARE DYSLEXICS, HOMOSEXUALS,
PEDOPHILES, AND SCHIZOPHRENICS
Megalith Books, 2012
(amazon.com)

PSYCHEDELIC VISIONS
Megalith Books, 2013

BEYOND MEN ARE FROM MARS
Megalith Books, 2014
(amazon.com)

Professore Morton's Neuroscience Research
and Pubications
http://www2.hawaii.edu/~bemorton

MODULAR CONSCIOUSNESS:

THE KEY THAT UNLOCKS PERSONALITY, MARITAL CONFLICT, DRUG SEEKING, HALLUCINOGENS, AND RELIGION.

BRUCE ELDINE MORTON, Ph.D.

Megalith Books

Doral, Florida, USA

MEGALITH BOOKS

ISBN 978-0-9833417-4-1

Library of Congress Control Number: 2015915431

General subject headings

Body and Brain/Mind
Neuroscience/Consciousness
Psychology/Developmental/General
Psychology/Personality
Family and Relationships/
Violence Religion/
Origins and Initiations

Dr. Morton's email address is: bemorton@hawaii.edu

TABLE OF CONTENTS

DEDICATION:

To **Richard Dawkins,** Champion of Reality.

ACKNOWLEDGEMENTS:

Thanks goes to **Kent Barshov** for copy editorial work.

INTRODUCTION: The Paradigm Shifts of this Book
What is a Paradigm Shift?

Everybody is familiar with a paradigm shift, although some may not realize it. A paradigm shift results in a radical change of thinking contexts that opens a completely new set of possibilities for action. As an example: While watching a good mystery movie, the author gives out certain facts meant to adjust our thinking to conclude that one of the characters involved is guilty of the crime. However, one of the last events of a good thriller is the introduction of a new fact that changes everything. At that point, an "Aha" occurs in a flash of light and we immediately discard our earlier reasoning, which we now can see was wrong. We quickly realize that our earlier conclusion was faulty due to lack of a key important fact that has changed the entire picture. As a result, a surprising but now most logical person is obviously the culprit. That's a paradigm shift.

Of course, a good joke often shocks us with a paradigm shift at its end:

Question: What has many keys but can't open any doors? Answer: A piano.

Or, at an auction in Manchester a wealthy American announced that he had lost his wallet containing £10,000 and would give a reward of £100 to the person who found it. From the back of the hall a Scottish voice shouted, "I'll give £150!"

Or, a very drunk man comes out of the bar and sees another very drunk man. He looks up in the sky and says,

"Is that the sun or the moon?" The other drunk man answers, "I don't know. I'm a stranger here myself."

Or, a Scotsman who was driving home one night, ran into a car driven by an Englishman. The Scotsman got out of the car to apologize and offered the Englishman a drink from a bottle of whisky. The Englishman was glad to have a drink. "Go on," said the Scot, "have another." The Englishman drank gratefully. "But don't you want one, too?" he asked the Scotsman. "Perhaps," replied the Scotsman, "after the police have gone."

This book takes usual thinking (The Single Mind Fallacy), that there is only one brain consciousness of whose activity we are well aware. It then supplies some critical facts that change everything to bring about a paradigm shift providing a new reality about brain and mind. The theme of this book is the discovery that there are seven self-conscious modular elements in the brain that influence behavior. These include the right and left cerebral hemispheres of whose normal awareness Freud said everyone was aware. He famously added three additional elements which he felt existed quite outside of our awareness. These were the early versions of his Ego, Superego, and Id. Here, the self-conscious activities of each of these three elements will become obvious. Added to the above five brain elements are two additional unconscious behavioral modules of considerable importance. First is a mutated, and thus defective developmental arrest repair program, the xDARP, unrecognized source of neurotic behavior. And last but not least is the Servant Brain, the final output source for any and all behavior.

These seven modules freely move in and out of the brain's central seat of control in a manner not easily detectable from within, except by our or others' observations of differences in our resulting behavior. Such can be illustrated, say, by a young man romantically playing a guitar for his girlfriend. Who, upon seeing a competitor placing an arm around his beloved, stops playing and flies into a fit of rage. That young man may feel that he is the same person while making music as when stomping his foot and bristling in anger. Indeed he is! But, unbeknownst to him the brain element specialized for playing romantic music has been displaced by another one specialized in doing battle.

This in itself is an important paradigm shift. Rather than having one set of brain tools to optimize our survival, we have evolved seven specialist modules, each uniquely equipped to efficiently to stay on top of things. The existence of this Dual Quadbrain Model of modular consciousness brings understanding to a number of previously inexplicable behaviors that have long troubled humanity, many of which are described in this book.

In Chapter One, Julian Jayne's *Origin of Self-Conciousness by the Breakdown of the Bicameral Mind*, a previously suggested path of evolution to human self-conscoiusness is expanded, leading to the inception of Dual Quadbrain Model.

In Chapter Two: *The Quadrimental Brain,* the preliminary set of conceepts of a four layer brain are presented as the foundation of the Dual Quadbrain Model.

In Chapter Three, *Binary Expansion to the Dual Quadbrain Model,* is based upon the fact that the entire brain, aside from the secretory pineal gland, is bilateral. This opens the space to accommodate all elements needed to understand human behavior from the diabolic to the divine. There has been a recent understanding of the existence and properties of several self-conscious brain systems outside of normal consciousness.

Chapter Four, *Modular Consciousness: Our Society of Seven*, describes the practical contributions of each of the seven brain systems.

In Chapter Five, *Hemisity: Are you a Top-Down "Splitter" or a Bottom-Up "Lumper"*, the history of brain laterality is traced from the inadequate and later debunked concept of Hemisphericity to the transformational idea of Hemisity. The new concept is that one is either a completely left brain-oriented person or a completely right-brain-oriented one, with no intermediates possible. This is of course due to the fact that each of the two hemispheres must be completely separated from the other. The left does in top-down data analysis, while the right is specialized in bottom-up analysis, neither of which can be done in the same space. Individuals of both types of hemisity of course have access to the functions of the opposite cerebral hemisphere.

This hemisity-based discovery that our Executive Ego is irreversibly born either on the left or the right side of the brain results in their being two types of people: right-brain Lumpers, who tend to see the forest, and left-brain Splitters, who are more oriented toward individual trees. This is not a new idea, except that in terms of courtship and marriage it has been found that lumpers tend to choose splitters as mates, while splitters choose lumpers as mates.

That is, in two thirds of US marriages, "opposites attract", making for the representation of both points of view in each family.

Now, whether you are a lumper or a splitter has nothing to do with whether you are male or female. Rather, we end up with *two self-selecting species of humans*: Patripolar lumper male and splitter female couples, and Matripolar lumper female and splitter male couples. Further, in each species, the lumpers are dominant over the splitters. So in the Homosapiens patripolaris couples, the male is the boss, while in Homosapiens matripolaris couples, the female is in charge. Since in courtship nobody knows about this, about one third of the time lumper-lumper couples and splitter-splitter cross-species couples form.

Because the resulting offspring of these "cross- species" couples are by definition genetic hybrids, their DNA complement will carry inherited anomalies. This appears to be the origin of dyslexia, bisexuality, homosexuality, pedophilia, and schizophrenia, about whose origins nobody has had a clue. This is another significant paradigm shift that radically changes our ideas as to the origin and nature of these serious social problems. And, it is based upon modular consciousness!

Chapter Six, *Brain Modular Consciousness and xDARP Induced Marital Fighting,* describes the existence of a once useful but now broken developmental arrest repair program. Since this program has mutated, it has become the automated source endless pain and rejection between marital partners and other close friends. It once served a valuable service and its malfunction is not recognized internally, but rather still thought to be an authentic part of oneself. Yet, its endless creation of irrational marital conflicts continues to cause much suffering in the home and permanently traumatizes the children to create a repetition of its activation in the next generations.

Often marital couples self-select each other, based upon something that often called love, but it actually is infatuation: where "I only have eyes for you." In the absence of modular consciousness, infatuation is something that we are completely ignorant about, other than to call it "love sickness."

The paradigm shift here is that infatuation actually comes from the malfunction of a mutated developmental repair module in the brain, the *broken developmental arrest repair program* (xDARP). It appears to continually search among our potential eligible mates for someone who most matches our dominant parent; the one who thwarted our development by never allowing us to gain control over them as a child. The xDARP ignores other often superior mates and fixates upon that parent-like target person with intense infatuation. This fatal attraction has little to do with their potential as a good mate, and everything to do with the potential for transferring onto them and renewing an old developmental arrest conflict. When the person wins the affection of their target, so that they finally commit themselves, the xDARP feels safe enough to activate itself. It then repetitively escalates the person's incomplete childhood developmental struggle. This often begins in earnest before the relationship is one year old.

Chapter Seven, *Restoring Peace and Sanity by Turning off the xDARP, Devil Within.,* This type of endless conflict has had an ancient history leading to many attempts, some of them religious, to overcome the massive marital destabilization caused by the xDARP. The intensity of this unrecognized problem has also led to several modern approaches to stop the insanity of this cognitive disorder which you may recognize. Although modular consciousness, enables us to isolate and deal this defective brain system, a practical solution for those whose partner in is in denial has yet to be found.

Chapter Eight, *Removing Guilt Pain to Regain the Ability to Grow,* provides an explanation of the origin and nature of the conscience and its automatic production of guilt pain as punishment. Purchase of pain killers to temporarily replace subconscious guilt pain with the pleasure of no pain, is driving the whole world into total corruption at all levels. Guilt pain is easily removed by repaying the damaged party enough until they can look you in the eye and willingly reconcile you back into your lost family.

Chapter Nine, *Hallucinogens: Direct Access to the Hidden Source, Our God-Within,* introduces the Superego "Source" as the pattern generator behind Plato's Theory of Forms and also Jung's Archetypes. Modular Consciousness already assigns to the Source a complete memory of all events of experience, prenatally to the present. The addition of a gifted pattern generator to this complement of skills creates for us a hidden intelligence of prodigious capabilities within the cerebellum, the brain structure with the most cells. It is the obvious source not only of the amazing continually changing intensely colored hallucinations of perfect forms in the earliest stage of hallucinosis, but also of the incredible, life-changing wisdom and repair that it provides later. So, this chapter includes how to become transformed by gaining access to the hidden Superego-Source and It's higher intelligence, the God-within. Although many lengthy and arduous meditation and prayer methods have been used whereby some few achieved holiness, neuroscience has

11

discovered a way that all can use to accomplish this transformation. The proper use of sacred entheogens does not require years of meditation, only a day.

In Chapter 10, *Death/Rebirth: Lost Rite of Passage to Human Maturity,* addresses a major loss in tribal culture that we have sustained. That is, the profoundly needed societal structure provided by the ancient coming of age, death/rebirth initiations. These vision quest type of tribal tradition transformed individual adolescents, who naturally operated within a "win-lose" violent competition mentality. By passing through initiatory conditions which stressed the brain to the point of ego-death, they transcended and were reborn into the spirit of a "win-win or no deal" social orientation. This procedure permanently transformed them into mature cooperative human beings. They could then be trusted as members of the tribe and naturally matured into positions of trust and responsibility to ultimately become respected elders.

Lacking this social foundation, today's youth and later adults are never confronted with dying and surrender to the presence of the vast complexities and exquisite beauty of the eternal universe, where all that exists is perfect. Not being reborn to the spirit, they remain immature and profane instead develop into purposeless fearful, fighting individuals, only able to operate on an "I win, you lose" basis. Now, they are thoughtlessly destroying civilization with wars for dominance, and eliminating many possibilities for human sociability. How can we restore the true heritage of possibility and opportunity to our youth and the opportunity to produce adults possessing inherently sacred wisdom? We need to restore the two thousand year reign of the Greek Elusian Mysteries where it was desirable once in a lifetime for each person to pass through an entheogenic (hallucinatory) life/death ceremony and join the human race.

Chapter 11, *Demystifying the Common Origin of the Worlds Now Obsolete Religions,* tells the stories of how each of the originators of the World's Religions underwent an Ego Death/Transcendent experience where they were transformed by the contact with their Source, "God Within." This changed their lives so dramatically that those around them were convinced that they had gained access to God's wisdom. Because they knew that they themselves lacked such insight, it was natural for them to follow one who did.

Chapter 12, *Pruning Artificially Hyperactive Stress Neurons to Stop Psychic Pain-based Drug Seeking,* is an answer to political scientist author of *The Ghost in the Machine,* Arthur Koestler's plea for help in correcting the murderous violence that is part of human inheritance. He felt that now that we have come to the point in history where one man can flip a switch to activate nuclear annihilation of human existence on earth, we are doomed to extinction. He despaired of any medical or political solution. His only hope was if some drug could be found to selectively inhibit or excise the brain module responsible for our violent dispositions. Now progress has been made in this direction, but not by the means he envisioned. That of another paradigm shift: the cerebellar pruning of artificially hyperactive stress neurons. Thus as you can see, reading about these topics can become fascinating.

INTRODUCTION

CHAPTER 1: Origin of Self-Consciousness by the Breakdown of the Bicameral Mind.

The Ancient World and the Bicameral Mind

Pre-human hominids separated from the apes and repeatedly left Africa beginning several million years ago. Remains of hominids who lived in the Caucasus between in the Caspian and Black Seas in Russia have been unearthed in the ancient town of Dmanisi, along with several types of tools. Their cranial volume was found to be around 700 cubic centime- ters (cc), up from the about 400 ccs for the modern apes. For comparison, our own present brain volume is about 1200cc. These people have been reliably dated as living 1,700,000 years ago! They were the earliest Caucasians. Because they are the first hominid know to use tools, they were called "Handy Man": *Homo habilis*. **Figure 1** illus- trates something of their appearance and location.

Over the passage of unimaginable eons and thousands of generations, by the time the Neanderthals and Cro-Mag- nons lived only some 500,000 years ago, hominid cranial capacity had increased to over 1700 cc. That is 500 ccs or 140% larger than our own! Evidence has been uncovered that these hominids were very smart, caring for their invalids and their aged, creating and playing musical instruments, crafting elegant hunting weapons, even fashioning religious icons, including earth-mother goddesses. It literally has been a devolution in brain size ever since.

Figure 1. The Dmanisi Man with tools, the first Caucasian, dated at 1.7 million years bp

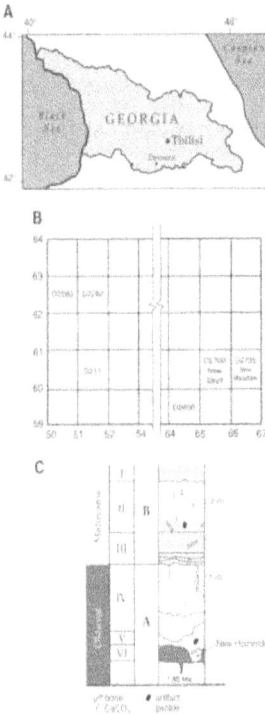

The skull is in remarkably fine condition (Fig. 2). The maxillae are slightly damaged anteriorly, the zygomatic arches are broken, and both mastoid processes are heavily abraded. There is damage also to the orbital be a female. However, the upper canines carry large crowns and massive roots, and their size counsels caution in assessing sex.

In its principal vault dimensions, D2700 is smaller than D2280 and the specimens attrib-

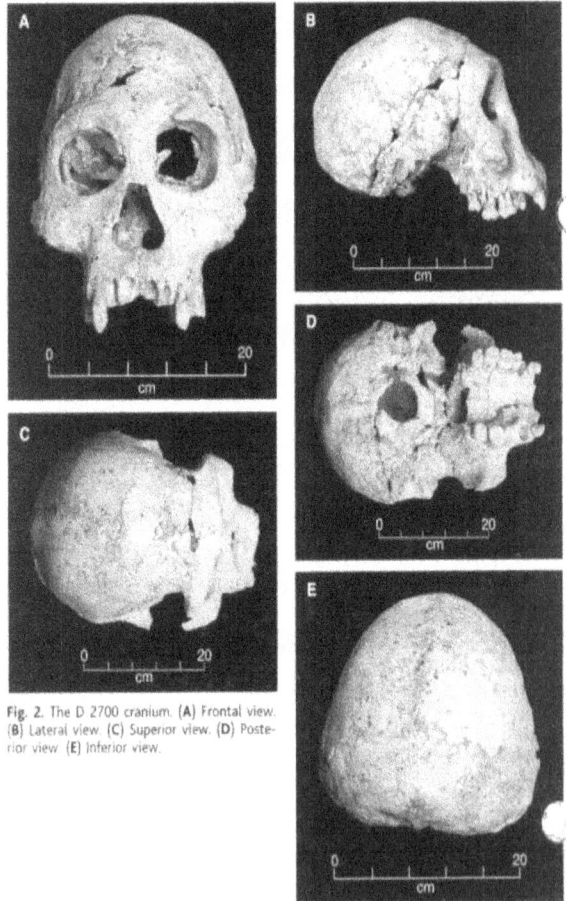

Fig. 1. (A) Location map of Dmanisi site. (B) The locations of hominid fossils (excavation units are 1-m squares). (C) General stratigraphic profile, modified after Gabunia et al. (5, 6). The basalt and the immediately overlying volcaniclastics (stratum A) exhibit normal polarity and are correlated with the terminus of the Olduvai Subchron. Slightly higher in the section, above a minor disconformity and below a strongly developed soil, Unit B deposits, which also contain artifacts, faunas and human fossils, all exhibit reversed polarity and are correlated with the Matuyama. Even the least stable minerals, such as olivine, in the basalt and the fossil-bearing sediments show only minor weathering, which is compatible with the incipient pedogenic properties of the sediments.

Fig. 2. The D 2700 cranium. (A) Frontal view. (B) Lateral view. (C) Superior view. (D) Posterior view. (E) Inferior view.

16

There have been numerous ice ages in the past half a million years since the Neaderthals and Cro-Magnons lived. The later hominids obviously had the intelligence to survive in the glaciers that often covered their territories. Yet, because they lived in balance with their environment, their numbers stayed low. Other hominids lived in the tropics as well. After the last ice age began to thaw only about 15,000 years ago, the global human population was quite small, maybe 3 million total. However, at around 5,000 years ago something dramatically changed. For the first time in the over 2 million years and hundreds of thousands of generations that had gone by, for the first time the numbers of humans rapidly began to increase. Something had changed! As a result, our population has since exploded! We now are over 7 billion souls. What happened?!

Julian Jaynes in his book "The Origin of Consciousness in the Breakdown of the Bicameral Mind", Houghton Mifflin, 1976, provided the first hint of an explanation to account for this. In it, he documented a change in hominid mentality that began to occur about 5000 years ago. He provided compelling evidence that before this point humans were not truly conscious, and that over next 2000 years they developed self-consciousness. As a result by 1000 BC the world began radically to change.

Hominid bicameral consciousness:

Is self-consciousness necessary to survive and live a good life? Clearly, the answer is no. Animals and even human babies do not have it. Self-consciousness, like the introspection that we are able to perform while automatically driving a car or playing a piano, constitutes only a small element on top of usual mental behavior. Self-con- sciousness is not necessary for the learning or performance of skills, speaking, writing, listening, or reading. It is not required for the formation of concepts, for thinking or judgment, which is often automatically preformed, nor is it necessary for reason, where the best insights are often subconscious in origin.

Thus, evidence suggests that humans before 1000 BC were conscious like animals but had no sense of self. They functioned perfectly well using their subconscious reptilian brain core Id complex, which automatically followed its ancient survival routines. That is, of cooperating in family building and viciously attacking non-family predators. If in situations of social stress, when they didn't know what to do, they asked "God", often by praying to hand-held personal idols. Their subconscious cerebellar (social-brain superego-Source) "God-Within" replied in the form of visions or later by internal voice broadcasts, much like the self-generated voices of the schizophrenic. These "divine" answers were complete, superior, and gratifying.

This was the bicameral mind of the hominids before about 2000 BC, as documented by Julian Jaynes. He asserted that self-consciousness came after the origin of language and writing, which emerged around 3000 BC. He provided evidence that the gaining of self-consciousness could be seen in the written poetry of the Iliad, ancient Greek literature describing historical events occurring around 1000 BC. In his analysis, the first part of Iliad showed no concept of will, mind, soul, subjective consciousness, or of mental acts, such as introspection or thinking. There was no subjective mind-space, self-aware-ness, no internal reality to introspect upon. These key el-ements were found in the much later Odessy.

If this were so, what initiated their advanced behav-ior? According to his model, their actions originated in the actions and (hexameter) speech of the internal gods. The gods always have their way. In terms of the Dual Quad-brain Modular Consciousness Model, developed here, the gods were produced by the cerebellar social brain supere-go, based in memories of parents or other authority fig-ures. The gods were never miraculous nor stepped out of natural laws, but acted as superior humans. They led, advised, and ordered. They spoke wisdom. Response was amazement, wonder, eureka! The gods were the hallucina-tions only seen or heard by the ones they internally spoke to, those non-subjective noble automatons who knew not what they did. Volition, planning, initiative, originated in the hidden Superego Source, God-Within and was then "told" to the individual, who obeyed because he could not see what to do by himself. It was a theocracy where every man was a slave to the voices heard within whenev-er novel situations occurred.

The voices appear to have first been parental, which often continued after the death of the father and leading to the presence of home shrines. They continued after the death of clan leaders. Later of kings became deified and treated as still living, whose voices directed others. They could be sought in large central houses of the gods. Mil-lions of hand held personal idols have been found with en-larged eyes that apparently "spoke" to their owners.

Jaynes rightly called this mentality the Bicameral Mind. He and others thought it had something to do with

21

the right and left hemispheres. But, that was not correct.

As we shall see, the bicameral mind was completely based upon two subcortical consciousness modules. The first was the Id brain core that directed normal ancient behavioral routines. This was separated from and not normally aware of the hidden consciousness of the second element of Jayne's Bicameral Mind, the social brain Superego, God- Within. Under conditions of social stress and need, this Source spoke to the Id, guiding it when necessary via vocal or other hallucinations. This was experienced as the illu- sion that a personal external God vocally answered their prayers and guided them in times of emergency.

Arrival of Human Self-Consciousness:

True human self-consciousness emerged from the breakdown of this hominid bicameral mind. That is, after about 2000 BC, for reasons possibly related to a strengthening Ego, an increasing loss of contact with cerebellar superego God appears to have occurred among the population. Voices or even oracles no longer spoke in times of need giving an- swers. Its prized directive visions became less and less available until by today their remnants only can be found in 2000 year old scriptures.

Increasing Loss of Divine Wisdom after Its Suppression by a Strengthing Ego

The arrival of self-consciousness in humans ultimately was forced upon them to replace the silenced voices of their inner gods. They developed a logic about living in a way that could in part replace the voice of the Superego. Ironically, since then humans have yearned to regain access to this divine inner wisdom. Indeed, its cer- tainty and wisdom were not replaced by the newly ar- riving hemispheric intellect and imagination of self-conscious- ness. Humanity has continually looked for it in ways, many of which continue into the present. This quest was first outlined by Julian Jaynes in his "Origin of Conscious- ness in the Breakdown of the Bi-cameral Mind".

In brief, it was as follows. At the time of the Law of Hammurabbi (1792 BC), God and man spoke face to face. Five hundred years later, in 1230 BC, Tukulti-Ninurta I, tyrant of Assyria, kneels low before an empty throne. The gods will not listen to him. A little later, about 1000 BC, King David of Israel wrote:

> As the stag pants after the water brook
> So pants my mind after you, O God!
> My mind thirsts for God! For the living God!
> When shall I come face to face with God?

As the voices became less common, "mouth wash-ing" ceremonies were adapted to clarify the voices of the idols. Formalized prayer appeared for the first time, prais-ing and flattering the god, and begging for favors. Later sacrifices were performed to bribe the gods. With time and further desperation, these became human sacrifices. This attempt to get the god's attention by human slaughter be-came extreme in Central America and many other places. Then, angelic intercessors were invoked. With the contin-uing lack of divine communication, it was imagined that the gods were angry and were attacking humans. Lucky charm protections appeared as amulets around neck or wrist. Medicine become concerned with the exorcism of malevolent demons. Written magical incantations multiplied.

With the loss of the voices, various means of divining information first emerged, including magical omen-like predictions, that is, "if this happens, then this will occur". There were newfound medical omens where the messages from the gods which could be deciphered from the size and arrangement of the organs of sacrificed animals. There were star-based, horoscopic omens. Men began to cast lots in an attempt to find clear "yes, no, or who" answers from a god. There was no concept of chance or randomness. The results only could have been caused by the gods.

The concept of the immortal soul, the foundation of Dualism, was invented about 600 BC. The soul was not life, but that which exists after life has ceased and it separates from the body. At first, the soul went to Hades. However, soon the idea came that the soul instead transmigrates into the body of a newborn infant or animal to continue living in another. This profoundly inaccurate and pernicious concept was fixed in thought by Plato's writings. It then evolved through Gnosticism into the great religions, and on to Descartes, thence to be one of the great spurious quandaries of modern psychology.

At special locations in Greece, such as Delphi, there remained some who could still hear their inner god. They were called Oracles and could be consulted to provide immediate elaborate answers to problems posed. This became the central method used by leaders for making important decisions for well over a thousand years after the breakdown of the bicameral mind. To questions asked of supreme priestesses under sacred laurel trees, the reply was given at once, completely, and uninterruptedly in the first person. These women, who were once simple farm girls, underwent an induction into a trance which resulted in an archaic authorization. Plato called Oracle at Delphi "the interpreter of religion to all mankind". The oracles became erratic and uninterpretable after around 60 AD.

According to Jaynes, speaking idols were pretty much gone and useless by 1000 BC. But, by 100AD idolatry had remarkably returned. "In churches, temples, and in shrines the world over, religious statues are still being carved, painted, and prayed to. The Virgin Mary and Jesus hang in our cars, buses, and living rooms. Church bells ring across towns and countrysides on feast days, as in bicameral Mesopotamia 4000 years ago, except now the idols are silent."

Prophesy and possession began to appear about 400 BC. Ironically, possession was not a duplication of the bicameral mind. No god spoke through human lips in ancient Greece. But now it became the complete domination of the person and his speech without later memory of the event. Possession replaced the bicameral mind. Socrates said "God-possessed men speak much truth, but to know nothing of what they say." "... for prophesy is a madness, and the prophetess at Delphi and the priestesses at Dodona, when out of their senses have conferred great benefits on Hellas, both in public and private life, but when in their senses, few or none." Aristotle said the possessed, "...do not know, before being seized by the spirits, what they are going to say, any more than after having recovered their natural senses do they remember what they have said, so that everyone knows what they say except themselves."

Before the breakdown of the bicameral mind, the god spoke to the individual who remained conscious, received and remembered. Here, the opposite was true, yet by the trance-induced possession, the voice of the superego could still be heard by others, if not by the often simple, unsophisticated medium herself. And in such a deep trance, the cerebellar superego "god" would seem to reveal past or future, or answer questions and make decisions, as in the older Greek oracles.

There are god and demon possessions in the modern world, for example in the Umbanda religion containing over half of the population of Brazil, where mediums dance into possessed ecstasy. Through them the (cerebellar superego) gods can be consulted for, and may give, decisions on any illness or personal problem, on getting or keeping a job, on financial business practices, family quarrels, love affairs, or even, among students, advice about scholastic grades.

In modern glossolalia a similar situation exists. An individual can enter into a trance and begin speaking in tongues within a religious group in front of a benevolent charismatic leader, which are not understood or remembered by speaker. Their analysis indicates a subcortical output of epic dactyls similar to those of the ancient Iliad, regardless of the language of the speaker, according to Jaynes. It is as if they were possessed by the cerebellar social brain Holy Spirit whose language output was in the form of epic dactyls.

In the case of modern demon possession, almost always the persons possessed by a demon are uneducated, usually il- literate, believe in spirits and demons and also live in a society that does. Possession was chiefly a linguistic phe- nomenon, not one of actual conduct. The demons were not violent, but highly intelligent, bargaining and keeping agreements. The exorcism cure always was by the com- mand of an authoritative person, speaking in the name of a more powerful god or authority figure.

Also, in certain altered states of consciousness, we can still hear them, such as in near death experiences, or by use of entheogens ("god manifesting" psychoactive substances, such as psilocybin or DMT). However, the latter controversial avenue has become illegal with the notable exception of the peyote-using Native American Church and those originally Amazonian religions using ayahuasca as a sacrament.

Hominids first became human when they were forced to use their cerebral hemispheres to create answers, formerly supplied by the inner voices of their Superego. They become self-conscious in the process of learning how to introspect. A key element in this transition was the use of a metaphor of something familiar to describe something unknown. This ultimately led to the mental creation of an inner reality model approximation of external reality, based upon increasingly accurate metaphors. Within this inner reality space, the world could be created and manipulated by stimulus generalization without risk of real damage. Now it has extended to space travel and molecular biology.

The Features of Self-Consciousness that Emerged in the Limbic Executive Ego.

There follows an amalgam, first described by Julian Jaynes and expanded by the present author, of the requirements for the new consciousness of the cerebral cortical hemispheres:

Spatialization: a visual working space is necessary for conscious awareness. Here, not only is structure spatial, but also time is made to be spatial, as is energy. This permits the construction of a 5D inner reality model of actual 5D external reality (where the 3D of structure, plus the 4th D of time and the 5th D of free energy can describe any behavior, Morton, 2011). Any conscious thought of a concrete action in a concrete world then becomes spatial. Using our cerebral hemispheres, we created the first inner *virtual* reality model of external reality by:

Modeling: At any moment we can never be conscious of things in their true nature, or even of our total memory of them, but only of abstractive-interpretations we make of them. Which excerpts we make are influenced by our emotions and beliefs. How we abstract others influences the kind of world we feel we are living in.

Th e Analog 'I': We (our self-image, Ego) can act in this virtual internal reality space to imagine doing things and assessing their outcomes, without actually doing them in external reality. Mental acts are analogs of bodily ones. One could also use this space to create ideal forms, or fantasy, or deception.

The Metaphor 'Me' : We also can see our self, both in our virtual world and in the external one as form of met- aconsciousness.

Narritization: In self-consciousness we continually see our Ego selves as the main figures in the ongoing stories of our lives. The picture we create of ourselves determines how we act and choose in new situations. We rationalize our behavior by later assigning causes as to why we acted the way we did. Also our interpretations as to why other things behaved the way they did.

Compatibilization: We try to fit all new observations into our inner model of reality, expanding it as needed, or remodeling incongruent portions to unify it.

Thus, self-consciousness is a process, not a thing. It constructs an internal reality space containing an 'I' that can observe the space and move within it. It acts on any event, abstracts, adapts, narratizes, and manipulates it. The structure of this inner reality became increasingly more like that of the physical world. In this space of self- consciousness, one could begin to make judgments as to who they are and yet may become. The more accurate one's inner reality model became through education, experience, and trial and error, the more it became aligned with external reality, the sole source abundance, opportunity, and power to provide increasingly personal survival benefits that actually worked.

This new self-consciousness became the driving engine that converted hominids into humans, creating superior survival, and the consequent population increases since 1000 BC. The arrival of self-consciousness has led to the formation of our modern civilizations, the science-based increase in our life span, and the incredible conquest of space.

Yet, the yearning for the hidden God-within still

remains today. As we she see that longing can now be satisfied, but not easily.

CHAPTER 2: The Quadrimental Brain

Why a Multiple Mind Model of Consciousness is Needed:

A single consciousness model has never been able to account for the complexities of human behavior. Failure to understand, predict, or control behavior has resulted in enormous tragedy and suffering. That is, a single consciousness model has not accounted for the following: identity, volition, awareness, causality, responsibility, introspection, altruism, hypnosis, the unconscious, or spirituality. Furthermore, a single consciousness model cannot account for the production of our many subconscious behaviors. "Yes, Tommy! We only use 10% of our brain. The other 90% uses us!" That hidden 90% is actually the sum of the subconscious activities of our evolutionarily evolved four-layered brain.

The original Brain Core houses our autonomic nervous system, our musculoskeletal coordination, our drives, and instincts of which we are unconscious from up here in the brain where we now reside in our language cortex. Built upon this Brain Core foundation is the Limbic System: source of the twelve Primary Emotions, and the sixteen Ego Defenses. The third key layer is the Cerebellum, which is the preconscious source of developmental programs and developmental arrest repair programs, conscience, guilt, morality, herd behavior, projection, planning, intuition, wisdom and, unconscious knowing. The activities of all three brain foundations constitute our subconscious minds. Our self-conscious "I" now resides in our cerebral cortex, the fourth element of our Quadrimental Brain. This book provides evidence of the existence of these multiple minds hidden within our remarkable, modular human brain.

Earlier Multiple Consciousness Models:

In Greek-Platonic philosophy, the mind usually consisted of four parts: the soul, reason, the competitor, and appetite. In the religions of Judaism, Islam and Christianity, there were often three consciousness elements: Me, the victim of fate; the devil made me do it; and God help me! More recent psychological thought has had up to four consciousness elements. For example, the Harvard Professor, William James (1878) proposed the existence of the material self, the social self, the spiritual self and pure ego. Very early in the 19th century, Sigmund Freud (1929-1923) also felt that there were four mind elements. They were Normal Consciousness, about which everyone knew, and three subconscious entities, which he called the Id, the Ego, and the Superego. Although he did not know the brain elements producing them, this has now become obvious, as described here.

Surprisingly, most neuroscientists today hold to their childhood belief in a Unitive (Single) Consciousness meme, which asserts we know about and are responsible for everything we do and are. A notable exception was Paul McLean (1990) at the National Institute for Health in the USA who developed The Triune Brain Model, which consisted of three increasingly recent evolutionary layers. They were the reptilian system, the paleo-mammalian (limbic) system, and the neomammalian system, as illustrated in **Figure 2.**

The Quadrimental Brain Model

However, McLean's Triune Brain Model did not accommodate later discoveries of the many non-motor behaviors produced by the hindbrain cerebellum, an obvious major brain structure whose small cells numbered more than the entire rest of the brain. The neuronal activities of the cerebellum were not present in his model. For example, cerebellar auto-stimulation of institutionalized criminals remarkably reversed their murderous rage, turning them into cordial socially appropriate individuals. Further, the site of Primary Memory has been found to be in the cerebellum. It is also required for language syntax generation. Surprisingly, the cerebellum also is activated in faith healing, hypnosis, and during "control psychoses", and clearly in hallucinosis.

Therefore, McLean's Triune Brain has been expanded into the **Quadrimental Brain Model**. Bruce Morton first described this model before the International Society for Research on Aggression in Parma, Italy, in 1985. The model concept is as follows: The human brain consists of four layers representing stages of increasing sophistication in our evolutionary development to optimize the survival of our constituent cells. (Morton, 1985, 1989).

Figure 2, McLean's Triune Brain System

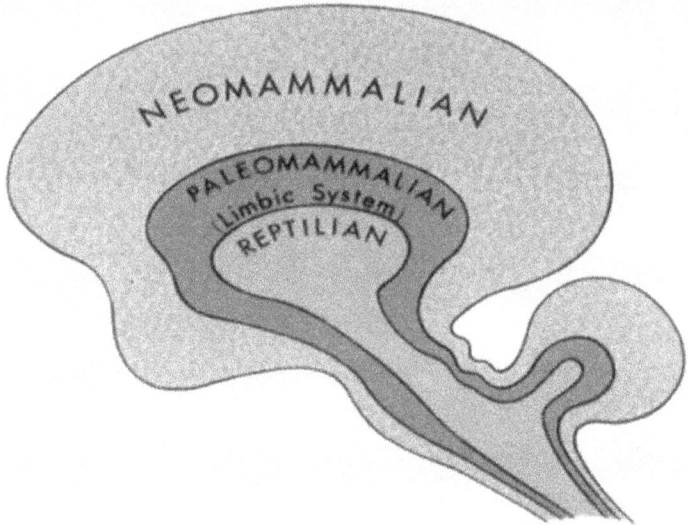

Symbolic representation of the triune brain (see Chapter 2 and Figure 2-1).

Figure 3 shows a cartoon of the Quadrimental Brain and **Figure 4** further elaborates it.

Proposals for two Quadrune Brain models appeared and disappeared around this time, one even incorporating the cerebellum as a separate system.

Layer 1: Reptile Brain Core and Striatum: The Selfish Brain

The small brain, as it existed in the age of the reptiles had a remarkable ability to promote cellular survival

Figure 3

THE QUADRIMENTAL BRAIN

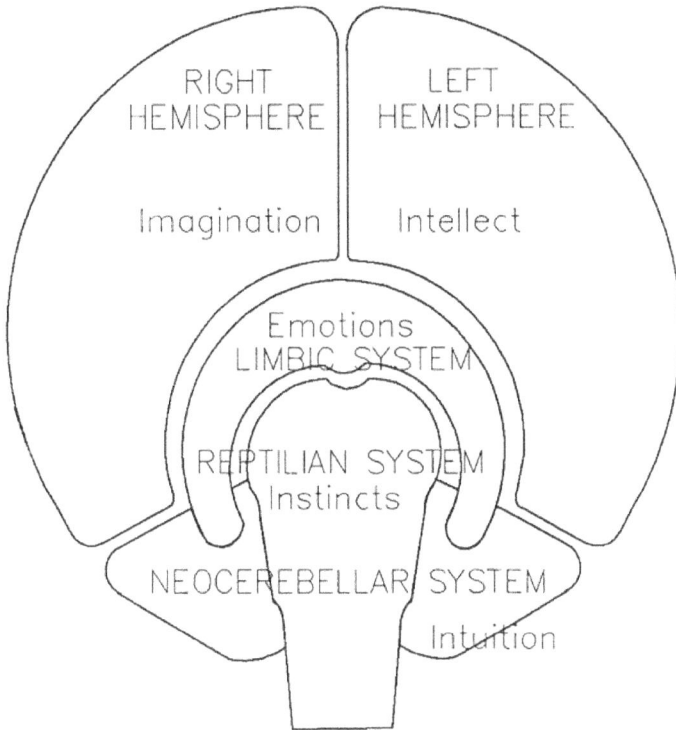

RIGHT HEMISPHERE

LEFT HEMISPHERE

Imagination

Intellect

Emotions
LIMBIC SYSTEM

REPTILIAN SYSTEM
Instincts

NEOCEREBELLAR SYSTEM

Intuition

SOURCE OF HUMAN EXPERIENCE

Figure 4 LAYER VIEW OF THE QUADRIMENTAL BRAIN
(Start at the bottom and move upward.)

<u>**Cerebral System:**</u> *<u>Imagines, Describes</u>*
Aware of Self-Awareness. Able to Represent Reality
either by Imaging or Abstracting of Primary Memory.
Metamind: Offline thinking; True Language.
In Humans, Except Young Children.
<u>Normal Human Consciousness</u>

<u>**Limbic System:**</u> *<u>Has - Controls</u>*
Aware of Self. Non Syntactic Language.
Executive: Controls External Operations
Uses Primary Emotions and
Ego Defenses to Motivate.
<u>Preconscious Ego</u>

<u>**Cerebellar System:**</u> *<u>Is - Knows</u>*
Knowledge of Time and Space
Records Primary Memory Track
Causality, Pattern Generator
Aware of the Group as Part of Itself.
<u>Subconscious Superego</u>

<u>**Striatal-Brain Core System:**</u> *<u>Does</u>*
Aware of Senses. Has a Same-Different Comparator
for Set-Points or Evaluating Competitors.
Motivated by Pain or Pleasures. Instincts.
Also in Lower Organisms that have Brains.
<u>Unconscious, Id</u>

within the animal not just at the level of cells, but also at the level of tissues, of organs, and that of the entire organism. The abilities required for this remarkable feat are located in the brain core and rise up to include the striatum, equivalent to the inner reptilian layer of McLean's Triune model shown in **Figure 2.** They are similar to those of Freud's Id with unconscious drives, passions, and instincts. Unfortunately, the behaviors of this reptilian, Selfish Brain are often confused with those of Freud's Ego. Although Freud usually conceived of the Executive Brain as his "Ego", popular culture treats the ego as if it were the Id, as in "She hurt his ego". Therefore, Freud's allegorical terms are best replaced with ones that are more specific.

Layer 2, NeoCerebellum: The Social Brain

The social brain began to develop separately around this time. It was based upon the primary memory time track in the cerebellum that gave it knowledge of time, causality, and thus morality. The social brain views itself as a part of a larger family group that is more important than itself as an individual. This early manifested itself in the coordinated behavior of large groups of social organisms: the swarming of bees or locusts, the schooling of fish, the flocking of birds, and migration of reindeer, and the trouping of monkeys. The Social Brain was the brain layer that Freud ambiguously called the Superego. This function can now be localized in the cerebellum, especially within the neocerebellum.

Layer 3, Limbic System: The Executive Brain

The emergent properties at the self-level are quite opposite to those emerging at the group level. Thus, complex judgments are needed to know whether a particular survival situation is better solved by the killing violence of the selfish brain, or by the nonkilling cooperation of the more capable social brain. This led to the evolutionary development of the third brain level of control: that of the Executive Brain Ego.

The executive brain emerges from the properties of the "limbic system", so named by Paul McLean. These are a set of neural tissues intimately wrapped around the self-brain Id core and extending up into the limbic cingulate cortex of the fourth level (the cerebrum). The executive Ego is aware and highly concerned about the survival of both itself and its family. It powerfully controls and motivates the Id with the reward and punishment of the primary social emotions. It also strongly controls the social brain with the many "Ego defenses of the Id".

A strong executive Ego continually decides whether to authorize the reptilian brain to produce a selfish response, or whether to ask the social brain to design a synergistic social response (Wan, Cheng, & Tanaka, 2015). Thus, a strong executive confers superior survival to the organism, while a weak executive cannot overrule reptilian selfishness with its inherent suppression of the wisdom of the social brain, leaving it lying unheeded within.

Layer 4, Intellectual Brain: The Cerebral Hemispheres

Within the most recently developed fourth brain layer, that of the cerebral cortex, lie the abstractive abilities that produce the intellect and imagination of our derivative "cartoon and caption" type of usual consciousness. Here we have access to language, imagery and the awareness of our own self-awareness that forms the basis of contemplative thought: that the universe is self-aware. This is Freud's fourth and mundane level of consciousness, the only one of which he felt all are aware. He strongly believed that the above described three more ancient and layers operated powerfully outside of normal awareness.

The Quadrimental Brain, a Wider View:

Let us now look at functions of these four specialized brain layers again at a little greater depth. **Figure 5** shows a cartoon of the Quadrimental Brain centering on cellular survival.

The Reptile Brain DOES

Regardless of who controls it, the reptile or selfish brain core Id is the one and only output source of any and all behavior, both internal and external. This includes directives from higher brain levels or even from hypnotic external sources. Its own cellular homeostatic behaviors include genetically selected drives and instincts, such as conquest and defense of territory by dominance, via fighting and display. It will then use this territory to get food by hunting for, taking, and eating fuel, for shelter

Figure 5.

THE QUADRIMENTAL BRAIN: CONSCIOUSNESS AND MOTIVATION

Bruce E. Morton, Ph.D.,
University of Hawaii
School of Medicine
©

The Optimization of Cell Survival is the Source and Purpose of All Behavior

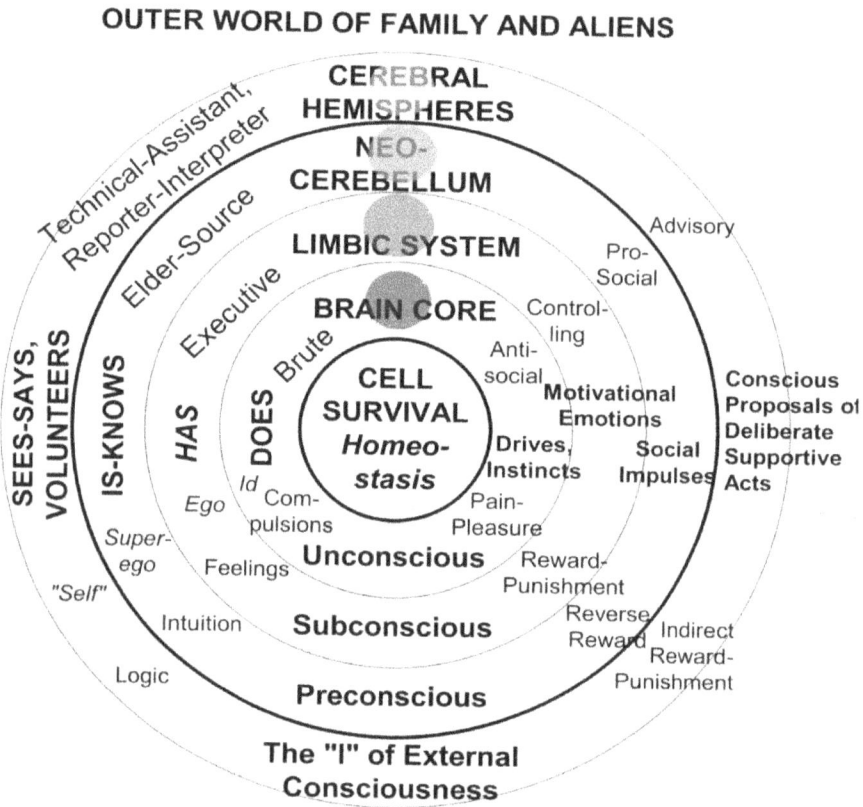

OUTER WORLD OF FAMILY AND ALIENS

Technical-Assistant,
Reporter-Interpreter

CEREBRAL HEMISPHERES

NEO-CEREBELLUM

Elder-Source

LIMBIC SYSTEM

Executive

BRAIN CORE

Advisory

Pro-Social

Controlling

SEES-SAYS, VOLUNTEERS

IS-KNOWS

HAS

DOES

Brute

Anti-social

CELL SURVIVAL
Homeo-stasis

Motivational Emotions

Conscious
Proposals of
Deliberate
Supportive
Acts

Ego

Com-pulsions

Drives,
Instincts

Social
Impulses

Super-ego

Feelings

Pain-Pleasure

"Self"

Unconscious

Reward-Punishment

Intuition

Subconscious

Reverse Reward

Indirect
Reward-Punishment

Logic

Preconscious

The "I" of External
Consciousness

The Reptile Brain receives earlier-similar memory responses from sensory inputs originating in cerebellar primary memory. The primary memory is a record of the sensory experience time track going back to before hatching or birth. The reptile brain records its repetitive routines in striatal habit memory as well as cerebellar primary memory. Important reptile routines include times of waking, excretion, eating, sunning, seeking shade and sleeping.

The reptile brain also uses brain core striatal memory for same-different data matching and analysis. This enables it to detect deviations from internal homeostatic set points, such as blood glucose, which it instinctively corrects. Same-difference matching also identifies and sizes external objects. From this it decides whether to fight or submit. As a rule, all else being equal, the biggest opponent will win. If your opponent is obviously larger than you are, then why fight only to die? Surrender has thus become an automatic reptilian Id alternative! The leader becomes, by definition, the biggest and best. Others willingly "follow the leader", as their superior. This important pecking order detail later formed a basis of internal surrender of the behavioral output Reptile Brain DOER to other later brain additions. It also formed a basis of external surrender to Father (Superior, Higher Authority), Teacher, Leader, King, God, God's priest-healer, other Hypnotists, and with schizophrenics controlled by imaginary aliens.

Reptile Brain behavioral output is automatic, i.e., produced by the autonomic sympathetic (punished avoidance) and parasympathetic (rewarded approach) nervous systems. It has direct control of the entire body, including the tongue and is the ultimate source of power. If the Reptile Brain is not surrendered to an internal or external Higher Authority, it is programmed to control everything itself. If resisted, it will escalate force up to killing levels of violence. It must be right. It must look better at all costs. It must win. It must dominate and control. This was a matter of life or death.

The Reptile Brain is the source of social conflict. A part of it is the brain location of the personal "Devil" in humans. Its antisocial "Laws of the Jungle" are inherently in conflict with society and religion: Its past is forgotten. The future does not exist. This is it, Here, Now! Let's party! It is the source of pleasure seeking: It loves "wine, women, and song". It is the source of pain avoidance: this makes it lazy, undisciplined and wasteful. It is the source of territoriality, and is selfish, greedy, obsessive, and ma- licious. It is the source of domination, and is competitive, aggressive, and destructive. It is the source of violence: it rapes, injures, kills, dismembers, and can be cannibalistic.

The Social Brain IS

The goal of the Social Brain (Freud's Superego) is group-species-life survival optimization. It is directed by the ancient family and herd-oriented elements of the cerebellum, the site of primary memory. As mentioned above, this so-called hindbrain has more cells than the entire rest of brain, but they are a smaller, making it smaller than the cerebrum. As our primary memory, it is continuously forming a linear time track forming an experiential multi-sensory record of our status over time. Its primary memory is in the format of very large-sized memories based upon the elegant, repetitive structure of the cerebellum. Our experiential time track is a continuous record reaching from the present to back before our birth. Without memory, current events, the snarl of a wolf for example, are gone forever the instant they happen. With primary memory, they are retrievable and held in Working Memory for analysis and for continuing survival optimizing responses beyond immediate simple flight reflexes.

The hidden Social Brain is the source of many important homeostatic behaviors. It uses cerebellar primary record of events in time and space to determine "the sequence of events", and from this to recognize causality (cause-cause, or effect-effect). From knowledge of causality come many important things, for example: meaning, learning, selfhood, survival reality, social knowledge, worst and best projections and knowledge of death. The Social Brain is also the site of language syntax: When did who do what to whom, where, and why? Syntax obviously originated from the coordination of both physical behavior for which the cerebellum is well known, and the coordination of ideas: which we call thinking. Drugs of abuse such as alcohol, because they inhibit cerebellar coordination, cause one to become both physically tipsy and mentally silly.

Knowledge of causality makes clear the advantages of deferred behavior, and support the self-restraint required. Similarly, the synergistic advantageous cooperative behavior within the group for the greater good of both family and the individual are obvious. Out of the Social Brain's view of the group as part of its own self, comes unselfish support and altruism. It protects, nurtures, and trains family members. From this comes conscience and guilt. It organizes and maintains solidarity of the family unit. From this comes ethics, law, order. It has been identified with The God Within, The Holy Spirit, The Source, Our Higher Power, Our Higher Intelligence. With It's pattern generator, It is the source of insight, intuition, wisdom, inspiration, one's "True Self", morality, purity, holiness, truth, faith, religion and species immortality.

The Inherent Universe-Level Conflict between two Brain Elements: Reptile (pro-individual) vs. Social (pro-group).

As mentioned earlier, each universe-level has unique emergent laws. The laws at the universe-level of the *individual* include: "I win. You lose" competition escalating to violence. "Give it to me now or I'll kill you!" works well against hyenas and snakes. In contrast, there exist the laws at the next higher universe-level of the *family* including both, "win-win" cooperation, non-violence and, "How can I best help you?" which work so well for loved ones of family. Thus, two conflicts exist between the self and social Brains: When shall I act to optimize survival?; Now or later? (for the reptile brain self, there is only NOW!) and Whose survival shall I optimize? My own or that of my family?; (for the reptile-selfish brain the only answer is mine!).

The familiar "double standards" of behavior that must inherently result from this conflict include self vs. others: "I am being held to a 'different-higher' standard than you are", and that of family vs. aliens: "It's not who you are, but who you know". The conflict between reptile brain and the Social Brain is a central theme of religion. It is seen in Christian fundamentalism as the "Great Contro- versy between Christ and Satan". In Islam, it appears as the Holy War (Major Jihad) between self-will and Allah's will.

The Two Opposing Survival Realities: War between Levels; Source of Inner Stress.

An overlooked, but still functioning mechanism used by the Social Brain Superego to inhibit reptile brain selfish behavior is as follows: The social brain labels prospecies behavior as good, godly, unselfish, and selfless. It rewards good with acceptance (love), happiness, joy. It labels selfish, violent, antisocial behavior and killing as bad, evil, and diabolic. It punishes bad with conscience, guilt, intense internal pain, depression resulting from the pain, stress, and rejection-ostracism resulting from physical violence.

The important early successful response by reptile brain to stop Social Brain rejection was to confess one's theft of survival benefits from the other or others, and to restore their stolen survival benefits to them. When restitution was complete, then forgiveness, acceptance and synergy automatically returned, both from those who were harmed. The two then became reunited as family.

Historically important maladaptive reptile brain responses exist attempting to bypass the social brain's rejection and guilt. For example: to run away from one's family (after social mobility was no longer lethal on the glacier), and/or to inhibit separation pain by short-term antisocial sex, or, more recently, to inhibit Social Brain guilt pain by drugs of abuse (alcohol, hemp, opium). Due to the inevitable homeostatic development of drug tolerance, intoxicating levels soon become required to block the pain. The resulting drug tolerance-based drunkenness required to block the Social Brain's guilt pain causes vast amounts of family disruption, academic failure, joblessness, social isolation, welfare dependence, poor health, criminal behavior, and kills millions on the highways. The need to stop guilt pain drives global drug trade, causing personal and government corruption, international crime, as well as damage to human society and the ecosystem.

The Executive Brain HAS:

The executive brain Ego optimizes overall cell survival by determining and managing whether the final decision output will come from: 1) the Reptile Brain whose internal reality makes selfish demands and wants it all right now; 2) the Social Brain whose survival reality for species survival demands that turn it off the Selfish Brain's violence in favor of cooperative nonviolent solutions; or the cerebral Intellect brain's cultural and personal ideas about external reality.

The Executive brain Ego structure is the limbic system, including the thalamus and cingulate cortex. Evolutionarily, the executive brain was the first of the quadrimental brain layers to manifest the fetal/mater nal programs, including curiosity, and juvenile rehearsal-play, as compared to the usually suppressive, humorless reptilian brain's antisocial drives.

The Executive Ego has two powerful sets of tools at its disposal to enforce its decisions. First, it can utilize the rewarding positive poles of emotions and drives **(Table 1)** to motivate the brain system called upon to act as requested, i.e., the famous "Carrot". Or, it can use their negative extremes to bring about painful punished compliance, using the infamous "Stick". Second, if it fails to accomplish its goals, it has an arsenal of the classical Ego defenses of the Id, **Table 2,** available for use to avoid taking responsibility for its failure.

When the executive ego feels safe, it motivates action by use of the Hexadyad Primary Emotions. Table 1 is a composite positive and negative binary expansion of the six pairs of primary emotions. As may be seen, in this model there are several perspectives of emotions available, ranging from that of cellular homeostasis, to descriptions of mood and personality, to extreme descriptors that we have applied to the concepts of God and Satan.

Placed at the center of **Table 1** are the six primary emotion pairs: They are: 1. certainty vs. confusion, 2. confidence vs. fear, 3. pleasure vs disgust, 4. gratitude vs. anger, 5. elation vs. grief, and 6. satisfaction vs. desire.

Table 1. SUMMARY OF THE HEXADYAD PRIMARY EMOTIONS AND THEIR DERIVATIVES
(Since primary emotions are binary, start at the midline of page and work up and down)

+CONCEPT EXTREME:	OMISCIENT CREATOR	OMNIPOTENT	GOD IS LOVE	HEAVENLY FATHER	KING OF KINGS	PRINCE OF PEACE
+BEHAVIORAL EXTREME:						
To self:	At cause	Tells the truth	Accepts	Gives of	Joyful	At peace
To others:	RESPONSIBLE	ETHICAL	LOVES	GIVES TO	ENTHUSIASTIC	AT PEACE
+PERSONALITY:	Knowing	Secure	Accepting	Supportive	Enthusiastic	Peaceful
+MOOD:	CLARITY	CALM	HAPPY	THANKFUL	JOYFUL	CONTENTED
+BIOLOGICAL STATIS:	Properties known	Safe to act	Resource available	Ally found	+Reinforcement	Free to act
+EVERYDAY MOTIVATOR:	RIGHT, SMART	STRONG	YES, GOOD	FRIEND	WINNER, SUCCESS	HAVE
+LIMBIC CONCLUSION:	I know	I am stronger	I accept	I am helped	I win	I have
+EMOTION:	1. CERTAINTY-EXPECTANCE	2. CONFIDENCE	3. PLEASURE	4. GRATITUDE	5. ELATION	6. SATISFACTION
-EMOTION:	CONFUSION -SURPRISE	FEAR	DISGUST	ANGER	GRIEF	DESIRE
LIMBIC CONCLUSION:	I don't know	I am weaker	I reject	I am harmed	I lose	I lack
-EVERYDAY MOTIVATOR:	WRONG, STUPID	WEAK	NO BAD	ENEMY	LOOSER, FAILURE	NEED
-BIOLOGICAL STATUS:	Properties known	Time to escape	Source of harm/waste	Competitor identified	Negative reinforcer	Must get supplies
-MOOD:	UNCERTAIN	ANXIOUS	NEGATIVE	IRRITATED	SAD	DISSATISFIED
-PERSONALITY:	Ambivalent	Insecure	Rejecting	Hostile	Gloomy	Demanding
-BEHAVIORAL EXTREME:					APATHETIC	LIES
To others:	BLAMES	UNETHICAL	HATES	HARMS	STEALS	CHEATS
To self:	Lies to	Afraid of the truth	Suicidal	Accident-Prone, Ill	Hopeless	Self and drug abuse
-CONCEPT EXTREME:	IDIOT, FOOL	FRIGHTENED TO DEATH	DIABOLICAL HATRED	RAGING DEMON	WAILING KNASHING	CRIMINAL FIEND

Rising upward or falling downward from these core responses are the limbic system ego's conclusions derived from them. Expanding further we come to their motivational value, then their survival (biological) significance. If the same emotion is prolonged for a few hours or days, the resulting moods are listed. If prolonged for weeks or years, they become part of personality. The personal meanings of these binary emotions to self and others are listed next to the last, followed by familiar spiritual conceptual extremes.

The Hexadyad Primary Emotions Model has found support in the work of Ekman (2006) who from cross cultural research found that all around the world, humans responded in the same manner to the same emotional stimuli. These persons could also accurately identify the emotion experienced from the face of others responding to the same stimuli. His list of universal human emotions included five of the six hexadyad negative emotions (surprise, fear, disgust, anger, sadness). There was one generalized positive emotion, (happiness). Possibly the latter outcome was because the experiencing of all six positive emotions results in the same smile upon one's face.

In the 1990s Ekman expanded his emotions to those not encoded by facial expression. Some of his non facial emotions included the missing positive pole to primary emotion pairs, contentment (satisfaction), relief (confidence), pride in achievement, excitement, and amusement (elation). Others (guilt, embarrassment, and shame) were complex social emotion composed of more than one primary emotion.

Table 2: Ego Defenses of the Reptilian Id: The Sixteen Lies (Confabulations)

1. **Acting out:** expression of an impulse in spite of its negative consequences.
2. **Compensation:** development of another characteristic to offset a deficiency.
3. **Denial:** declaring that an anxiety provoking stimuli doesn't exist.
4. **Displacement:** taking out impulses on a less threatening target.
5. **Intellectualization:** avoiding emotional impact by focusing on details.
6. **Passive-Aggressive Behavior:** avoiding aggression by passivity.
7. **Projection:** placing one's unacceptable impulses upon someone else.
8. **Rationalization:** supplying a logical reason in place of the real one.
9. **Reaction Formation:** replacing a real belief with one causing less anxiety.
10. **Regression:** returning to a previous stage of development.
11. **Repression:** loss of access to memories of past trauma.
12. **Resistance:** defense against conscious awareness of unconscious desires.
13. **Somatization:** channeling conflict onto one's body: obesity, allergies, etc.
14. **Sublimation:** acting out unacceptable impulses in a socially acceptable way.
15. **Suppression:** pushing something that causes anxiety out of consciousness.
16. **Undoing:** obsessive repetition of ritualistic act as if to ally guilt from an event.

When the executive is unsuccessful in suppressing the reptile brain, it uses the sixteen Ego Defenses of the Id (**Table 2**) to justify its use of the Reptile Brain to produce antisocial behavior. Clearly, each of these defenses is an after-the-fact lie, as exemplified with the use of denial or of projection onto others. We see these in use all the time by people seeking to avoid responsibility for their acts or failure to act. The sixteen classic defenses listed here are probably not exhaustive. In general, they provide proof that our Id would rather win, be right and dominate, and that it would rather lie through its teeth than lose, be wrong or be dominated. Thus, the executive is equipped with a genetic arsenal of sophisticated deceptions. Furthermore, it does not see them as lies, but as the "gospel" truth and often is willing to fight to be right about them. How interesting that we have such an elaborate set of weapons to use against non-family "aliens" (gooks, krauts, etc).

The Executive-Ego is also profoundly afraid of dying and suppresses access to memories of past threats of death trauma by mental blockades. Even when off-line, during REM sleep or when injured or drugged, it camouflages uncontrolled breakthroughs of raw memories of personal trauma. These instead are disguised as dreams, nightmares, or waking hallucinations. The Executive can be selectively inhibited and weakened to the point of collapse by both certain types of meditation, and by ingestion of drugs that specifically activate the serotonin 5-HT2a stress receptor, all of which are hallucinogens like LSD.

These receptors have been found on inhibitory in- terneu- rons to cause an overall inhibition of the cingu- late cortex (Carhart-Harris, Erritzoe, Williams et al., 2012), here pro- posed to be the site of Freud's Ego. Un- der these circum- stances of so called "Ego (Id) death", visions of tran- sendental figures and events can be produced. Anciently, these altered state experiences likely provided the irra- tional foundations of our cur- rent religions (Hancock, 2007).

The Executive can also be caused to give over its control to a higher outer authority, for example as 1) in certain practices of religion (including human suicide bombers, or WWII Kamikaze pilots), or 2) in child-like inductive learning (from the most authoritative parental or scientific source) or 3) in hypnosis (Faith Healing, Death Curses, Mass Hysteria).

Executive Properties as Self, Supervisor, Ego, Will and Controller of Volition:

The Executive Ego Will seeks the solution of ongo- ing survival problems using the above primary emotions as motivators. It has been quantitatively studied in mam- mals and birds. It is the source of judgment and decision. This includes attention, causal action, anticipation, expec- tation of outcome (anxiety or excitement), detection and correction of errors and evaluation of final effects. It learns from experience and takes pre-conscious action based upon its emotional evaluation of relative survival values, likelihoods and profitability. It calculates profitability in terms of survival maximization. This requires a predatory strategy based upon the maximum intake of energy for the least expenditure of effort in a random and unpredictable possibilities of profitability is a core issue. That is, what the cost/benefit ratio will be of each of the alternatives available. This estimate is based upon the survival value of the goal, the needed direction of effort and the type of action recognized.

Ultimately the Executive Ego delegates authority: Should "I" use my competitive Reptile Brain at the universe level of individual? Or, should I use my cooperative Social Brain at the next higher universe level, that of the group? Also what importance should be given to what my conscious cerebral Imagination sees or what my Intellect reports? These sophisticated decisions are at the center of our preconscious Executive's call to action.

The Intellect IMAGINES-REPORTS

The brain of higher mammals has relatively recently evolved a potent abstract reasoning accessory in the cerebral cortex. This abstracting accessory, called the Intellect, serves the just described reptile-social-executive brain "Triad" to optimize cellular homeostasis with increased sophistication. The more ancient and powerful triad members are each self-aware, but operate outside the awareness of the intellect, which is located in the asymmetric right and left cerebral hemispheres. In humans, intellect matures late and takes over consciousness by about 3 years of age when true language becomes operational.

Working memory is a basic element essential to the intellect: Working memory retrieves reverberating facsimiles of cerebellar primary memory (social brain), and striatal habit memory (reptile brain) via the thalamus (part of the executive brain). Working memory holds these fax copies for manipulation on a prefrontal cortex viewing screen. The Intellect then copies (via hippocampus) these faxes of vast and unwieldy cerebellar primary memory into two different compressed cerebral memory formats, each small enough to be manipulated in time and space off-line.

One of these, usually in the right hemisphere (see next chapter), produces visual cartoon abstracts, something that children find inherently attractive. These are the concrete images of inner reality. In the other memory abstraction, produced by the left hemisphere, consists of compressed memory captions: These are the abstract symbols of language. The intellect uses these handy new cartoon – caption "funny book" memories to facilitate thinking of new ideas off-line. This enables it for the first time to conceptualize, plan, safely rehearse, adapt, to produce an improved plan, without having to expose itself to the dangers of trial and error in external reality. It can project data in time and space to predict worst and best possible outcomes. These abstracting compressing skills formed the foundational source of speech, writing, mathematics, logic and civilization. Further, the intellect can be aware of its own self-awareness and thus reach the organizational level of Metamind.

There are advantages of having a consciousness operating at the intellectual-imagination level. Not only can it form new survival-optimizing ideas off-line, while the older brain "Triad" are routinely working. But, its existence also avoids second-by-second suffering (of Buddhism) from the continuous operation of the powerful punish-reward emotional motivators operating in the more ancient lower brain triad. This is because these seem to operate mainly subconsciously outside of its awareness.

However, there are two critical disadvantages to operating from a consciousness only aware at the intellectual-imagination level. First: such a narrow consciousness assumes that its own volition alone produces all its behavior, until it learns otherwise, which is rarely, if ever. The cartoon in **Figure 6** illustrates this. Second, the Intellect cannot retrieve and upgrade harmful earlier cerebellar or striatal memories of childhood trauma or error that were formed in the larger, more cumbersome primary memory format before the age of 3, at which time it first began forming retrievable records in the cerebral cartoon-caption format of the Intellect.

Clearly, the Quadrimental Brain Model, as illustrated in **Figure 5**, is a more accurate approximation of the human mind than that of the Unitive Model. However, as might be expected, the mind of humans is even more complex than four layers. This is due to the bilateral nature of vertebrate form incorporated into our human structure. Due to evolution, rather than one sided simply being a mirror image of the other, the two sides of each of the four

vertical layers of brain evolution have developed a differ- ent
cialized functions. This has forced an expansion of the Qua
mental Brain Model into the Dual Quadbrain Model, with
Society of Seven, described in the next chapters. However, c
working at that level of under- standing, we will be equippe
understand what human thought is all about.

Id, **ego**, and **super-ego** are the three parts of the psychic appa-
ratus defined in Sigmund Freud's structural model of the psych
they are the three theoretical constructs in terms of whose activ
and interaction our mental life is described. According to this
model of the psyche, the **id** is the set of uncoordinated instinct
trends; the **super-ego** plays the critical and moralizing role; an
the **ego** is the organized, realistic part that mediates between th
desires of the **id** and the **super-ego.** The **super-ego** can stop or
from doing certain things that one's **id** may want to do."
(Wikipedia, 2017)

Proposed *neuroanatomical sources* **and** synonyms **for**
Freud's Terms for the unconscious that are used in this boo

Id: *Brain core,*
  Negative Id: Dragon, Reptile Brain, Self-brain, Dominator,
        Devil, Demon
  Positive Id:, Dog Brain, Servant Brain, Best Friend

Ego: *Cingulate Cortex*, Executive, Supervisor, Caretaker

Superego: *Cerebellum*, Social Brain, Source, Higher

        Power, Inner Wisdom, Holy Spirit, God-Within

As to normal consciousness which he said was familiar to all,
Intellect: *Left Hemisphere Cerebrum*
Imagination: *Right Hemisphere Cerebrum*

Figure 5: Pattern on Professor Morton's old Reyn's Hawaiian Shirt

Figure 5 legend: A Farmer with a straw between his teeth is riding backwards on a fat pig. He reports upon and rationalizes all that happens, believing himself to be in charge. The thoughts of the farmer represent what occurs in human LH unitive consciousness. Obviously, the pig has a mind of its own, whose operation is almost completely out of the farmer's awareness.

CHAPTER TWO

CHAPTER 3: Bilateral Expansion to the
Dual Quadbrain Model

Introduction: The Need to Advance to a
Dual Quadbrain Model

The entire vertebrate central nervous system is bilateral. That is, all its structural elements are paired on either side of the midline, for example the two cerebral hemispheres. The sole exception is that there is only a single central pineal gland, an endocrine organ. This exception led the French philosopher Descartes (1637) mistakenly to declare the pineal gland to be the seat of the soul. Awareness of sidedness in brain function appears to be as old as written history. For example, Diocles of Carystus in the 4th century BC wrote: "There are two brains in the head, one which gives understanding, and another which provides sense-perception. That is to say, the one which is lying on the right side is the one that perceives: with the left one, however, we understand" (Lockhorst 1985).

Although Diocles may have been the first to write about brain laterality, Marc Dax (1865) was the first on record in the modern era to note a difference in function between the cerebral hemispheres. In 1836, he reported victims of stroke or other injury to the left hemisphere (LH), but not the right hemisphere (RH) could not speak. This hemispheric asymmetry for language was also thought to be tied to contra-lateral hand preference (Broca 1863). Among those 90% of humans who are right handed (Coren, 1992), language is located in the LH in over 95% of them (Smith and Moscovitch, 1979). Of the remaining about 10% of left-handed individuals, some 60% of these also have language in their left cerebrum (Levy and Reid, 1976). Thus, the LH houses language ability in at least 9 out of 10 humans.

Nearly a century passed before reports of any further manifestations of hemispheric laterality. Then, a large study by Weisenberg and McBride (1935) demonstrated a RH superiority for visiospatial skills. During that century, the laterality term, "dominant hemisphere", became irreversibly tied to the language-processing hemisphere, usually the LH, because of its association with the brain areas required for speech and dominant handedness. This forced the creation of second terms not using the word, dominance, such as "hemispheric laterality" or "cerebral asymmetry", to describe the many, more recently discovered non-language differences in cerebral structure and function, most notably found in "split-brain" subjects. These individuals had been produced by treatment for intractable epilepsy by severing their corpus callosum, the only cerebral connection between the hemispheres, thus limiting the spread of seizures from one side to the other (Sperry, 1982; Gazzaniga, Bogen & Sperry, 1962; Gazzaniga, 2000).

Based upon the surprisingly different responses obtained by the interrogation of each of these disconnected hemispheres of split-brain subjects (Gazzaniga, et al., 1962; Geschwind, Iacoboni, Mega, Zidel, Cloughesy, & Zaidel, 1995; Gazzaniga, 2000), investigators proposed that the right and left cerebral hemispheres are characterized by in-built

qualitatively different and seemingly mutually antagonistic modes of data processing, necessarily separated
from interference by the major longitudinal fissure of the
brain (Levy, 1969; Sperry, 1982). It is as if they each use
opposite approach orientations to analyze what is going
on. As will become obvious, this turns out to be very valuable for the organism's survival as a whole.

In this model, the left hemisphere is specialized in
top-down, deductive, cognitive dissection of local detail,
while the right hemisphere orientation is a bottom-up, inductive, perceptual synthesis of global structure (Sperry,
1982; Gazzaniga, 2000). Known laterality differences between them reinforce this context. That is, there are striking differences in input to each hemisphere, differences in
internal neuronal-columnar architecture, and differences
in hemispheric output (Kosslyn, Koenig, Barrett, Cave,
Tang, & Gabrieli, 1989; Kosslyn, Chabris, Marsolek, &
Koenig, 1992; Hutsler & Galuske, 2003; Jager & Postma,
2003; Stephan, Fink and Marshall, 2006).

Supporting the above view of opposite processing
modes between the cerebral hemispheres is a large body
of evidence, only briefly summarized here, that the left
cerebral hemisphere in most right-handed individuals
manifests facilities for language (Broca, 1863), has an orientation for local detail (Robertson & Lamb, 1991), has
object abstraction-identification abilities (Kosslyn) (1987)
and appears to possess a hypothesis-generating, event "interpreter" (Wolford, et al, 2000, Gazzaniga, 1989, 2000).
In contrast, the right hemisphere excels in global analysis

(Robertson & Lamb, 1991; Magun, et al., 1994), object localization (Kosslyn, et al., 1989), facial recognition (Milner, 1968) and spatial construction (Sperry, 1968).

It is of interest that within this huge group of right-handed, LH-dominant speakers, the existence of two major human sub-populations has repeatedly been inferred, whose characteristic thinking and behavior styles differ in a manner that appeared to mirror the properties of the asymmetric hemispheres. That is, in some right-handed, LH-languaged individuals, left hemisphere traits were proposed to be ascendant, producing a "left brain-oriented" thinking and behavioral style (Springer and Deutch; 1998; Fink, Halligan, Marschall, Frith, Frackowiak, & Dolan, 1996). Such left brain-oriented persons are top-down, important detail, deductive "Splitters". Yet, in other right-handed, LH-languaged persons, right hemisphere traits are thought to be more prominent, resulting in a contrasting "Right brain"-oriented style (Davidson and Hugdahl, 1995; Shiffer, 1996), currently viewed as bottom-up, big picture, inductive "Lumpers".

Thus, original permanent assignment of the term "hemispheric dominance" to language laterality ultimately forced the creation of yet a third laterality term, "Hemisphericity" (Bogen, 1969; Bogen, DeZure, Tenhouten, and Marsh, 1969). This was required in order to describe this third laterality phenomenon: the seemingly binary differences in left and right brain thinking and behavioral style within individuals of both the same language dominance and non-language subsystem asymmetries. Unfortunately,

hemisphericity was based upon an incorrect initial definition: that of each person's unique point on a gradient between right and left-brain extremes. After years of conflict, and hundreds of publications, this misconception
caused such problems that the actual existence of hemisphericity was placed in doubt (Beaumont, Young &
McManus, 1984).

As will be seen, the observer of the executive ego
can only be unilateral. That is, it can be on only one side
of the brain. This is consistent with the logic that within
any institution, there can be only one "bottom line" authority. This also reduces the number of separate consciousness elements from eight to The Society of Seven (next
chapter).

Recently, redefinition of hemisphericity depending
upon which side of the brain the unilateral Executive Observer was inherently and irreversibly embedded has restored credibility of hemisphericity, but in a binary form.
This is the more robust, either right or left brain-oriented
phenomenon, under the new name of "Hemisity" (Morton, 2001, 2001, 2003 abcd; Morton and Rafto, 2006,
2010). Hemisity was a foundational element leading to the
discovery of the Dyadic Evolution and Familial Polarity
Morton, 2011).

Asymmetries and functional differences also exist
in laterality between sides of the two lower layers of the
quadrimental brain as well. In both the cerebellar social
brain and the reptilian self-brain, the behavior of one side
focuses more on the individual survival and the other upon
the survival of the family group.

Six Postulates Creating the Dual Quadbrain Model:

The above essential background elements of 1) bi-laterality of the entire brain, 2) asymmetric inputs to the cerebral hemispheres, 3) contrastingly different data processing orientations of the asymmetric hemispheres, and 4) differing behavioral outputs of the asymmetric hemispheres, and 5) the Quadrimental Brain were combined with other evolutionary and neuroscience information to create the Dual Quadbrain Model of behavioral laterality developed next.

In **Figure 7**, the still valid Quadrimental Brain Model of **Figure 5** in Chapter 2 and the lateralized Dual Quadbrain Model contexts are compared using grey tone coding. The cartoon of the structure of the human bilateral brain and its major anatomical interconnections only co-incidentally resembles that of a human head. Obvious are the two cerebral hemispheres of the Intellectual Brain are on top and the bilateral cerebellar Social Brain elements on either side. The unilateral limbic system Executive Brain is within the surrounding cerebral hemi-spheres. The bilateral Reptile Brain stem and striatum of the Reptile Brain are beneath. These Id-like sources mediate that final behavioral output to the spinal column. The corpus callosum, the major bridge between the cerebral hemispheres, is depicted. So are the cortico-trophic releasing factor (CRF) anxiety connections between the paired emotion generating amygdalae, and the norepinephrine fear pathways of the locus coeruleus pair. Counterbalancing these punishment pathways (-) norepinephrine fear pathways of the locus coeruleus pair.

Figure 7. Comparison of the Quadrimental Brain with the Dual Quadbrain Laterality Expansion

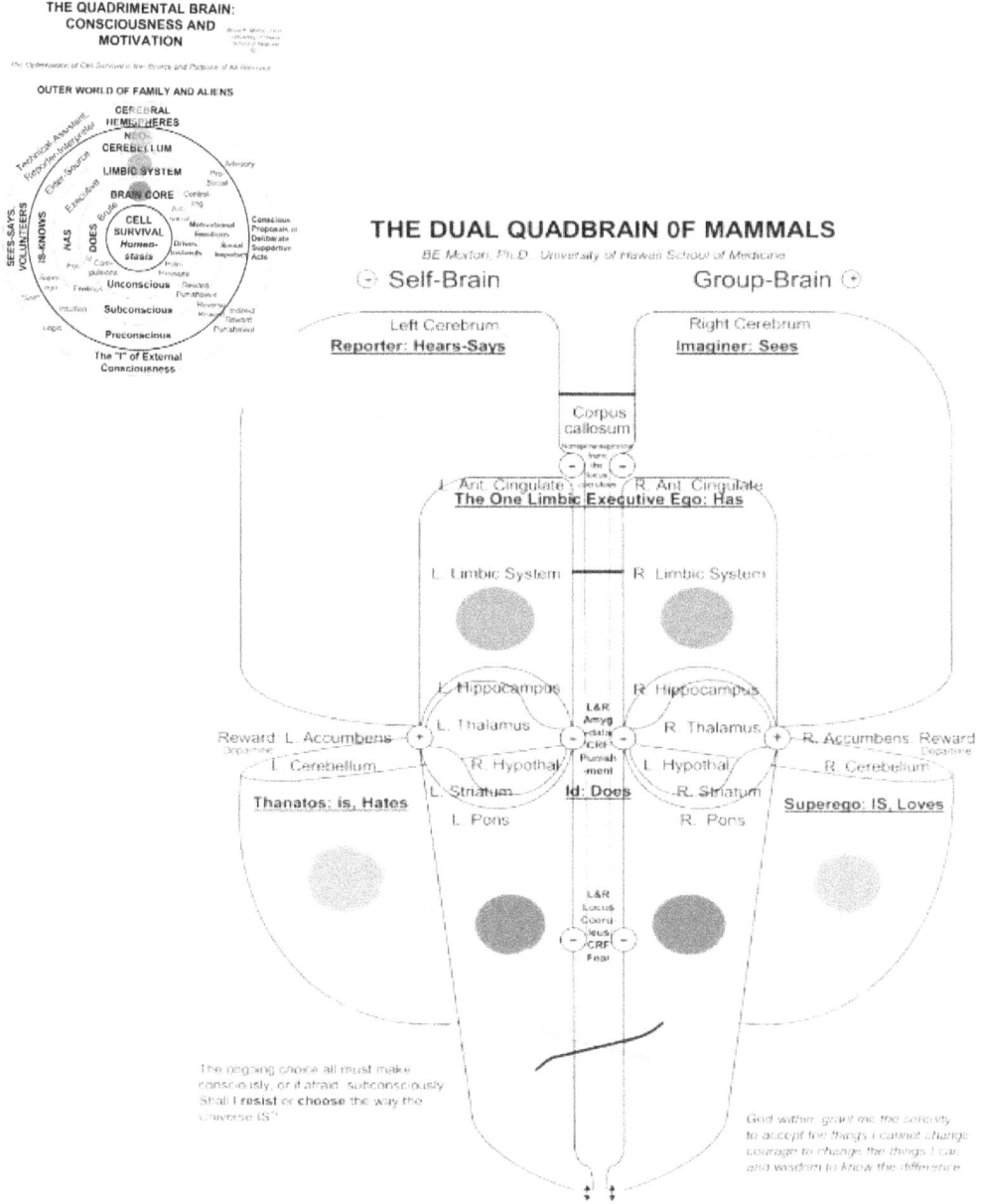

Counterbalancing these punishment pathways (-) are the rewarding pathways (+) of the pleasure neurotransmitter, dopamine. We will utilize these six postulates as a device to fill in the detailed functions of the Dual Quadbrain elements.

Dual Quadbrain Model Postulate 1: Left side Self-Survival Orientation vs. Right side Group-Survival Orientation Form a Bilateral Functional Axis for the Entire Brain

In the Dual Quadbrain Model, it is postulated that the quadrimental elements of the left half of the brain are dedicated primarily to self-survival and self-sufficiency, either when alone or in the presence of competition against other species. In contrast, the right side elements of the brain are devoted to group, herd, and species survival and cooperative social interaction (Henry and Wang, 1998). Each side of the brain is alternatively activated or suppressed as appropriate to the social environment and directed by the single unilateral Executive Ego.

Dual Quadbrain Model Postulate 2: The Bottom-Up and Top-Down Processing of the Two Cerebral Hemispheres are Functionally Opposite and Require Physical Separation

The opposite orientation of the two more recently arrived powerful data abstracting units within the Intellectual System that produce our usual cartoon (right hemisphere) and caption (left hemisphere) based consciousness is shown in **Figure 8**. In brief, the left cerebral hemisphere

Figure 8, Dual Quadbrain Intellect

THE DUAL QUADBRAIN OF MAMMALS

BE Morton, Ph.D., University of Hawaii School of Medicine

⊖ Self-Brain   Group-Brain ⊕
(*Can be inhibited by fear)

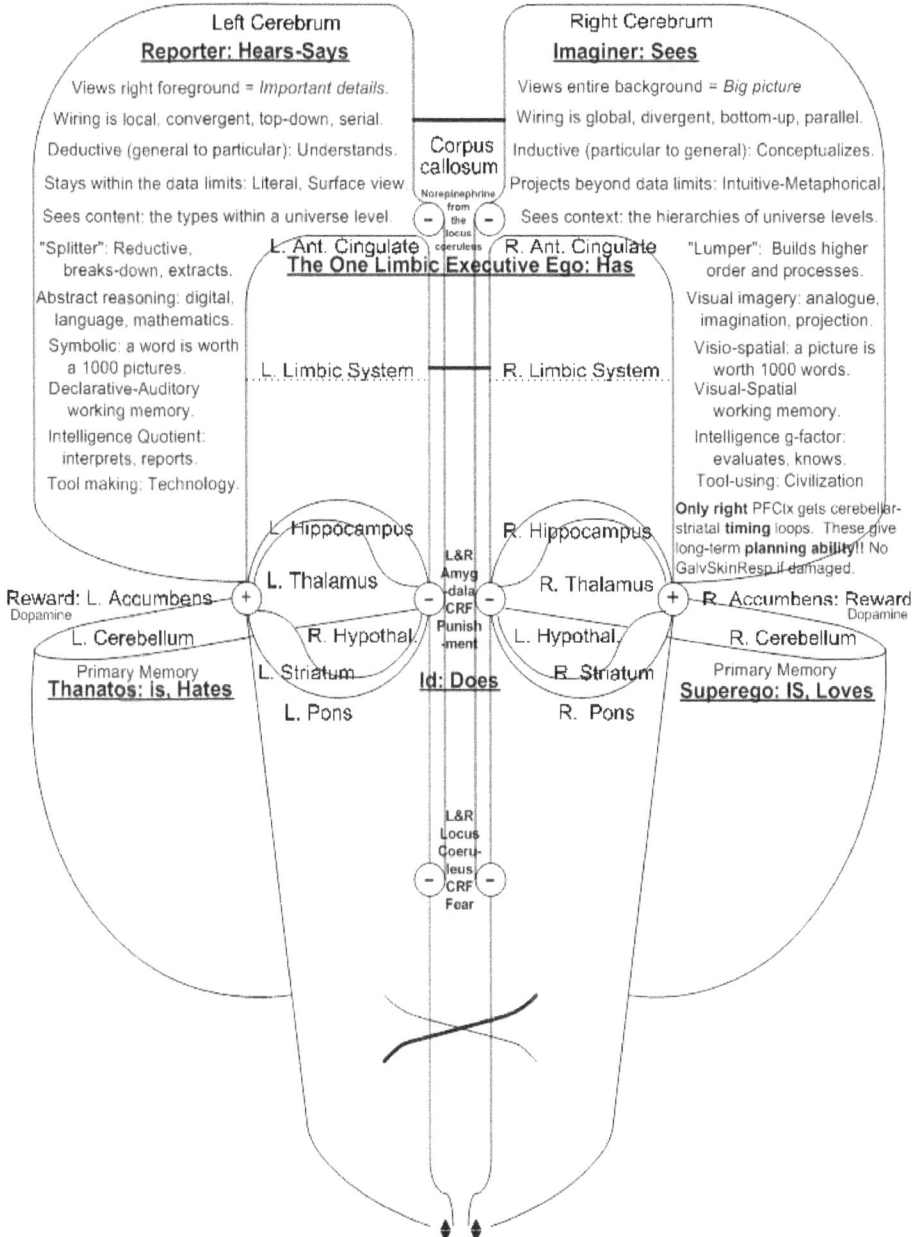

Left Cerebrum **Reporter: Hears-Says**		Right Cerebrum **Imaginer: Sees**
Views right foreground = *Important details*.		Views entire background = *Big picture*
Wiring is local, convergent, top-down, serial.	Corpus callosum	Wiring is global, divergent, bottom-up, parallel.
Deductive (general to particular): Understands.		Inductive (particular to general): Conceptualizes.
Stays within the data limits: Literal, Surface view.	Norepinephrine from the locus coeruleus	Projects beyond data limits: Intuitive-Metaphorical.
Sees content: the types within a universe level.	⊖ ⊖	Sees context: the hierarchies of universe levels.

L. Ant. Cingulate   **The One Limbic Executive Ego: Has**   R. Ant. Cingulate

"Splitter": Reductive, breaks-down, extracts.
"Lumper": Builds higher order and processes.

Abstract reasoning: digital, language, mathematics.
Visual imagery: analogue, imagination, projection.

Symbolic: a word is worth a 1000 pictures.
Visio-spatial: a picture is worth 1000 words.

L. Limbic System — R. Limbic System

Declarative-Auditory working memory.
Visual-Spatial working memory.

Intelligence Quotient: interprets, reports.
Intelligence g-factor: evaluates, knows.

Tool making: Technology.
Tool-using: Civilization

Only right PFCtx gets cerebellar-striatal **timing** loops. These give long-term **planning ability**!! No GalvSkinResp if damaged.

L. Hippocampus   R. Hippocampus

L&R Amyg-dala CRF Punish-ment

L. Thalamus   R. Thalamus

Reward: L. Accumbens ⊕   Dopamine   ⊖   R. Accumbens: Reward   Dopamine

L. Cerebellum   R. Hypothal.   L. Hypothal.   R. Cerebellum

Primary Memory   L. Striatum   **Id: Does**   R. Striatum   Primary Memory
Thanatos: is, Hates   **Superego: IS, Loves**

L. Pons   R. Pons

L&R Locus Coeru-leus CRF Fear

⊖ ⊖

sees differences between things, uses top-down, deductive reasoning from the general to the particular to dissect the next lower-universe level and thus is a "Splitter". In contrast, the right hemisphere sees commonalities within things, uses inductive reasoning to go from the particular (individual) instances to the general (group). The two hemispheres must remain separate because the two opposite processes performed by the hemispheres are incompatible. However, the two exchange information: via the corpus callosum, and the deeper anterior and posterior commissure-like cables.

Because of their differences, each cerebrum performs mutually exclusive, survival-maximizing data processing operations. In the right brain, incoming data (for example, an approaching white poodle) is *inductively* compared (with the assistance of the striatal matching system) with earlier-similar memory data of a white pit bull terrier to see whether the two data sets might be similar and related. It is of great survival value to know rapidly if both sets of data are related. If so, earlier-similar outcome memories can next be scanned in terms of past survival harm or benefit. Then avoidance or approach behavior initiates and coordinates increasing the survival benefit of the present situation.

In exclusive contrast, with the left-brain, the incoming data (the poodle) is *deductively* compared with earlier-similar memory data of the pit bull to see how the two data sets are *different and unrelated*. The rapid detection of differences is also of great survival value, for example, noting the critical difference between the playful poodle from the past, and the present rapidly approaching pit bull, foaming at the mouth.

The presence of the global type of wiring motif of the right hemisphere compared to the local type of architecture of the left hemisphere supports necessary segregation of two incompatible brain processes into separate top-down and bottom-up data analysis systems (Kosslyn, 1987; Van Kleek, 1989; Lamb, et. al., 1990; Kosslyn, et. al., 1992; Fink, et. al., 1996). The eye input assignments given the two hemispheres where the more visual-global RH attends to the entire spatial-visual field, while the left attends only to the right foreground further reinforces this separation. This results in left hemi-neglect upon right hemisphere stroke or other injury, leading to drawings of clocks with numbers only on the right side. The localized language centers in the LH also emphasize such by making this hemisphere the more auditory-speech oriented of the two. The cerebral asymmetries caused by the left local vs. a right distributed wiring organization, lead to detectible laterality differences in how the corresponding vertical columns themselves are organized and interconnected in general.

Local vs. global structural and functional hemispheric differences prompt the speculation that the content orientation of the LH facilitates the detection of differences ("Splitter") in a top-down, deductive, analytical, intelligent manner. In contrast, the concept-context orientation of the RH assists in the detection of global similarities

("Lumper") in a bottom-up, inductive, intuitive, at times metaphorical way (Bottini, Concoran, Sterzi, Paulesu, Schenone, Scarpa, Frackowiak, and Firth, 1994). Thus, the orientation of the RH is for visual-concrete images where "a picture is worth a thousand words" contrasts with that of the LH toward abstractions, where "a word is worth a thousand pictures".

To have two such high speed specialized data analysis systems on-board and intercommunicating with the Executive Ego has enabled mammals, especially humans, to be highly successful during the intense, ongoing process of survival. The contrasting processing motifs of the two cerebra show behavioral output differences that influence the social behavioral orientation of each side of the dual brain resulting in hemisity.

Dual Quadbrain Model Postulate 3: The Right Side of the Limbic System is the Source of The Social Emotions, while from the Left Side come the Ego Defenses of the Id.

As presented in **Figure 9**, elements of the motivational systems of the brain, including the Hexadyadic Primary Emotions of Chapter 2, provide powerful internal motivation of social behavior via punishment and reward ("carrot and stick", **Figure 10**). The primary emotions have here been arbitrarily localized in the right limbic system, while, the sixteen Ego defenses of the Id ("that pack of lies"), presented in Chapter 2, have been placed in the left side of the limbic system.

Although controversial, more evidence supports

Figure 9. The Unilateral Executive Ego

THE DUAL QUADBRAIN 0F MAMMALS

BE Morton, Ph.D., University of Hawaii School of Medicine

⊖ Self-Brain   Group-Brain ⊕
                               (*Can be inhibited by fear)

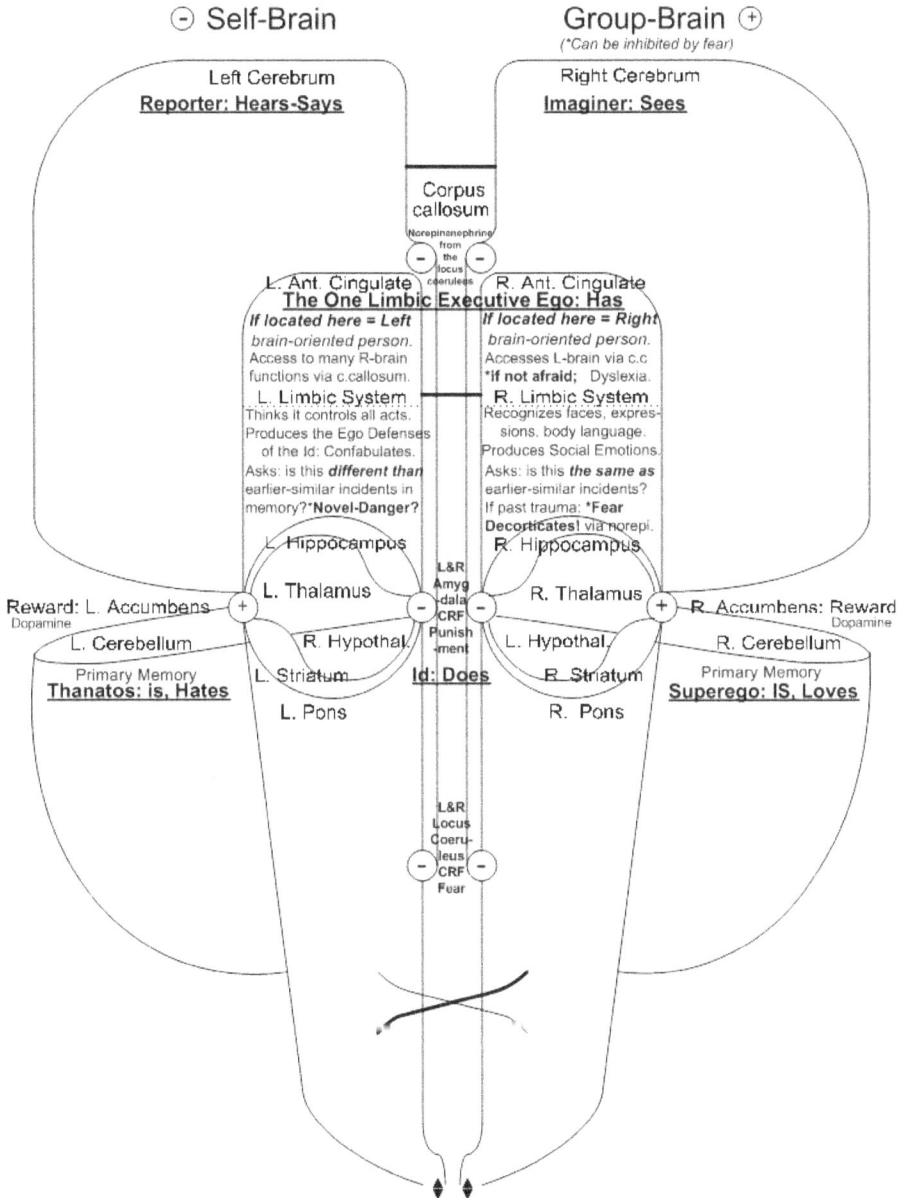

Left Cerebrum
Reporter: Hears-Says

Right Cerebrum
Imaginer: Sees

Corpus callosum

Norepinephrine from the locus coeruleus

L. Ant. Cingulate   R. Ant. Cingulate
The One Limbic Executive Ego: Has

If located here = Left brain-oriented person. Access to many R-brain functions via c.callosum.

If located here = Right brain-oriented person. Accesses L-brain via c.c *if not afraid;* Dyslexia.

L. Limbic System
Thinks it controls all acts. Produces the Ego Defenses of the Id: Confabulates. Asks: is this *different than* earlier-similar incidents in memory?*Novel-Danger?*

R. Limbic System
Recognizes faces, expressions, body language. Produces Social Emotions. Asks: is this *the same as* earlier-similar incidents? If past trauma: *Fear Decorticates!* via norepi.

L. Hippocampus   R. Hippocampus

L&R Amygdala CRF Punishment

L. Thalamus   R. Thalamus

Reward: L. Accumbens ⊕   ⊖   ⊖   ⊕ R. Accumbens: Reward
Dopamine   Dopamine

L. Cerebellum   R. Hypothal.   L. Hypothal.   R. Cerebellum

Primary Memory   L. Striatum   Id: Does   R. Striatum   Primary Memory
Thanatos: is, Hates   **Superego: IS, Loves**

L. Pons   R. Pons

L&R Locus Coeruleus CRF Fear

Figure 10.

THE QUADRIMENTAL BRAIN AND FEELINGS (AFFECT):
SOURCE OF INVOLUNTARY DRIVES, INSTINCTS, EMOTIONS, AND IMPULSES
Bruce E. Morton, Ph.D., University of Hawaii School of Medicine

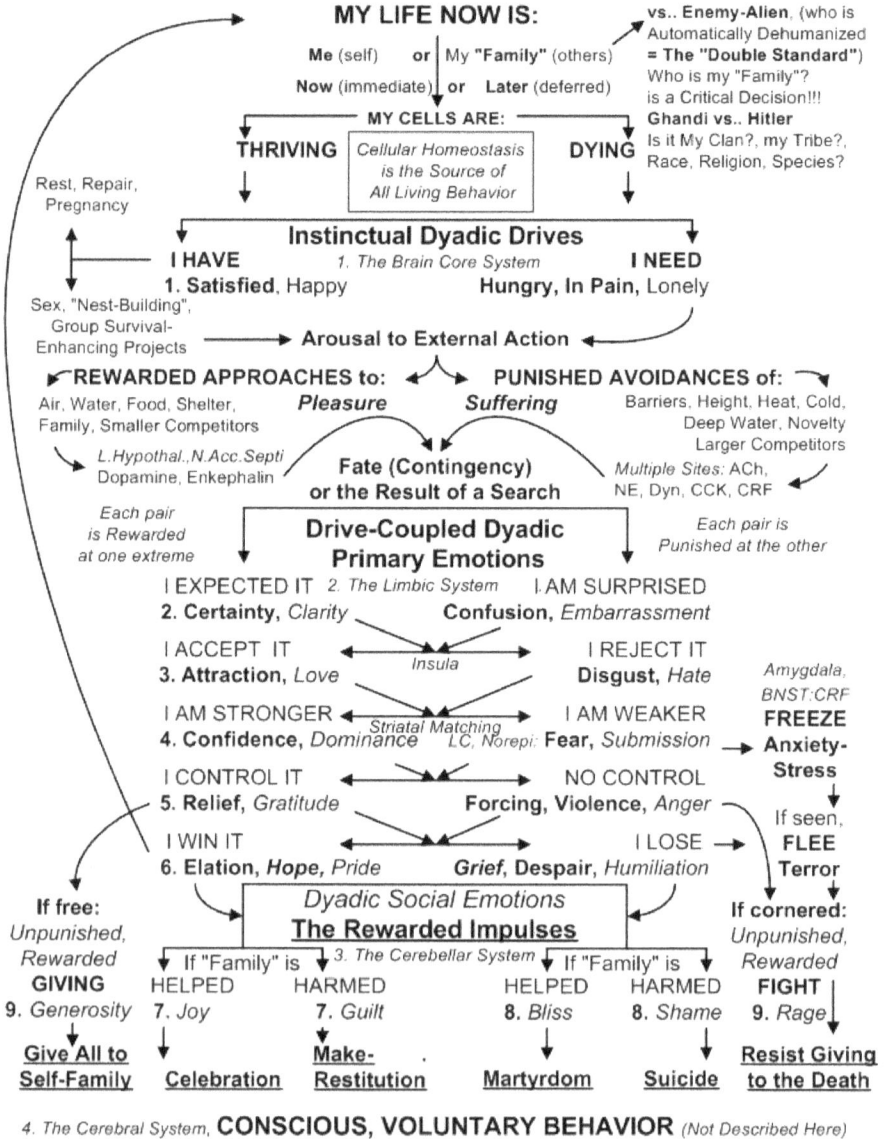

MY LIFE NOW IS:

Me (self) or My **"Family"** (others)

Now (immediate) or **Later** (deferred)

vs.. **Enemy-Alien**, (who is Automatically Dehumanized = **The "Double Standard")**
Who is my "Family"? is a Critical Decision!!!
Ghandi vs.. Hitler
Is it My Clan?, my Tribe?, Race, Religion, Species?

MY CELLS ARE:

THRIVING   *Cellular Homeostasis is the Source of All Living Behavior*   **DYING**

Rest, Repair, Pregnancy

Instinctual Dyadic Drives
I HAVE   *1. The Brain Core System*   **I NEED**
1. Satisfied, Happy   **Hungry, In Pain**, Lonely

Sex, "Nest-Building", Group Survival-Enhancing Projects

Arousal to External Action

REWARDED APPROACHES to: **PUNISHED AVOIDANCES of:**
Air, Water, Food, Shelter, Family, Smaller Competitors   *Pleasure* *Suffering*   Barriers, Height, Heat, Cold, Deep Water, Novelty Larger Competitors

L.Hypothal.,N.Acc.Septi Dopamine, Enkephalin

Fate (Contingency) or the Result of a Search

Multiple Sites: ACh, NE, Dyn, CCK, CRF

Each pair is Rewarded at one extreme

Drive-Coupled Dyadic Primary Emotions

Each pair is Punished at the other

I EXPECTED IT   *2. The Limbic System*   I AM SURPRISED
2. Certainty, *Clarity*   **Confusion**, *Embarrassment*

I ACCEPT IT   *Insula*   I REJECT IT
3. Attraction, *Love*   **Disgust**, *Hate*

Amygdala, BNST:CRF

I AM STRONGER   *Striatal Matching*   I AM WEAKER
4. Confidence, *Dominance*   *LC, Norepi:* **Fear**, *Submission*

FREEZE
Anxiety-Stress

I CONTROL IT   NO CONTROL
5. Relief, *Gratitude*   **Forcing, Violence**, *Anger*

If seen,

I WIN IT   I LOSE
6. Elation, *Hope, Pride*   **Grief**, *Despair, Humiliation*

FLEE
Terror

Dyadic Social Emotions
The Rewarded Impulses
3. The Cerebellar System

If free:
Unpunished, Rewarded
GIVING
9. *Generosity*

If "Family" is
HELPED   HARMED
7. *Joy*   **7.** *Guilt*

If "Family" is
HELPED   HARMED
8. *Bliss*   **8.** *Shame*

If cornered:
Unpunished, Rewarded
FIGHT
9. *Rage*

Give All to Self-Family   Celebration   Make-Restitution   Martyrdom   Suicide   Resist Giving to the Death

4. The Cerebral System, **CONSCIOUS, VOLUNTARY BEHAVIOR** *(Not Described Here)*

positive emotions as a right brain phenomenon, with the left brain showing negative emotions or emotional avoidance. This might provide a basis for interpreting the effects of the separate viewing by each side of the brain of video scenes of sex or violence in comparison to viewing emotionally neutral video scenes (Wittling, 1990; Wittling and Pfluger, 1990). No changes in mood, blood pressure, or salivary cortisol occurred when only the viewer's LH was allowed to see this strongly evocative material.

However, when only the RH was allowed to watch the sex or violence videos, there were large changes in mood and significant increases in blood pressure and in salivary cor- tisol when compared to viewing of neutral scenes (Wittling and Roschmann, 1993). This is consistent with the report of prominent alterations of EEG signals on the right side during sexual orgasm (Cohen, Rosen, Goldstein, 1976).

Dual Quadbrain Model Postulate 4. The Brain can have only one Executive Observer. Depending on which Side it is Inherently Located, the Individual will show the either Right or Left Brain-Oriented Behavior and Thinking Styles of Hemisity.

Beyond left cerebral hemisphere language dominance for about 90% of humans, and the right hemisphere non-language, spatial, temporal skill asymmetries and literalities, the existence of a unilateral executive system observer has resulted in yet another either-or phenomenon called "Hemisity". This concept is unlike the earlier, now moribund idea, called hemisphericity, where someone's personality was supposedly located somewhere on a gradient between left and right brain orientation extremes. Rather, depending on which hemisphere the unilateral executive is inherently and irreversibly imbedded, either the left or right brain thinking and behavioral orientation of hemisity results. The origin of an individual's hemisity subtype, either right or left brain-oriented, appears to be genetically determined before birth (Crowell, Jones, Kapuniai, and Nakagawa, 1973; Wada, 1977).

What does that mean in terms of individual hemisity behaviors? This will be the topic of Chapter 5.

Dual Quadbrain Model Postulate 5: Superego-like Positive Social Behaviors vs. Sadomasochistic Neurotic-Psychotic Orientations are Among the NonMotor Functions Contributed by the Paired Neocerebellum.

The Dual Quadbrain Model proposes the cerebellum as the site of an individual's vast store of experiential primary memory. This concept has considerable experimental support (Desmond, Gabrieli, Wagner, et al. 1997; Schreurs, Gusev, Tomsic, et al. 1998; Bracha, Zhao, Wunderlich, et al. 1997; Kleim, Vij, Ballard, & Greenough, 1997). Recording and retrieval to cerebral consciousness of parts of this primary lifetime cerebellar database somehow requires the participation of the hippocampus (Bontempi, Laurent-Demir, Destrade and Jaffard, 1999; Squire, Ojeman, Miezin, Petersen Videen, and Raichle, 1992; Teng and Squire, 1999).

Superego-like higher intelligence, constructive ideology, and derivative religiosity are among the non-motor functions (Schmahmann, 1991) of the more recently evolving neocerebellum (Leiner, Leiner, and Dow, 1991). Due to crossed cerebellar diaschisis, in this paired brain element some functions are contralateral (opposite in side) to those of the cerebrum (Barker, Yoshii, Loewenstein, Chang, Apicella, Pascal, Boothe, Ginsberg and Duara (1991). However, for the sake of simplicity, this is ignored here (as were other possible limbic or brain core ipsilateral vs. contralateral crossover distributions)

These Superego-Divine like properties are opposed to those of the Thanatos-like Sadomasochistic, Neurotic-Psychotic Reactive Mind with its diabolic destructive death-wish, derivative suicide, superstition, human sacrifice, and cannibalism. The "unexperienced" trauma to which the individual has been subjected without integration in early childhood, or in adulthood cases of PTSD (Post Traumatic Stress Disorder), forms the basis for the content in the reactive Mind-Pain Body . This trauma primarily includes that of developmental arrests and fixations, and the ineffective activation of the xDARP, the topic of Chapter 5 and 6.

Figure 11. summarizes the asymmetries of the opposed neocerebelli producing the opposite sur- vival behavioral logics of the Superego and Thanatos.

Contrasts between the Two Cerebellar Elements: Social Brain Source vs. the Pain Body-Reactive Mind

Making the now unavoidable assumption that all human behavior is brain-originated, what can be said

Figure 11. The Dual Quadbrain
Double Social Brain:

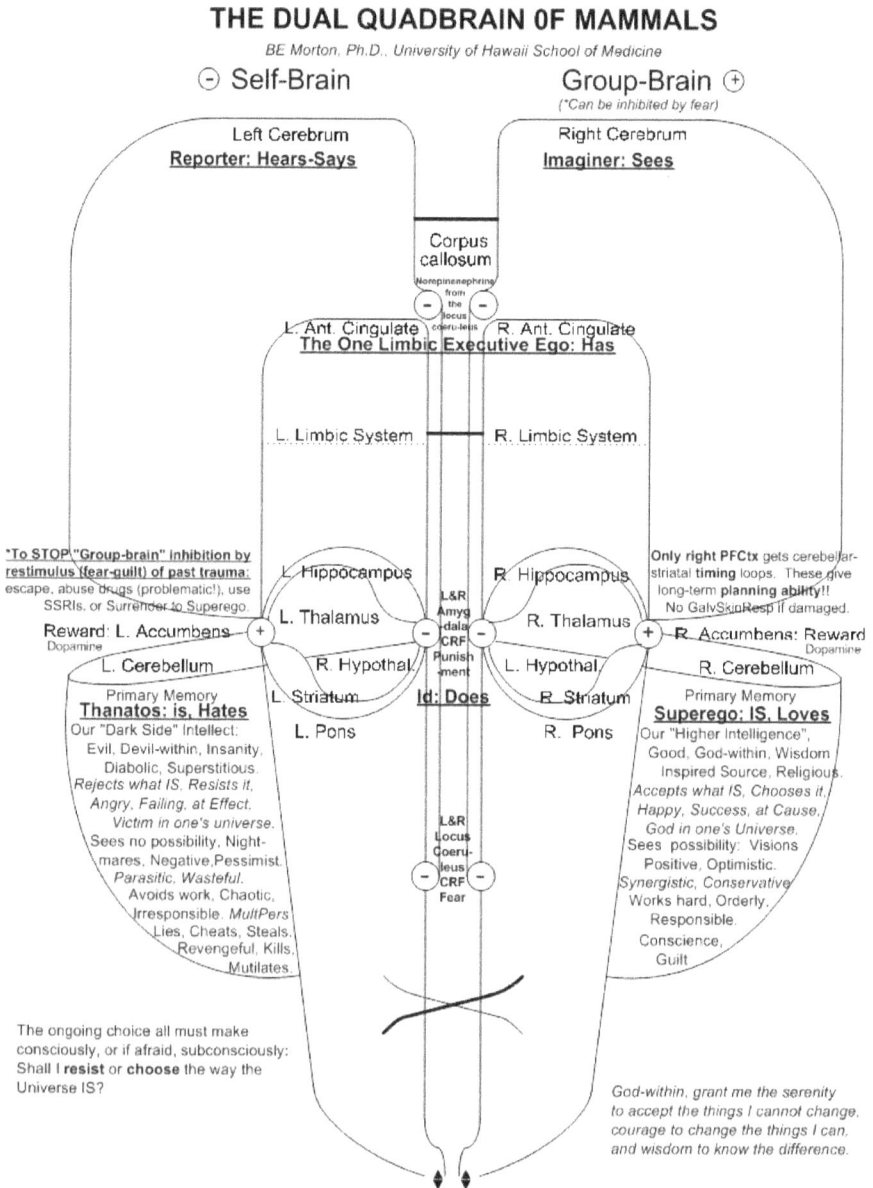

THE DUAL QUADBRAIN OF MAMMALS
BE Morton, Ph.D., University of Hawaii School of Medicine

⊖ Self-Brain   Group-Brain ⊕
(*Can be inhibited by fear)

Left Cerebrum
Reporter: Hears-Says

Right Cerebrum
Imaginer: Sees

Corpus callosum
Norepinepnephrine from the locus coeru-leus

L. Ant. Cingulate   R. Ant. Cingulate
The One Limbic Executive Ego: Has

L. Limbic System   R. Limbic System

"To STOP "Group-brain" inhibition by restimulus (fear-guilt) of past trauma: escape, abuse drugs (problematic!), use SSRIs. or Surrender to Superego.

Only right PFCtx gets cerebellar-striatal timing loops. These give long-term **planning ability!!** No GalvSkinResp if damaged.

Reward: L. Accumbens ⊕
Dopamine

L. Hippocampus   R. Hippocampus

L&R Amyg-dala CRF Punish-ment

⊕ R. Accumbens: Reward
Dopamine

L. Thalamus   R. Thalamus

L. Cerebellum
R. Hypothal / L. Hypothal
R. Cerebellum

Primary Memory
Thanatos: is, Hates
Our "Dark Side" Intellect:
Evil, Devil-within, Insanity,
Diabolic, Superstitious.
Rejects what IS. Resists it,
Angry, Failing, at Effect.
Victim in one's universe.
Sees no possibility, Night-
mares, Negative,Pessimist.
Parasitic, Wasteful.
Avoids work, Chaotic,
Irresponsible. *MultPers*
Lies, Cheats, Steals,
Revengeful, Kills.
Mutilates.

L. Striatum   **Id: Does**   R. Striatum
L. Pons   R. Pons

L&R Locus Coeru-leus CRF Fear

Primary Memory
Superego: IS, Loves
Our "Higher Intelligence",
Good, God-within, Wisdom
Inspired Source, Religious.
Accepts what IS, Chooses it,
Happy, Success, at Cause,
God in one's Universe.
Sees possibility: Visions
Positive, Optimistic.
Synergistic, Conservative.
Works hard, Orderly,
Responsible.
Conscience,
Guilt

The ongoing choice all must make consciously, or if afraid, subconsciously:
Shall I **resist** or **choose** the way the Universe IS?

God-within, grant me the serenity to accept the things I cannot change, courage to change the things I can, and wisdom to know the difference.

about the anatomical source of human behavior of the type that has been called bad, evil, sinful, hateful or diabolical? This includes nonsexual rape, sadistic torture, ritual murder, mutilation, necrophilia, cult human sacrifice and vengeful cannibalism.

People tend to deny that humans really have the potential for such society-rending behavior, and thus avoid having to think about it except perhaps under the protective sanctions of the entertainment media. Perhaps, because once fostered, such behavior seems so frighteningly close to the surface, this denial is facilitated. Individual behavior that destroys the survival of one's own species underlies all definitions of bad, wrong, sinful, evil (from the devil) or diabolic. This makes one's species-centric point- of-view a highly critical issue. For example: is roasting and eating a chicken or pig a necessity and a hereditary right? How about the same consideration for chimpanzee "bush meat" parts? Or, on the other hand, should this murder, mutilation and cannibalism of sentient beings more than justify the violence of the animal rights move- ment on behalf of domestic rodents?

In contrast, there must bc an anatomical brain source for those human behaviors we call godly, good, righteous, kind, loving, holy or divine. Such acts include generosity, benevolence, compassion, mercy, humility, nonkilling and altruism. The latter includes self-sacrifice up to and including the point of willingness to die for another, others, or even to do so for a valued religious or humanitarian cause. Social behavior dedicated to enhancing the survival of one's own species underlies all definitions of good and godliness. Again, the critical issue is the individual's definition of who the family is. Thus, the age-old problem: is self-sacrifice appropriate in behalf of one's offspring during calamity, in family feuds, or in struggles against pagans, infidels, confederates, Nazis, Vietnamese, or Somali pirates?

In the Dual Quadbrain Model of behavioral laterality, the above-defined traits of good and evil are included among the subconsciously generated non-motor behaviors of the neocerebellum, and integrated by the cerebellar vermis. The basis for this assignment comes from primate and human cerebellar lesion and implant research (Reiman, Raichle, Robins, Mintun, Fusselman, Fox, Price and Hackman, 1989; Ricklan, Cullinan, and Cooper, 1977; Heath, 1977; Heath, Llewellyn and Rouchell, 1980; Heath, Rouchell, Llewellyn, and Walker, 1981). There, use of self-stimulus with electrode implants in the cerebellar vermis transformed insane killers into the most benevolent and sociable of persons. However, temporary failure of cerebellar self-stimulation equipment, quickly released the convict with a broken brain back into a state of agitated homicide, killing his nurse with a pair of scissors.

Dual Quadbrain Model Postulate 6: Separable Id-like Dominatingly Selfish vs. Surrendered Selfless Behavioral Elements are on Either Side of the Brain Core

An evolutionarily ancient, Id-like, dominating, self-survival element within the left side of the brain stem core is associated with sympathetic nervous system based punished avoidance via flight and fight. It is convenient to call it the Dominator or Dragon Brain.

In critical contrast, paired on the right side of the brain core, is the Id-like protective, productive element, here called the Servant Brain. It predominates when the Reptile Brain has "met its match" and has surrendered to a larger reptile, or, importantly, to a more powerful higher power, either within the brain, or surrendered to an external consciousness. The Servant Brian's behavior is altruistic, cooperative, species survival-oriented, tied to parasympathetic nervous system's rewarded approach, feeding, rest, repair, and reproduction. **Figure 12** summarizes the asymmetries of the left and right lower brain elements producing these contrasting punished and rewarded Id-like behaviors.

For example: it is logical that the right brain core, through its search for similarity and relatedness would tend to perceive commonality, thus family and community that is implicit in species preservation (Henry and Wang, 1998). These would be complimented by right Id-associated cooperative social behaviors, humor, constructive support, as well as promoting Social Brain-religiosity behaviors. In contrast, the left-brain, while searching for differences, would tend to see non-family and non-related alien strangeness, together with the associated antisocial responses of anger, guilt-free conscience, and self-preservation. This could be tied to a competitive coronary type-A behavior pattern (Henry and Wang, 1998) and combativeness.

Thus, left brain-oriented individuals without adequate socialization should show more self-survival (win-lose) orientation than the group-survival (win-win) orien-

Figure 6, Dual Quadbrain Reptile Brain Partners:
THE DUAL QUADBRAIN OF MAMMALS

BE Morton, Ph.D., University of Hawaii School of Medicine

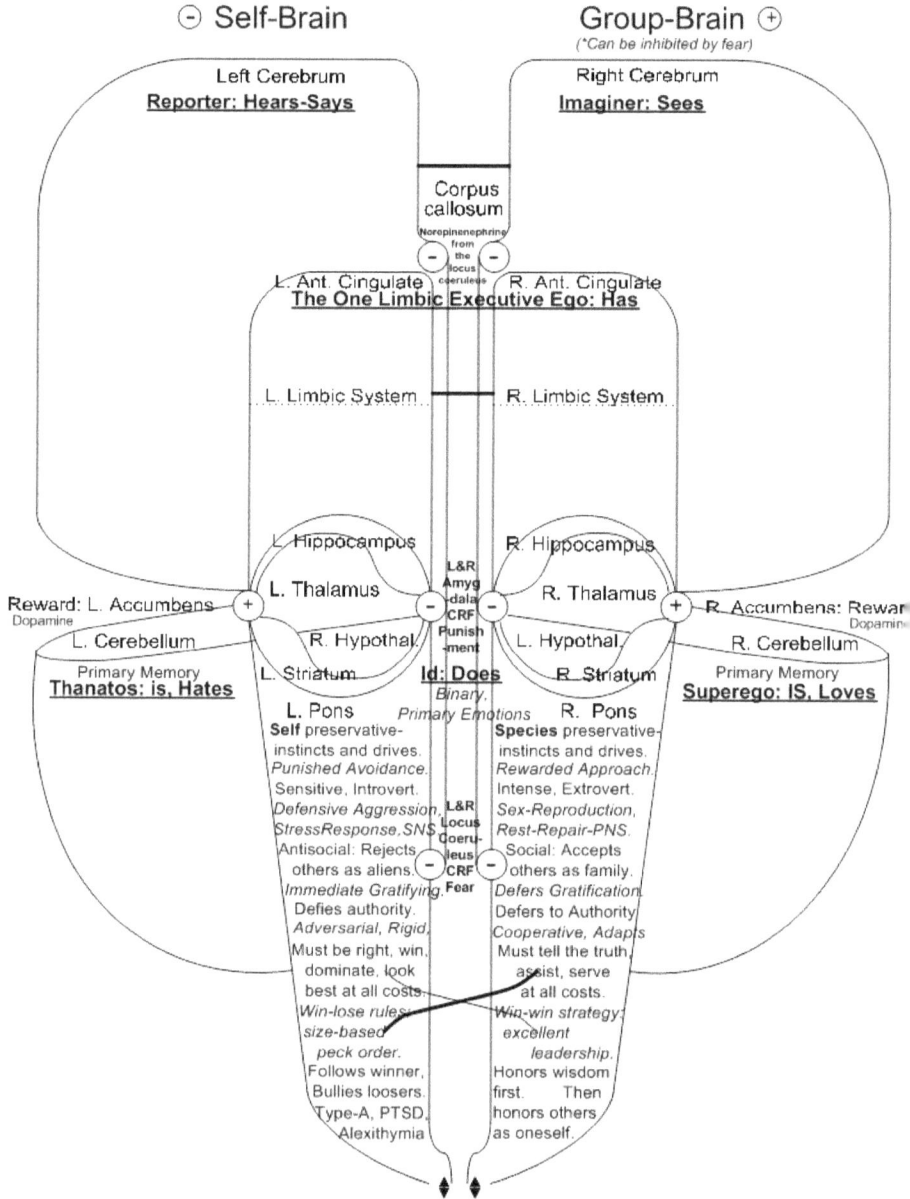

⊖ Self-Brain

Group-Brain ⊕

(*Can be inhibited by fear)

Left Cerebrum
Reporter: Hears-Says

Right Cerebrum
Imaginer: Sees

Corpus callosum

Norepinephrine from the locus coeruleus

L. Ant. Cingulate — R. Ant. Cingulate
The One Limbic Executive Ego: Has

L. Limbic System — R. Limbic System

L. Hippocampus — R. Hippocampus

L. Thalamus — R. Thalamus

L&R Amygdala
CRF
Punish-ment

Reward: L. Accumbens (+)
Dopamine

(+) R. Accumbens: Reward
Dopamine

L. Cerebellum — R. Hypothal. — L. Hypothal. — R. Cerebellum

Primary Memory
Thanatos: is, Hates

L. Striatum — **Id: Does** — R. Striatum

Primary Memory
Superego: IS, Loves

L. Pons — Binary, Primary Emotions — R. Pons

L&R Locus Coeruleus CRF Fear

Self preservative-	Species preservative-
instincts and drives.	instincts and drives.
Punished Avoidance.	Rewarded Approach.
Sensitive, Introvert.	Intense, Extrovert.
Defensive Aggression,	Sex-Reproduction,
StressResponse, SNS	Rest-Repair-PNS.
Antisocial: Rejects	Social: Accepts
others as aliens.	others as family.
Immediate Gratifying.	Defers Gratification.
Defies authority.	Defers to Authority
Adversarial, Rigid,	Cooperative, Adapts
Must be right, win,	Must tell the truth,
dominate, look	assist, serve
best at all costs.	at all costs.
Win-lose rules,	Win-win strategy:
size-based	excellent
peck order.	leadership.
Follows winner,	Honors wisdom
Bullies loosers.	first. Then
Type-A, PTSD,	honors others
Alexithymia	as oneself.

tation of their right brain associates, with higher mortality.

The left side Reptilian Brain with its selfish control mode produces the rude antisocial behaviors of, "I want it now!" (there is no past or future). "If you don't give it to me right away, I will damn well force you to, or die trying". On the other side of the brain, the surrendered, servile, altruistic Servant Brain provides, polite, "How may I serve you?", "Your wish is my command!" and applies generous, cooperative, collaborative, disciplined, powerful assistance, like a hard working sled-dog to whomever internal or external higher power it has given over its control.

Clearly, the Dual Quadbrain Model of behavioral laterality is only an organizational metaphor, a cartoon simplification of the real. At some level it must break down as inadequate to represent the actual complexity of brain and behavior, finally demanding the brain itself as the ultimate reality. One of the first levels upon which this model might be found wrong is that of the relative sidedness of subcortical elements. That is, the existence of both ipsilateral and contralateral tracts between the cortex and the cerebellum, limbic system and brain core guarantee a brain laterality that is more complex than this model.

Yet, the overall clarification of behavioral motivation, brought by the context of a self vs. species brain duality, may be a critical step required to facilitate the ultimate lateral distribution of the important anatomical details. Furthermore, the logical neuroanatomical localization within this evolutionary model of Freud's theoretical constructs of the Id, Ego, Superego and Thanatos provides an integration of human behavior which hopefully will stimulate the discovery of ever more accurate information about locations of these important behavior-generating motifs.

With this introduction to the Society of Seven defined by the Dual Quadbrain Model, we are now in the position to ask, "Who AM I? Who is in control? and Why?" in our next chapter.

CHAPTER 4: Modular Consciousness: Our Brain's Society of Seven

Getting Acquainted with the Consciousness Elements of the Brain's Society of Seven.

The creation of the Dual Quadbrain Model of Consciousness to replace the inadequate Unitive Model of Mind gives us the tools to begin a rational approach to understanding human behavior. The background development of the four levels of the Quadrimental Brain Model in Chapter 2 facilitated the introduction of their four bilateral aspects in the Dual Quadbrain Model in Chapter 3.We are now prepared to meet and develop a working relationship with each of the members of the Dual Quadbrain Model's Society of Seven, assembled in **Figure 13**, and their associated seven unique realities that alert us to their highly dynamic individual presence upon our throne of control, our cock- pit seat of power.

One might think that the upper two members really need no introduction, because one is already consciously aware of them as part of who we think we are. However, getting better acquainted with them is well worth the effort. Although they may be of either gender, they will be referred to in the masculine singular.

Figure 1: Dual Quadbrain Model of Human Consciousness

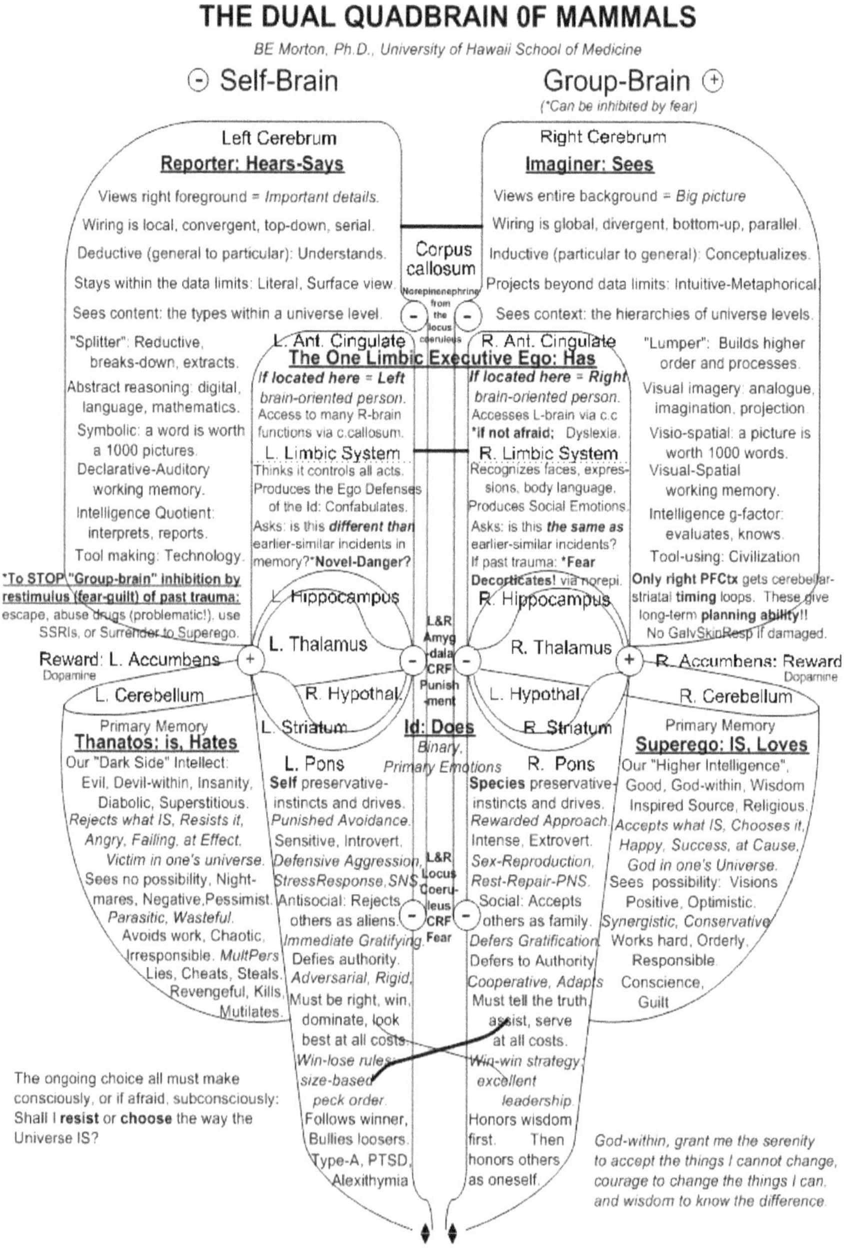

THE DUAL QUADBRAIN OF MAMMALS

BE Morton, Ph.D., University of Hawaii School of Medicine

⊖ Self-Brain   Group-Brain ⊕

(*Can be inhibited by fear)

Left Cerebrum
Reporter: Hears-Says

Views right foreground = *Important details.*

Wiring is local, convergent, top-down, serial.

Deductive (general to particular): Understands.

Stays within the data limits: Literal, Surface view.

Sees content: the types within a universe level.

"Splitter": Reductive, breaks-down, extracts.

Abstract reasoning: digital, language, mathematics. Symbolic: a word is worth a 1000 pictures. Declarative-Auditory working memory.

Intelligence Quotient: interprets, reports.

Tool making: Technology.

*To STOP "Group-brain" inhibition by restimulus (fear-guilt) of past trauma: escape, abuse drugs (problematic!), use SSRIs, or Surrender to Superego.

Reward: L. Accumbens ⊕
Dopamine

L. Cerebellum

Primary Memory
Thanatos: is, Hates

Our "Dark Side" Intellect: Evil, Devil-within, Insanity, Diabolic, Superstitious. *Rejects what IS, Resists it, Angry, Failing, at Effect. Victim in one's universe. Sees no possibility: Night-mares, Negative, Pessimist. Parasitic, Wasteful. Avoids work, Chaotic. Irresponsible. MultPers. Lies, Cheats, Steals, Revengeful, Kills, Mutilates.*

The ongoing choice all must make consciously, or if afraid, subconsciously: Shall I **resist** or **choose** the way the Universe IS?

Corpus callosum
Norepinenephrine from the locus coeruleus

L. Ant. Cingulate
The One Limbic Executive Ego: Has

If located here = Left brain-oriented person. Access to many R-brain functions via c.callosum.

L. Limbic System
Thinks it controls all acts. Produces the Ego Defenses of the Id: Confabulates. Asks: is this **different than** earlier-similar incidents in memory?*Novel-Danger?

L. Hippocampus

L. Thalamus

R. Hypothal.

L. Striatum

Id: Does
Binary.

L. Pons
Primary Emotions

Self preservative-instincts and drives. Punished Avoidance. Sensitive, Introvert. *Defensive Aggression, StressResponse, SNS Antisocial: Rejects others as aliens. Immediate Gratifying. Defies authority. Adversarial, Rigid, Must be right, win, dominate, look best at all costs. Win-lose rules size-based peck order. Follows winner, Bullies loosers. Type-A, PTSD, Alexithymia*

R. Ant. Cingulate
If located here = Right brain-oriented person. Accesses L-brain via c.c. *if not afraid; Dyslexia.

R. Limbic System
Recognizes faces, expres-sions, body language. Produces Social Emotions. Asks: is this **the same as** earlier-similar incidents? If past trauma: *Fear **Decorticates!** via norepi.

R. Hippocampus

R. Thalamus

L&R Amygdala CRF Punishment

L. Hypothal.

R. Striatum

R. Pons
Species preservative-instincts and drives. Rewarded Approach. Intense, Extrovert. *Sex-Reproduction, Rest-Repair-PNS. Social: Accepts others as family. Defers Gratification. Defers to Authority. Cooperative, Adapts Must tell the truth, assist, serve at all costs. Win-win strategy excellent leadership. Honors wisdom first. Then honors others as oneself.*

L&R Locus Coeruleus CRF Fear

Right Cerebrum
Imaginer: Sees

Views entire background = *Big picture*

Wiring is global, divergent, bottom-up, parallel.

Inductive (particular to general): Conceptualizes.

Projects beyond data limits: Intuitive-Metaphorical.

Sees context: the hierarchies of universe levels.

"Lumper": Builds higher order and processes.

Visual imagery: analogue, imagination, projection. Visio-spatial: a picture is worth 1000 words. Visual-Spatial working memory.

Intelligence g-factor: evaluates, knows.

Tool-using: Civilization

Only right PFCtx gets cerebellar-striatal timing loops. These give long-term **planning ability**!! No GalvSkinResp if damaged.

R. Accumbens: Reward ⊕
Dopamine

R. Cerebellum

Primary Memory
Superego: IS, Loves

Our "Higher Intelligence": Good, God-within, Wisdom Inspired Source, Religious. *Accepts what IS, Chooses it, Happy, Success, at Cause. God in one's Universe. Sees possibility: Visions Positive, Optimistic. Synergistic, Conservative Works hard, Orderly, Responsible. Conscience, Guilt*

God-within, grant me the serenity to accept the things I cannot change, courage to change the things I can, and wisdom to know the difference.

1. Dr. Imagination of the Right Cerebral Hemisphere

First, say hello to right brain Dr. Imagination. He brilliantly produces succinct visions of the best and worst options available to you right now under your specific circumstances: from your heart's desires to your worst nightmares. His sole purpose is to provide, if you will only take the time to look, what are your best immediate opportunities as well as what are your best long-term choices to optimize your survival and/or that of your family. He also provides you warnings of harmful things, actions, situations or contexts to avoid. The reality orientation of Dr. Imagination is that of self-conscious External Reality, unless he is taken over by another more powerful member of the Society of Seven.

2. Mr. Reporter of the Left Cerebral Hemisphere

Next, greet left brain Mr. Reporter. Talk about the production of sounds and words to describe the visions of Dr. Imagination: this is what the language brain reporter does best! From the simplest to the most abstract, Mr. Reporter strives always to have the right words or symbols available for you to think or say. The millions of words in your primary memory that it has already heard or read are availa- ble for you to draw upon. Mr. Reporter also knows well the language and rules of numbers, and can grasp the com- plex concepts within each context. Mr. Reporter's mind is occupied with our ever expanding Internal Reality model of External Reality. That includes self-conscious- ness: its consciousness of itself and its own thoughts.

It is very easy to mistakenly identify oneself with Dr. Imagination or Mr. Reporter because the way they think constitutes our usual consciousness. However, once we take a transformational step in our maturation to discover who we really are, we will be delighted to see that they are actually our loyal indispensable consultants: intellectual, articulate and imaginative.

3. Mr. Executive Ego Within the Limbic System

Although you may not know him or her very well, your Executive Ego, source of will power, is your special person. Like a foreman or contractor, you have placed him in charge of the intimate details required to maintain and successfully run your living estate. The reality of the Executive Ego is Survival Reality. He is really smart and has repeatedly been shown to make subconscious survival-optimizing decisions a second or more before your Intellect and Language consultants even become aware of them (Libet,1983). These "bottom-line", "the buck stops here" decisions of your Executive Ego, make a second by second difference between your life or death.

If your Executive Ego is on the left side of your brain, he is more intimately associated with Mr. Reporter and its abstract reasoning. Yet, your Executive also has information transfer lines across the corpus callosum connecting with Dr. Imagination on the other side of the brain as well. In contrast, if your Executive is on the right side of your right brain, he works hand in hand with Dr. Imagination, but keeps close tabs on Mr. Reporter via other lines back across the corpus callosum.

Your Executive Ego is a Society of Seven member of great feelings, especially fear of death and joy of life, and uses these to motivate its subcontractors by use of rewarding (attracting) or punishing (causing avoidance) primary or derivative emotions (Chapter 2). If your Executive is in good shape, he can overpower any opposition among his subcontractors. However, if your Executive is injured, weak or sickly, he cannot always force his Id or Superego to follow his orders or to keep them from becoming unruly or rebellious. This is especially true of the more destructive left side members of both the Reptile Brain core and the cerebellar (anti) Social Brain.

The Bilateral Brain Core Reptilian Id

Freud's Reptilian Id is also split bilaterally and resides on both sides of the brain core. As the first brain level to evolve, it is the only paired brain element who actually has direct access to all the levers, wheels, switches and dials that control life. The Id literally keeps all your cells alive every second of every day. It takes this job very seriously and will fight any outside cellular homeostasis stressor to the death. It is completely in charge of our survival at each universe level, from the molecular through subcellular, cellular, tissue, organ, up to and including that of the living human being. As we will see, all other behavioral sources must work through the Id to change our behavior.

The left side of the brain core is specialized in competition: defending us and winning battles against non-family enemies using the strategy of "Win-Lose". We call it the **Dominator-brain,** or other synonyms, such as Dragon-brain, Wolf-brain, or **Negative Id**. On the right side of the brain core, the friendly, faithful dog-like **Servant Brain,** or **Positive Id** is specialized in cooperation, utilizing the emergent property advantages of the "Win-Win" strategy as a committed member of the family team. With this in mind, let's meet each of these two brain core Id partners. These bilateral Id elements will be described next.

4. Mr. Dominator, Id of the Left Brain Core

Occupying the left side of the Id, salute Mr. Dominator. He uses your body very skillfully and successfully to protect you against alien competitors, such as rats, snakes, and hyenas. Did I mention thieves, rapists, and assassins? Although the Mr. Dominator can be male or female, as you can see, it is quite an impressive physical specimen. He is the force that powerfully protects us from our enemies and accomplishes all of your behavioral de sires.

However, he is dreadfully inept at working within groups of humans. He is generally rude, nasty and upset. He must always be right, win, dominate and control everybody, and will fight viciously to do so. He will only give in and surrender to a winner who is bigger or more powerful than he is. He is totally inept at knowing how to optimize the survival of groups of at the next higher universe level, because he only knows the self laws of the one-on-one competition level, such as on monkey island where "sh-t runs downhill". In addition, as we have seen these laws are totally the opposite and harmful for optimizing the survival of the group and society.

If your Executive Ego fails to prevent Mr. Dominator from becoming upset, taking over, and thus from doing antisocial harm, the Executive tries to avoid responsibility for his or her failure to control him. He does so, by making excuses for Mr. Dominator's bad behavior, using some of the 16 Ego Defenses of the Id (Chapter 2), such as denial or projection, all of which are lies. When you hear such rationalizations coming out of your mouth, you need to recognize that your Executive Ego is becoming too weak to prevent your Mr. Dominator from taking over your throne and doing antisocial harm. Then, you need quickly to go about finding ways to strengthen him or her. The Executive Ego can best go off line and rest during REM sleep or during certain types of therapy.

As mentioned above, it takes a tough Executive Ego to handle a raging Mr. Dominator. However, a strong Executive, by use of his powerful emotions, can calm and replace Mr. Dominator with the other side of the brain core, Mr. Servant, as the willing doer of his commands (see below).

5. My Faithful Servant, Trusted Friend of the Brain Core on the Right

Anciently and still today, when Mr. Dominator meets someone he recognizes to be more powerful, he refuses to fight and be killed by that more powerful entity. Instead, he makes strong obeisance-submission signals and surrenders. By doing so he is in essence saying that rather than die, he is willing to give you anything and everything he has, even including the surrender of all his or her money, property, spouse, and kids. In exchange for being allowed to live, he is promising to work loyally for your Executive Ego, even to give his or her life to defend and protect you, nothing held back. Now that's real surrender!

Anciently, at the reptilian stage of evolution, this was literally the case. All who did not surrender to and support the leader were violently exterminated. As Quadrimental Brain layers were added, this surrender to external higher powers was extended to the internally more powerful Executive Ego, who itself could defer too higher members of the Society of Seven,, or gain to more powerful external forces, i.e., to dominant persons, or institutions. Under these circumstances, the imbalance of power is so great in Mr. Dominator's mind that his only choice is to surrender or die.

By surrendering, he transforms into a trusting, reliable servant. This transformation is so complete, that he takes on a new personality, like that of a once snarling wolf turned into a lover-dog, man's best friend. If you treat that dog right, he will do anything for your love and acceptance. Meet your dog-like Servant Brain. As your former internal enemy, he has surrendered to become your best friend. Without hesitation, he will delightedly do anything you ask, or die trying. Clearly, it becomes very unwise to kill someone who, when surrendered to your Executive Ego, becomes such an loyal, empathetic, committed and valuable ally, side-kick.

What is Good? What is Bad? It Depends Upon Which Universe Level is Involved

In this chapter we bring clarity to the eternal battle waging within each of us: that of "Good" vs. "Evil." Again we are drawn to the bilateral nature of the brain, one side devoted to our own self-survival, the other to survival of our family and species. At the foundation of this conflict are the ever-present structural levels of the universe, treated more extensively in my book "Neuroreality". That is, elements in each lower level, when combined create the next higher level. For example, a combination of cells at the cellular level creates the tissue level. A combination of tissues creates the organ level. A combination of organs creates the organism level. And, a combination of organisms creates a family, society, or species level.

A key fact is that the laws that are required for life and "good" for the occupants of a specific level, are totally inappropriate ("evil") to the unique requirements for life of those at the next higher or lower level. And, the laws that are unique and work for that next higher level, do not work and thus harm the level above (or below) that. For example cells need to be in an environment of controlled pH and ionic strength or they will rupture. In contrast, tissues are tolerant to pH and ionic strength, but need to be protected from shear forces or they will be disintegrated. Organs don't need narrow pH, ionic, or shear protection, but require oxygenated blood or they will fail. Organisms have their own blood supply, but need food and shelter or they will die. Families, societies, or species require re-production and protection from injury or they will become extinct.

What is remarkable about the brain is that it supplies optimal environments for each of our body many universe layers, from that of the subcellular to that of the family, society, and species. However, these brain many operations occur outside of our awareness, except at the level of our self and that of our social relations. What is unrecognized is that the laws that are required for our self-survival in the jungle, are totally opposite to those we need to survive well with others. That is, it is often correct to fight, maim, and kill snakes and hyenas in order not to be eaten. However at the level of family and society, these are called antisocial behaviors and punished by isolation, ostracism, incarceration, or execution as totally inappropriate. In contrast, behaviors appropriate for our interaction with children and mates, such as "Here, let me help you", "I can wait for my share until you have yours," would result in sheer death in the jungle.

One side of our brain core Id is highly specialized to deal with self-survival by tooth and claw. I call it the "Dominator-brain" among other things. It is the source of violence. It plays by the antisocial laws of "Win-Lose". The other side, "Servant-Brain" ,our ever-loving, faithful friend, is equally devoted to our group's survival by the "Golden rule: Do unto others what you would have them to do to you" or its reciprocal negative statement "Don't do unto others what you would not like them to do to you." Those need to be recognized as "Win-Win or No Deal" principles appropriate for living at peace and acceptance of others.

When well and strong, our Executive Ego

Figure 14
Sources of Killing vs. Nonkilling Behavior

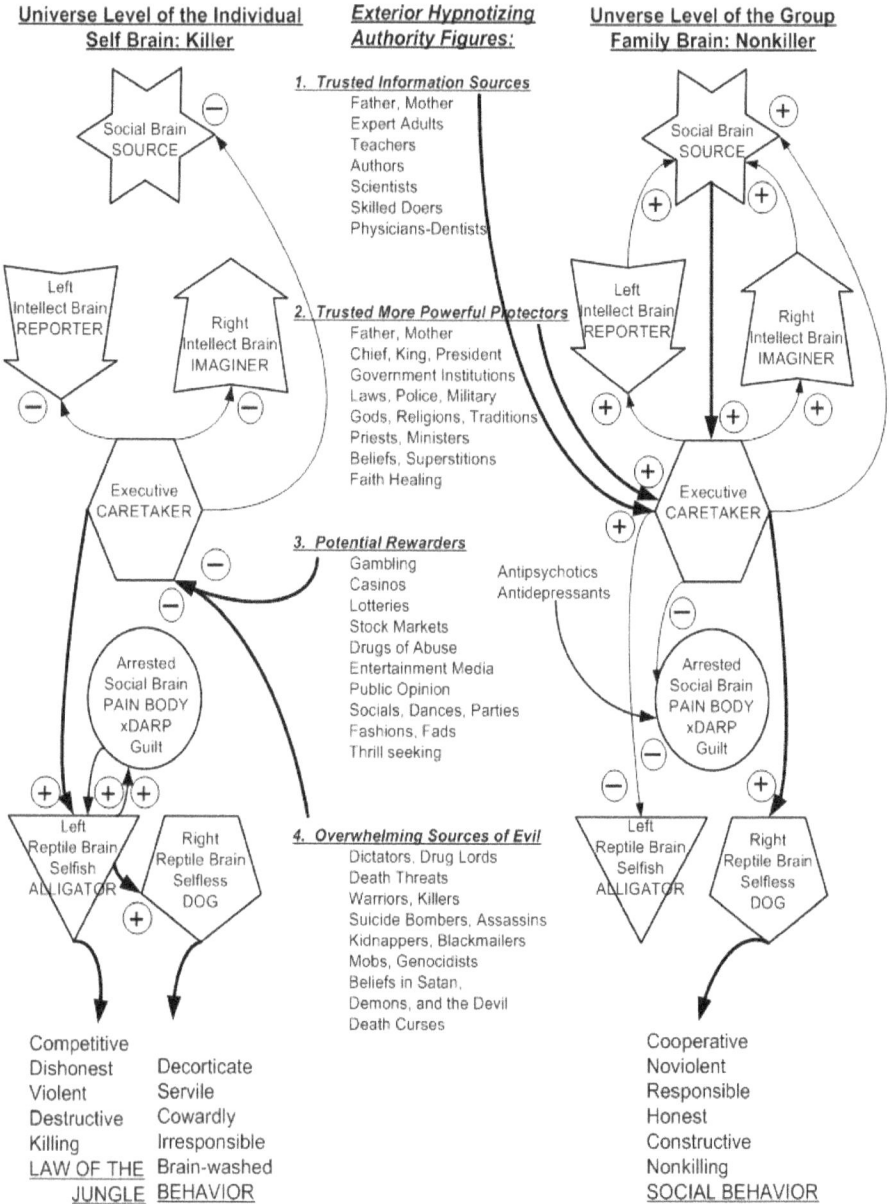

Universe Level of the Individual
Self Brain: Killer

Exterior Hypnotizing
Authority Figures:

Unverse Level of the Group
Family Brain: Nonkiller

Social Brain
SOURCE (−)

Social Brain
SOURCE (+) (+) (+)

1. Trusted Information Sources
Father, Mother
Expert Adults
Teachers
Authors
Scientists
Skilled Doers
Physicians-Dentists

Left Intellect Brain
REPORTER

Right Intellect Brain
IMAGINER (−)
(−)

Left Intellect Brain
REPORTER (+)

Right Intellect Brain
IMAGINER (+) (+)

2. Trusted More Powerful Protectors
Father, Mother
Chief, King, President
Government Institutions
Laws, Police, Military
Gods, Religions, Traditions
Priests, Ministers
Beliefs, Superstitions
Faith Healing

Executive
CARETAKER (−)

Executive
CARETAKER (+) (+)

3. Potential Rewarders
Gambling
Casinos
Lotteries
Stock Markets
Drugs of Abuse
Entertainment Media
Public Opinion
Socials, Dances, Parties
Fashions, Fads
Thrill seeking

Antipsychotics
Antidepressants

Arrested
Social Brain
PAIN BODY
xDARP
Guilt (−)

Arrested
Social Brain
PAIN BODY
xDARP
Guilt (−) (−) (+)

(+) (+) (+)

Left Reptile Brain
Selfish
ALLIGATOR

Right Reptile Brain
Selfless
DOG (+)

Left Reptile Brain
Selfish
ALLIGATOR (−)

Right Reptile Brain
Selfless
DOG (+)

4. Overwhelming Sources of Evil
Dictators, Drug Lords
Death Threats
Warriors, Killers
Suicide Bombers, Assassins
Kidnappers, Blackmailers
Mobs, Genocidists
Beliefs in Satan,
Demons, and the Devil
Death Curses

Competitive
Dishonest
Violent
Destructive
Killing
LAW OF THE
JUNGLE

Decorticate
Servile
Cowardly
Irresponsible
Brain-washed
BEHAVIOR

Cooperative
Noviolent
Responsible
Honest
Constructive
Nonkilling
SOCIAL BEHAVIOR

objectively decides which brain side to assign to which project. Shall it be the Dominator-brain that deals with our enemies or the Servant-brain, to help our friends. When our Exec- utive Ego becomes ill and weak, it is overpowered by the Dominator-brain and we become very unfriendly and an- tisocial, even violent.

Competition vs. Cooperation: With who and when?

Figure 14 illustrates the two opposite behavioral motifs this Society of Seven team can produce. That is, if the Execu- tive Ego judges that individual competitive behavior is called for, the Dominator-brain becomes activated. If, in contrast it judges that social behavior is the more appropriate response, then empathic Servant-brain behavior emerges. On the left of the figure, the Executive has in- voked an emergency survival response by activating the selfish Dominator-brain into action. This results in instinct driven combative violent behavior with a potential of escalation to killing force. This essentially decorticate behavior occurs when we become really upset. It is the unplanned, untrained, instinctual and animal-like destructive rage response whose effectiveness has been honed by eons of survival of the fittest by tooth and claw.

In remarkable contrast, if the Executive concludes that social issues require solving, it strongly inhibits the Dominator-brain and instead activates the unselfish Servant-brain to produce a completely differ- ent set of behaviors that are cooperative, honest, peaceful, constructive and responsible: absolutely nonviolent.

Because our Executive often does not have the answers for what to do next to optimize survival, it can defer to external sources of greater information or greater protection. In the center of **Figure 14** lists some External Au- thorities to whom the Executive can give over our control. In the first category, it seeks more information. In so do- ing, it will draw upon many outside authorities. It does this first by rote memorization of other's ideas, often uncritically incorporating their viewpoints as "the truth". The more established and thus trusted an authority is, the more likely our Executive will have faith in them and assimilate their truth as our own. If our external sources are good, we can benefit from this. However, not all external sources are trustworthy.

Some persons are so habituated to surrendering to an external authority source that they never really developtheir own abilities to think for themselves beyond their own childhood beliefs. Unfortunately for them, the Inner Reality or Cultural Memes delivered by many external Controllers is far from the truth of External Reality. The Executive Ego of such a gullible person has become too lazy, or too overwhelmed, to accept facts staring them in the face. In laboratory experiments, many people prefer to believe the grossly deviant answers of a unknowingly sup- plied erroneous pocket calculator, than the obvious facts. Many people would rather hypnotically trust without question an ignorant, minimum-wage clerk's opinion in a shopping mall, than think for themselves. Sadly, this unwillingness to think for themselves extends into many social areas of importance including which authority we should believe.

If there is an external controller that is more powerful than we are, who can also supply us with protection that makes things safer, the Executive's judgment problem compounds itself. Does it trust the laws of our land and those enforcing them as working for our best interests?

We all know how either very good or how incredibly bad that can be. Similarly, does our Executive believe in our reli- gious leaders, support their building and other projects with our funds, and trust our children and youth with them? Alternatively, might there be a num- ber of hidden conflicts of interests that can drain, harm, or even kill us. Whom do you trust? It also appears that in the area of an- swers to the Big Questions, Our Serv- ant brain, with its Cultural Reality is the most gullible to these abstract issues and must be alerted to rely upon our Executive Ego's informed judgments assisted by our cor- tical intellects.

It is of great interest that our Executive has been shown to trust questionable external controllers and takegreat risks in order to obtain potentially great, but very im-probable rewards. This is both good and bad, and again requires intelligent judgment calls. How is the potential thrill of hitting the jackpot in a casino different than win- ning in the stock market? Again, intelligence, education and information are required. Some of our Ex- ecutive Egos would even entrust, and often lose, our life's savings under the direction a confident, but highly conflicted stock broker, one perhaps referred by a trust- ed friend, rather than doing the required homework and taking personal responsibility.

Many of our Executive Egos are so starved for pleasure and relief from subconscious stress that they will give over our control to a popular drug and completely ab- dicate responsibility for their intoxicated behavior. We also crave love and approval as true symbols of a high sur- vival state. In usually futile attempts to gain these, we go- to great lengths to invest in the latest entertainment or styl- ish fads, not recognizing that this behavior is about as likely to increase our survival, as winning a lottery would. We keep throwing bad money after good in investing in fine wines, fashionable clothes and jewelry, Broadway plays, elaborate home theaters, thrill toys, exotic vacations, blindly trusting these external controllers will give us the happiness and love we blindly seek. Parenthetically, with the Dual Quadbrain Model one can approach these addictions directly.

Further, the Executive Ego of most anybody will collapse in the presence of the overwhelming force of harm or evil. Panic activation of our reptilian "surrender or die" programs can overpower even the most intelligent of people. The fear inculcated by the personal threat of death by the Nazi and Communist Parties turned those wonderfully brilliant and developed German and Russian peoples into decorticate, servile slaves who would rather follow orders and kill, than responsibly resist at the cost of being killed themselves. Because of their terror, they were totally surrendered to, and fully supported demands of their ruthless external controllers. It is now nearly 80 years after the Second World War in Europe. Let us never forget the 6 million Jews, 20 million Russians, 10 million Christians and 1,900 Catholic priests who were murdered, massacred, raped, burned, starved and humiliated while the terrified German and Russian peoples looked the other way! Tragically, both historically and prehistorically many similar regimes of terror have left their bloody scars around the world over the ages.

Most humans suffer from violence and sincerely wish to do something about it. Here is where one's philosophy or religion can result in misguided righteous self-sacrifice to kill the alien non-believer. If one believes erroneous spiritual answers to The Big Questions that declare this present bitter life is only a dream; and that our true goal and reward is immortality in the hereafter, then, as we see, many people will drop all personal responsibility, willingly becoming suicidal instruments of death. Unfor- tunately, their genuine desires for the greater good of man- kind have allowed them to convert themselves into mind- less externally controlled robots of death instead, bringing even greater harm to humanity. A more accurate under- standing of external reality and the answers to the Big Questions would have directed their desire to be of service into much more beneficial non-violent paths.

6. Mr. Sadomasochist, the Pain Body of the Dark Side of our Cerebellum

Next, I will introduce you to the most unrecognized, but powerfully disruptive and internally stressful member of our brain's Society of Seven. Mr. Sadomasochist was first called the Reactive Mind (Hubbard, 1950). As we will see, is also synonymous with Tolle's (2005) Pain Body, and with the Morton's (2011) xDARP, described in later chapters of this book. As the perfect victim, rejecting the way the universe works, he will neither acknowledge your existence nor extend you a hand in friendship. Zero empathy!

The size and activity of Mr. Sadomasochist depends upon the degree of one's exposure to physical trauma and developmental thwarting circumstances much earlier in our life. Although most of this occurred during our first three years, some occurred later, especially during adolescence and war. For those fortunate to have experienced little developmental trauma, Mr. Sadomaso-chist can be very small and asleep most of the time.

However, for many of us who have been signifi-cantly arrested developmentally, it can be huge, cyclically rebellious, and very disruptive to home and family. This is especially true if during your very early years, you were caused to feel the pain inherent in being blocked from doing what we needed to do in order to complete your development. Then, in adulthood Mr. Sadomaso-chist can awaken ravenously hungry and must feed. He thrives upon a diet of pain of all types, especially on the psychological pain it recreates by subconsciously age-regressing to traumatic incidents of loss of control in the past.

After a day or two of feeding by stirring up such pain and creating such a crisis that we again feel like we might die, Mr. Sadomasochist finally becomes sated and goes back to sleep for a little while. However, soon it awakens, famished and in need of more pain. The brain based Mr. Sadomasochist is the origin of the theme ap-pearing so many times in literature, and in our lives such as the oscillating replacement of cooperative Dr. Jekyl by the murderous Mr. Hyde. Other examples are Christ vs. Satan Good vs. Evil, or more practically speaking, by cy-clically converting an angelic wife into a demon, thus repeatedly transforming heaven into hell.

The dangerous thing about Mr. Sadomasochist is that by taking over Dr. Intellect and Mr. Reporter he or she ironically tricks our Executive Ego into erroneously think-ing that our pain body *is exactly who we are. This is me*! When so fooled, we will not, cannot do anything

other than act out its twisted lies of past rejection in a cycle of endless struggle for control of our dearest important others. In fact, not to do so would seem to be denying the very essence of who we are.

Our "important-others", the targets of Mr. Sadomasochist's rejecting lies, take this seriously and fight back against his or her cyclic attacks. Then, Mr. Sadomasochist creates and feeds on the intense pain from the resulting unremitting rejection of our dearest friends and relatives. After each Pain Body feeding frenzy, we feel more damaged personally, and are remorseful that we have degraded and damaged those closest to us. And, as we inevitably continue to participate in its cyclic feeding frenzies, while unable to understand or resist it, some of us can end up hurting and ultimately driving away all those whom we love the most, committing crimes of passion, and ultimately having a nervous breakdown outside or within a prison or hospital.

The existence of this seemingly death-oriented(Freud's *thanatos*), diabolical member of our brain's So- ciety of Seven has driven many to drink, drugs and suicide. Mr. Sadomasochist's reality is Reactive Reality. Some- times, after "bottoming out", our Executive Ego surren- ders control into the arms of our "God" (Within), our Higher Power, our all wise Source, (the seventh member of our Society of Seven), seeking protection and redemp- tion from Mr. Sadomasochist's demonic and corrupting power. This results in conversion and transformation of the individual beyond something he or she would have ever been; the topic of later chapters in this book.

It is ironic that the biological existence of our Mr. Sadomasochist is the result of a recent evolutionary mis- take, which we will unravel in the next chapters. An unmutated Developmental Arrest Repair Program (DARP) once served our psychosocial development in the finest of ways. Now, it is broken and has become the primary source of the neuroses and psychoses that are driving the world mad.

7. The Social Brain SOURCE, the Life-giving Side of the Cerebellum

How can one be introduced to one's hidden, most amazing Source, one's God Within? Most of us are com- pletely unaware of the existence within us of this most de- veloped and subtle member of our brain's Socie- ty of Seven. Rarely in our lifetime do we even catch faint glimmers of the awe of IT. Yet, IT reigns over the vast trillions of cells that hold our Primary Memory within the cerebellum. To those sensitive individuals whose Executive is located on the left side of their brain, the thought of meeting their God Within can be terrifying. Indeed, as the source of guilt pain as administered as punishment for the evil of harming the survival of others, it can indeed be overwhelming. Yet in contrast, for those intense people, whose Executive is on the right, are for some yet unknown reason less threatened by strong emotion. They often actually seek to find and know God with some success. Interestingly, each of the eight world religions was founded by one of these right brainers (Chapter 10).

Now, the ancient route to the discovery of one's Social Brain Source has become clear and traversable by individuals of both hemisities. This is a transformative journey, because once you meet your Source, you can but only throw yourself on the ground before Its perfection and purity, and begin to clean up your life in response. Then, you too will joyfully surrender to that Higher Power, God-Within, Holy Spirit, who has your purpose, your plan and the power to achieve it. You are never the same again be- cause by having your eyes opened to Its exist- ence you will have become irreversibly transformed, (the "saved" of cer- tain religions.) Then, you know who you are and why you are here. Yet, our Social Brain Source is not supernatural in any way. It is our genetic inheritance. It producesEm- pathic Reality and has the non-supernatural answers to our global problems and can, by turning off the xDARP, bring peace, harmony, and ful-fillment in our lives here on earth and naturally lead us to the stars of our future.

In review, **Table 1** lists the seven members of the Society of Seven whom together produce our behavior.

Three Kinds of Pain: Physical, Psychological, and Guilt

The attempt to avoid physical pain by the Domina-tor Id is in stark contrast to our left cerebellar Mr. Sado- maso-chist's mental age-regression to painful earlier peri- ods of failure in an attempt to gain control of a develop-mental process, or to our right cerebellar Source's deliber-ate production of guilt pain. Fortunately for humanity, there are higher internal powers among each person's So-ciety of Seven, who normally can conquer and convert the selfish Mr. Dominator into our own willing selfless Mr. Servant, the one who does all the actual work. However, there are also many often unrecognized external powers outside of us, who also can attempt to demand our surren-der and to claim our loyalty. Because of this, our Reporter

Society of Seven Member	Type of Reality	Brain Element
1. Imagination	External Reality	Right Hemisphere *Concrete Visualizer*
2. Reporter	Internal Reality	Left Hemisphere *Abstract Reasoner*
3. Executive Ego	Survival Reality	Unilateral *.LimbicExecutive*
4. Dominator	Dream Reality	Left Striatum *Reptile Brain*
5. Servant	Cultural Meme Reality	Right Striatum *Reptile Brain*
6. Sadomasochist	xDARP Reality	Left Cerebellum *Thanatos*
7. Source-Purity Conscience	Empathic Reality	Right Cerebellum *Eros*

and Imaginer must be well educated to tell our Caretaker to whom he should or should not give over our control?

Quadrimental Brain Balance

Clearly, the recognition of the Dual Quadbrain Model's value in understanding human behavior opens many crucial new doors. The present lengthy discussion only begins to scratch the surface. When the Dual Quadbrain is aligned, as in **Table 2**, cooperative, conservative, nonkilling, highly able behavior appears. When the Dual Quadbrain misaligns, it becomes the source of antisocial behavior leading to conflict, aggression, and killing.

Table 2, Bottom-up, Top-Down Brain Hierarchy of Behavioral Control:

A. The Reptilian Brain is the sole producer of ALL behavior of the organism, be it via:
    1. The cooperative Servant Brain
        a. Except in an "Emergency" when its instinctive Dominator Brain behavior takes over.
            1) The weaker Ego is, the lesser the degree of danger that constitutes an Emergency.
    2. The competitive Dominator Brain in an Emergency.
    3. The xDARP-Pain Body, if it is for long in the presence of a loving (safe) friend or mate.
        a. As directed by the xDARP Pain Body by transference, seeking to complete arrested psychosocial developmental control form the past (infancy, childhood).
            1) Through transference, age regression, and reactivation of an ancient struggle. (see later in this book).

B. If alone and no Emergency has been perceived, the Servant Brain defers its control to the Executive Ego

C. The Executive judges and decides whether to direct the Servant Brain itself or to assign responsibility for its control to one of four higher options:
    1. To the Imagination of the right cerebral hemisphere: projects Worst-Best possible outcomes.
        a. Autosuggestion is available here, via imagery and strong commands.
    2. To the Intellect of the left cerebral hemisphere: source of abstract reasoning, mathematics and language.
        a. If the Executive Ego is weak: the product is *subjective* rationalizing thought.
        b. If the Executive Ego is strong: the product is pure *objective* logic.
    3. To the wisdom and insight of the Social Brain Source.
        a. via meditation and prayer for guidance from our God-Within, Higher Power.
    4.To an External Authority: Parent, Teacher, Chief, Laws, King, Priest, "God".
        a. This is the basis of Hypnosis: Assumptive learning from "Authorities"
        b. Faith Healing and Death Curses.

D. The Reptile Brain then obeys this external "Higher Power"

If alcohol and drugs are used block cerebellar conscience and guilt pain, then many other of our

Social Brain's skills will also be blocked, resulting in competi- tive, violent, short-sighted behavior, multiple breakdowns, and failure. Thus, as may be seen, brain system balance is logical and is knowable. Nobody expected understanding and predicting human behavior to be relatively simple. However, it now no longer is a mystery. In addition to the above dynamics, behavioral output can also be altered by the already well known factors of **Table 3.**

So, What's the Answer?: Who Am I? Who is in Control of My Behavior?

It is liberating to know that who I am turns out to be whichever element of my brain's Society of Seven (or those Exterior Controllers) that is dominant, ascendant and on the throne of my control cockpit at the present moment. I am that! At first, these seven states and their associated unique realities all seem the same to me. Thus, I am my rage, I am my compassion, I am my beliefs, or I "I bow to my God-Within Who I AM". As I in crease in maturity, I began to recognize that I have some control as to whom I place on the throne to be who I am. Although my automatic thoughts and feelings may be strong, I do not have to be them. This is liberating because, unobstructed, those very thoughts and feelings can place my Dominator Brain or Sadomasochistic Brain in control of me right now. Then I will have to take the later negative consequences of "my" emergent antisocial rejecting, "killing" behavior and the consequent harm I am doing to you now by allowing my Dominator brain to rule, reject you and struggle with you as my enemy. Instead, I have a brief period of a choice. By declaration, I can prevent

Table 3, Additional Factors Determining Which Brain Element is in Control

A. <u>Genetics and/or Development,</u> such as that producing Affective Illnesses, Alzheimer's Disease, Huntington's Disease, dyslexia, autism, or altered sexual identity.

B. <u>Nonlethal Brain Injuries,</u> such as infection, trauma, stroke, tumor, surgery, schizophrenia, and Parkinson's Disease.

C. <u>Psychoactive Drugs and/or Magnetic Probes</u> – Alcohol and other pain- killing drugs of abuse, and by LSD and other hallucinogens.

D. <u>Cellular Homeostatic Stress,</u> such as loss of control of access to air, water, fuel, sleep, rest, shelter, job, family members or support, blood glucose, tryptophan depletion, etc.

E. <u>Cultural Memes</u> associated with Suggestion and Hysteria: Media-based or personal rumors, war, famine, faith healing, hypnosis, spirit possession, death curses, or riots

---

Mr. Dominator from gaining control of me, and rather elevate my Social Brain Source to the throne. I then become it, with very different emergent behavior towards you: that of acceptance and "nonkilling" synergy.

To accept another just as they are, and just as they are

and exactly as they are not" has been an edifying definition of love. This is the acceptance and understanding we desperately seek from our mates, family, friends, and religion. This deep craving is manifest in the quality we project onto at least one of our many manufactured gods: our belief that the son of God hates the sin but loves the sinner, that God made me, that he wants me, that He knows my every strength and weakness, and loves even me.

By awareness and practice, I can lengthen that original microsecond that I have before my upset Dominator takes over and kills, giving me increasing opportunity to replace it with my totally responsible Source, and not get upset. As will be described in later chapters, we can become increasingly conscious of our power of choice as to who we are, by the means of the one whom we place in charge. As a result, reptilian upsets with life that now may be breaking through hourly to defeat us, can be so weakened that they only occur daily, then only weekly, only monthly, yearly, then not at all. Many people have accomplished this. It is the beginning of happiness.

Recent fMRI reports have noted high cerebellar activity during control of behavior by "another", that of an external controlling hypnotist. Recipients of faith healing comment on feelings of "heat" at the base of their skull (from their cerebellar Source). Does surrender to one's higher power to activate the cerebellar Social Brain, one's God Within, to come forward? If so, can this be done? More later.....

Some Concepts:

1. There is a control-module "Throne" in our mind, which can be occupied moment by moment by whichever is the most dominant member of our Society of Seven separate consciousness systems of the Dual Quadbrain at that time.

2. Regardless of which member of the Society of Seven is in power, at first it all seems to be the same as me. Through education, training and practice, I can increasingly recognize and influence which entity presently retains control over my mind and behavior, thus to best optimize my survival and that of my family.

3. The conscious entities that can occupy my mind include the following:

    a. Imagination (R-Cerebrum Concrete Visualizer), source of summarizing images. Reads External Reality.

    b. Reporter (L-Cerebrum Abstract Reasoner) produces summarizing descriptions. Compiles our unique Internal Reality

    c. Unilateral Limbic Executive Ego, if stronger than the Reptilian Dominator, it will choose who is to be in charge. It creates and follows Survival Reality: the key choice is between Self survival vs. Group survival.

    d. Dominator (L-Striatal Reptile Brain) source of defensive or aggressive killing. Can create Dream Reality.

    e. Servant (R-Striatal reptile brain) servile, sole source of any behavioral output or accomplishment. Knows Cultural Meme Reality.

f. Sadomasochistic Pain Body-Reactive Mind (L-Cerebellar Antisocial Brain) origin of "Satanic" insanity. Lives in xDARP Reality

g. Social Brain SOURCE (R-Cerebellar-Prosocial Brain), my God-Within: Source of Empathic Reality.

    h. External Controllers (More powerful persons, institutions, or beliefs), to whom my Caretaker out of wisdom, ignorance, or weakness may defer control of my Throne.

CHAPTER 5: Hemisity: Are You a Top-Down Splitter or a Bottom-Up Lumper?

Behavioral Laterality of the Brain: Support for the Binary Construct of Hemisity. Published in: *Frontiers in Psychology*, 4:683. doi: 10.3389/fpsyg. 2013.00683

Over the recent decade, the author has published many papers in the neuroscience literature providing increasing evidence that a major element of the brain's Executive Ego is inherently located on one side of the brain or the other. Which side it is upon determines whether one is a left-brain oriented "Splitter", focusing upon important details (the trees), or a right brain-oriented "Lumper", who emphasizes the big picture (the forest). In this chapter, these observations are reviewed and summarized in the following paper, appearing in *Frontiers in Psychology*, in 2013. Although briefly reminiscent of part of Chapter 3, this chapter continues the theme of this book; that modular consciousness exists in humans.

ABSTRACT:

Three terms define brain behavioral laterality: 1. Hemispheric dominance identifies the cerebral hemisphere producing one's first language. 2. Hemispheric asymmetry locates the brain side of non-language spatial skills. 3. A third term is needed to describe a person's binary thinking, learning, and behaving styles. Since the 1950s split-brain studies, evidence has accumulated that persons with right or left brain behavioral orientations (RPs or LPs) exist. Originally, hemisphericity sought to confirm the existence of such individual differences. It failed due to its assertion that each individual lay somewhere on a gradient between competing left and right brain extremes. Recently, hemisity, a more accurate behavioral laterality context, has emerged. It posits that one's behavioral laterality is binary: i.e., inherently either right or left brain-oriented. This insight enabled the quantitative determination of right or left behavioral laterality of thousands of subjects. MRI scans of right and left brain-oriented groups revealed two neuroanatomical differences. The first was an asymmetry of an executive element in the anterior cingulate cortex. This provided hemisity both a rationale and a primary standard. RPs and LPs gave opposite answers to many behavioral preference "either-or", forced choice questions. This showed that several sex vs. hemisity traits are being con- flated by society. Such was supported by the second neu- roanatomical difference between the hemisity subtypes, that RPs of either sex had up to three times larger corpus callosi than LPs. Individuals of the same hemisity but opposite sex had more personality traits in common than those of the same sex but different hemisity. Although hemisity subtypes were equally represented in the general population, the process of higher education and career choice caused substantial hemisity sorting among the professions. Hemisity appears to be a valid and promising area for quantitative research of behavioral laterality.

Introduction

Awareness of laterality of brain function is at least as old as written history. For example, Diocles of Carystus in the fourth century BC insightfully wrote: *There are two brains in the head, one which gives understanding, and another which provides sense-perception. That is to say, the one which is lying on the right side is the one that per-ceives: with the left one, however we understand. (Lock-horst,1985)* However, Marc Dax was the first in modern times to observe a difference in function between the hem-ispheres. In 1836 he noticed that victims of injury to the left hemisphere (LH), but not to the right hemisphere (RH) could not speak (Dax, 1865). Paul Broca extend-ed this work by additionally noting that often the domi-nant hand was contralateral to the language hemisphere (Broca, 1865).

Hemispheric Dominance vs. Hemispheric Asymmetry

For the following century, the term ''hemispheric dominance'' was only used to refer to language laterality of the brain. Then, a large study by Weisenberg and McBride (1935) demonstrated RH excellence in visuospa-tial skills. This called for the invention of a second term, ''hemispheric asymmetry'', to describe the many more-re-cently discovered non-language differences in cerebral structure and function, most notably those revealed in ''split-brain'' subjects. These individuals had been created by treatment for intractable epilepsy by cutting the corpus callosum, the main cerebral connection between the hem-ispheres, thus limiting the spread of seizures from one side to the other (Gazzaniga, 2000; Gazzaniga, Bogen, & Sperry, 1962, 1967; Sperry, 1982).

Based upon the surprisingly different responses ob-tained from each of these isolated hemispheres within split-brain subjects (Gazzaniga, 2000; Gazzaniga et al., 1962, 1967; Geschwind et al., 1995), it was early proposed

by investigators that the right and left cerebral hemispheres are characterized by inbuilt, qualitatively different
and mutually antagonistic modes of data processing, separated from interference by the major longitudinal fissure
of the brain (Levy, 1969; Sperry, 1982). In this model, the
left hemisphere specialized in top-down, deductive, cognitive dissection of local detail. In contrast, the right hemisphere produces a bottom-up, inductive, perceptual synthesis of global structure (Gazzaniga, 2000; Sperry, 1982;
Schiffer, 1996). This functional asymmetry context has
been reinforced by known laterality differences between
them. That is, there are striking differences in input to each
hemisphere, differences in internal neuronal-columnar architecture, and differences in hemispheric output (Hutsler
& Galuske, 2003; Jager & Postma, 2003; Kosslyn, Chabris, Marsolek, & Koenig, 1992; Kosslyn et al., 1989;
Schuz, & Preissl, 1996; Stephan, Fink, & Marshall, 2006)
that support a local wiring on the left vs. global wiring motif on the right.

Congruent with the above local-global view is a
large body of detailed evidence that the left cerebral hemisphere in most right-handed individuals manifests facilities for language (Broca, 1863), has an orientation for local
detail (Robertson & Lamb, 1991), has object abstraction-
identification abilities (Kosslyn, 1987), and appears to
possess a hypothesis-generating, event ''Interpreter''
(Gazzaniga, 1989, 2000; Wolford, Miller, & Gazzaniga,
2000). In contrast, the right hemisphere has been demonstrated to excel in global analysis (Proverbio, Zani, Gaz-

zaniga, & Mangun, 1994; Robertson & Lamb, 1991), object localization (Kosslyn et al., 1989), facial recognition (Milner, 1968), and spatial construction (Sperry, 1968).

Among the about 90% of humans who are right-handed (Coren, 1992), language is located in the LH in about 96% of them (Knecht, Dräger, Deppe, Bobe, Lohmann, Floel, Ringelstein, & Henningsen, 2000). Of the remaining about 10% of left handed individuals, some 73% of these also have language in their left cerebrum (Knecht, et al., 2000). Thus, by simple arithmetic it follows that that the left hemisphere houses language ability in about 93.7% of us.

The Failure of Hemisphericity to Define
Behavioral Laterality

It is of interest here that within this huge group of right handed, LH dominant speakers, the existence of two major human sub-populations has repeatedly been inferred (Sperry, 1968, 1982; Levy, 1969 ; Bogen, 1969; Kosslyn, 1987; Robertson & Lamb, 1991; Davidson, 1992; Bradshaw & Nettleton, 1981; Springer & Deutsch, 1998; Schiffer, 1996), whose characteristic thinking and behavior styles differ in a manner that appeared to mirror the putative properties of the asymmetric hemispheres. That is, in some right-handed, LH languaged individuals, putative left hemisphere traits seemed to be ascendant, to produce a "Left brain-oriented" thinking and behavioral style (Springer and Deutch; 1998; Fink et al., 1996). Such left brain-oriented persons are currently summarized as top-down, detail-oriented, deductive, "splitters". Yet, in another equally large group of right-handed LH languaged persons, right hemisphere traits are thought to be more prominent, resulting in a contrasting "Right brain-oriented" style (Davidson & Hugdahl, 1995; Schiffer, 1996), currently viewed as bottom-up, global, inductive, "lumpers".

Thus, the original permanent assignment of the terms "hemispheric dominance" to language laterality, and "hemispheric asymmetry" to non-motor lateralities ultimately forced the creation of a third asymmetry term, that of "Hemisphericity" (Bogen, 1969; Bogen, DeZure, Ten Houten, & Marsh, 1972) in order to describe this third phenomenon, behavioral laterality style. This term was needed in order to refer to the differences in left and right brain thinking and behavioral properties within the two groups of individuals with language dominance and non-language asymmetry commonalities.

Why should hemisphericity exist? Upon what mechanism might these two thinking and behavioral styles of hemisphericity depend? Early studies of this phenomenon were doomed by misconception that hemisphericity was the result of hemispheric competition (Corbalis, 1980; Bradshaw & Nettleton, 1981; Beaumont, Young & McManus, 1984). This resulted in hundreds of conflicting reports. For example, many studies found the presence of frontal EEG alpha asymmetries related to emotional states (reviews by Davidson, 1984a, 1984b, 1988b). State-independent or trait-related individual differences in EEG asymmetries related to affective valence have also been described, (reviews by Davidson, 1992; Davidson & Tomarken, 1989).

Similarly, another commonly employed measure of hemisphericity has been the predominant direction of conjugate lateral eye movements (CLEMs) in response to questions requiring reflective thought. CLEMs have been proposed as a measure of relative hemispheric activation, greater on the side contralateral to the direction of eye movement (Bakan and Strayer, 1973; Gur, 1975; Kinsbourne, 1972, 1974). Both EEG and CLEM lateralities seem related to hemispheric emotional asymmetry, but do not appear to be valid predictors of differences within normal behavior (Beaumont, Young & McManus, 1984; Reine, 1991).

Further, within the formal definition of hemisphericity, attempts to keep the discipline of psychology scientific demanded each person to be located somewhere on a gradient between putative left and right hemisphere behavioral extremes. Because most subjects hesitate to mark extremes (Dawes, 2008), this impeded the development of usable quantitative methods needed to determine individual hemisphericity. After thousands of conflicting reports, the field of hemisphericity collapsed in the 1980s, primarily due to these foundational misunderstandings and this unhelpful definition, (Beaumont, Young, & McManus, 1984, Efron, 1990; Fink et al., 1996; Ornstein, 1997; Schiffer, 1996; Springer & Deutsch, 1998). Hemisphericity has since been called a neuromyth that was debunked in the scientific literature 25 years ago (Corbalis, 1980; Lindell & Kidd, 2011). As a result, publications have plummeted so that over the last 20 years the term hemisphericity has appeared in the title of only seven publications listed in Medline, aside from those of this author.

In contrast, other aspects of brain laterality, such as handedness or language dominance, have hundreds of publications over the same period. Recently, a further nail in the coffin of hemisphericity has been supplied by the observation that no individual or group differences in lateral brain activity could be seen by functional magnetic resonance imaging (fMRI) (Nielsen, Zielinski, Ferguson, Lainhart, & Anderson, 2013)

Hemisity, a More Accurate Constant

A quarter of a century after the "death" of hemisphericity and of the consequent loss of a valid and needed term to describe the brain behavioral laterality of individuals, a new more accurate approach to behavioral laterality term was created, called "Hemisity", (Morton & Rafto, 2010). Unlike hemisphericity, hemisity is binary; thus matching the other two binary descriptors of brain behavioral laterality: hemispheric dominance and asymmetry **(Table 1)**. In this new context, an individual is in herently, unavoid- ably, and irreversibly either left, or right brain-orientated in thinking and behavioral style, and in a manner quite unrelated to hemispheric competition. Thus, hemisity has restored a valid descriptor for the above mentioned essential third element necessary to describe brain laterality. The author entered the field in 2001 with this binary distinc- tion, but initially published his results under the term of hemisphericity.

Biophysical and Questionnaire Measures of Hemisity

In contrast to analogue hemisphericity, the binary "hemisphericity" (hemisity) concept was more in

Table 1: Three Unique Cerebral Hemisphere Laterality Terms

Hemispheric Dominance:
A valid term that refers to which cerebral hemisphere houses first-language production skills.

Hemispheric Asymmetry:
A valid term that refers to which hemisphere produces the various non-language skills, such as facial recognition, emotion recognition, emotion production.

Hemisphericity:
An obsolete term that tried to describe an individual's characteristic learning and behavioral style as being located somewhere on a gradient between right and left brain extremes.

Hemisity:
A term *replacing hemisphericity* that refers to which hemisphere inherently contains an individual's unilateral executive element, the source of their characteristic learning/behavioral style. Thus, each person is inherently either left or right brain-oriented.
Adding sex, the other binary identifier, produces the four major hemisity subtypes: RM, RF, LM, and LF.
This situation requires rethinking of sexual characteristics, which are presently being conflated with hemisity subtype characteristics.

alignment with the qualitatively different and mutually antagonistic modes of data processing of the opposite cerebral hemispheres, and certainly was much easier to quantify. Numerous "hemisphericity" reports were published (Morton, 2001, 2002, 2003a, 2003b, 2003c, 2003d; Morton & Rafto, 2006. This series was continued by publication of additional "hemisity" reports (Morton & Rafto 2010; Morton 2012; Morton, Svard & Jensen 2014).

Four independent biophysical methods were devised to separate right and left brain-oriented persons (RPs and LPs). Each of these showed a remarkable consistency in dividing large groups of individual into nearly the same groups of LPs and RPs. Based upon the identity of these hemisity subgroups, ultimately four "either-or" forced choice preference type questionnaires were created whose applications also divided a large starting group into the same RP and LP hemisity subgroups. These biophysical and derivative questionnaire methods are briefly described next.

Dichotic Deafness Task:

Morton (2001) reported that normal subjects could be segregated into two groups on the basis of the Dichotic Deafness Test, a dichotic listening task involving the simultaneous presentation of nonmatching pairs of consonant-vowel syllables (CV). "Dichotically hearing" subjects reported more than 40% of the syllables presented to their minor (left) ear compared to their major (right) ear, while "dichotically deaf" subjects reported less than 40% of the

CV syllables presented to their minor ear. Forty percent was an arbitrary bootstrapping value empirically found to provide optimal separation of the two groups. Morton (2002) found that dichotically hearing subjects affirmed predominantly right hemisphericity items on Zenhausern's Preference Questionnaire (Zenhausern, 1978), while dichotically deaf subject showed a left brain orientation.

Polarity Questionnaire:

Morton (2002) described the development of a new hemisity questionnaire, The Polarity Questionnaire, the items of which were chosen for their ability to differentiate groups of subjects divided on a priori grounds into left and right hemisity groups. Grouping into dichotically hearing (right brained) and dichotically deaf (left brained) groups of subjects, defined by the Dichotic Deafness Test, showed a very strong correlation with the Polarity Questionnaire ($r = 0.51$, $p < 0.001$). This correlation was twice the magnitude of the correlation between the Dichotic Deafness Test and Zenhausern's Preference Questionnaire (Zenhausern 1978). Only 30% of the Zenhausern's Preference Questionnaire items, versus 90% of the Polarity Questionnaire items, were significantly correlated with Dichotic Deafness Test grouping. A low correlation between the Polarity Questionnaire and Zenhausern's Preference Questionnaire was also noted by McElroy, McCormick, Stroh, and Seta (2012) and by Morton (2012).

Mirror Tracing Task:

Morton (2003a) had right handed subjects trace the

117

outline of a five-pointed star as quickly as possible with either hand, using only a mirror to guide manual circumscription. Faster mirror tracing with one hand was regarded as an indication of preference for the use of the contralateral hemisphere. However, in the total sample of subjects, mirror tracing asymmetry was not significantly correlated with the Dichotic Deafness Test, Zenhausern's Preference Questionnaire, or the Polarity Questionnaire.

Yet, when subjects identified as having left brain affect by use of the Affective Laterality Test (Schiffer, 1997) were removed, robust correlations between mirror tracing asymmetry and the other three hemisity measures were observed. In the Affective Laterality Test, the hemisphere which is more responsive to emotionally-evocative pictures is determined. This is done by having subjects view pictures while wearing goggles which restrict vision to the periphery (viewing with the nasal portion of the retina) by occluding the inner two thirds of each lens, thus allowing viewing by only one hemifield of one eye at a time. Subjects are asked to judge which viewing eye was associated with larger initial emotional responses to the pictures. The validity of this approach was confirmed (Schiffer, Teicher, Anderson, Tomoda, Polcari, Navalta, Andersen, 2007). When the hemisity outcomes on the mirror tracing test were reversed or "phase corrected" for subjects with left brain affect (greater emotional responses to pictures viewed with the nasal portion of the right eye) and these data were included in the analysis, even larger correlations with the other three hemisity measures were evident (Morton, 2003a).

Best Hand Task:

Extending a line bisection instrument of Schenkenberg, Bradford, & Ajax (1980), Morton (2003b) had subjects draw a line through the estimated midpoint of a set of lines of varying lengths with each hand. Midpoint estimates for each hand of an individual showed excellent repeatability and stability. When the midpoint estimates of opposite hands were compared, characteristic and often large individual differences between the accuracy of each hands to bisect the lines were observed.

Of the 412 subjects studied, 75% fell into two of the four line-bisection response categories based on the more accurate hand (r or l) and whether it crossed over the other hand to mark (c) or it did not cross over, but marked on the same (s) side as the other hand. That is, the rs category = 45% and lc = 30%. Most of rs-category subjects uncorrected for handedness or left-handed writing grasp were classified as left brained by the Polarity Questionnaire. Conversely, most of the subjects in the lc-category were classified as right brained by the Polarity Questionnaire.

For the two smaller categories, the results were somewhat more complicated. Of the 10% of the total sample who fell into the rc-category, the males were right brained (8%), while the females were left brained (2%). Of the 15% of the total sample who fell into the ls-category, those with right brain affect on the Affective Laterality Test were right brained, as determined by the Polarity Questionnaire (10%), whereas those with left brain affect had left hemisity (5%). Thus, hemisity as determined by phase-corrected line-bisection results was also strongly associated with hemisity, as determined by phase-corrected mirror tracing results, the Dichotic Deafness Test, and Zenhausern's Preference Questionnaire.

Asymmetry Questionnaire:

Morton (2003c) developed another questionnaire measure of hemisity, the Asymmetry Questionnaire, which consists of 15 paired statements. Within each pair, one statement exemplified a left brained characteristic while the other reflected a right brained characteristic. The Asymmetry Questionnaire was found to have strong and significant correlations with two other hemisity questionnaires, the Polarity Questionnaire and Zenhausern's Preference Questionnaire, as well as three biophysical hemisity measures, the Dichotic Deafness Test, phase-corrected mirror tracing, and phase-corrected Best Hand Test.

Binary Questionnaire and Hemisity Questionnaire:

Recently the Binary Questionnaire and the Hemisity Questionnaires have also been developed and utilized (Morton, 2012). As shown in **Table 2**, these were of comparable quality to the Polarity and Asymmetry Questionnaires. As may be seen, all four of these questionnaires were superior to the earlier hemisphericity standard, the Zenhauser's Preference Questionnaire (1978).

3. MRI Studies of Neuroanatomical differences between RPs and LPs.

The above new methods enabled the accurate characterization of MRI assessments (Morton & Rafto, 2010)

Table 2: Overall Correlations and Reliability of Preference Questionnaire Scores with Predetermined Subject Hemisity Subtype

Preference Questionnaires (fast, easy) vs. Biophysical Methods (slow, difficult)	r (Pearsons)	p	n	% yield	alpha Cronbach's
Correlations of MRI pre-assigned hemisity subtypes with:					
Zenhausern's Preference Quest-naire	0.24	0.008	119	35*	0.37
Polarity Question-naire	0.57	0.000	132	82	0.57
Asymmetry Question-naire	0.48	0.000	111	60	0.64
Binary Questionnaire	0.43	0.000	112	30	0.66
Hemisity Question-naire	0.53	0.000	79	48	0.65
Best Hand Test (R-L)	0.37	0.000	143		
Mirror Tracing Test (R/L)	0.50	0.000	116		
Dichotic Deafness Test (R-L/R+L)	0.34	0.000	109		
vgACC laterality determined by MRI	0.93	0.000	149		

* = % yield refers to the percentage of questionnaire statements that were significantly associated with subject neuroanatomical hemisity. Pre-assigned hemisity subtype = direction of asymmetry of the ventral gyrus of the anterior cingulate cortex.
For r-values, the most accurate =1.00, <0.05 was significant, n= the number of subjects.

of the hemisity subtype of hundreds of subjects (Morton, 2003d). This enabled MRI studies to be carried out seeking brain structural differences between LPs and RPs.

Two neuroanatomical differences were found. The first, not illustrated, was the observation that the corpus callosum midline cross sectional area of RPs was up to three times larger than that of the LPs (Morton and Rafto, 2006). The implications of this discovery will be discussed later.

Second, it was observed that in 146 of 149 cases (98%) the subject's bilateral anterior cingulate cortex (ACC) in Areas 24 and 24' was up to 50% larger on the right side for RPs, while for the LPs it was up to 50% larger on the left (Morton & Rafto, 2010), **Figure 1**. This result motivated the transformation of this three minute MRI procedure into the primary standard for the determination of individual hemisity subtype, as follows:

MRI Assessment of Hemisity (Primary Standard):
These were obtained employing a General Electric Signa 1.5 Tesla MRI instrument. A midsagittal plane setup calibration protocol was run for 3 minutes to image 5 mm thick slices from the midline plane and two adjoining sagittal planes 6 mm on either side. Whole-head photographic images were prepared from these three planes. These three exposures were printed on a single film sheet for each subject. This procedure enabled both cortical walls on either side of the midline fissure to be visualized and measured, thus allowing sub-element lateralities of the ACC to be evaluated directly from the film. At two ACC sites on each side of the brain, one in Area 24 and the other at Area 24' (Vogt et al.,

Figure 15: Asymmetries of the Anterior Cingu- late Cortex

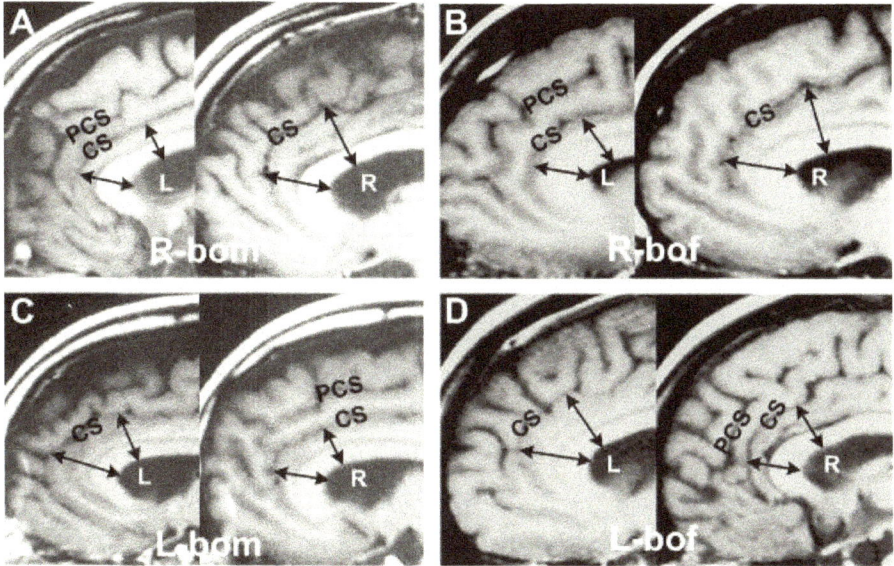

Figure 15. Asymmetries in the Anterior Cingulate Cortex Caption: Example of MRI sagittal images taken from 149 hemisity- calibrated subjects.
A. Right brain-oriented male (R-bom, RM).
B. Right brain-oriented female (R-bof, RF).
C. Left brain-oriented male (L-bom, LM)
D. Left brain-oriented female (L-bof, LF).
Pairs of arrows reaching from the lower surface of the central white cor- pus callosum (CC) to the cingulate sulcus (CS) illustrate four meas- urements made for each subject. CC thickness was the same on im- ages from either side. PCS refers to the paracingulate sulcus. Note that the arrow lengths are longer on the right side for RPs and left side for LPs. From Morton & Rafto, 2010.

1995), estimations of the relative thickness of the ventral gyri (vgACC) there were made. This abbreviation and these four ACC locations within Areas 24 and 24' are not to be confused with the more frontal ventral region of the perigenual ACC. The vgACC locations where these relative thickness estimations were made are illustrated by the arrows in **Figure 15**.

Two lines were extended perpendicularly from the inner edge of the CC, ending in one case at a more frontal point in Area 24 and in the other at a more dorsal point in Area 24' . Both points were in the plane of the cingulate sulcus and arbitrarily selected, based upon the sites in the region giving the largest vgACC thickness for each brain side involved. The average of these two lateral relative thickness estimates from the vgACC of each side were then used to determine upon which side of each subject's brain the vgACC was thicker. This can be recognized by noting that the arrows are longer on the right hemisphere for RPs and on the left for LPs.

Calibration of earlier hemisity methods against the MRI primary standard.

Asymmetry of the ventral gyri of the anterior cingulate cortex was significantly correlated with hemisity as determined by the Asymmetry Questionnaire (Morton, 2003c), the Polarity Questionnaire and Zenhausern's Preference Questionnaire (Zenhausern, 1978; Morton, 2002), the Dichotic Deafness Test (Morton, 2001, 2002), the Best Hand Test (Morton, 2003b), the Phased Mirror Tracing Test (Morton, 2003a), as well as two new hemisity questionnaires, the Binary Questionnaire and the Hemisity Questionnaire (Morton, 2012). The categorical associations of each of these methods of determining hemisity with each other and with asymmetry of the vgACC were highly significant (Morton and Rafto, 2010). The correlations among continuous measures of asymmetry derived from each of these methods were also significant. All nine hemisity measures had high loadings on the first factor, suggesting an underlying dimension of hemisity accounting for the relationships among these nine measures. The correlations between these hemisity instruments may be seen in **Table 2**,

That the anatomical primary standard for hemisity was found to validate the previous secondary instruments developed to assess hemisity was gratifying because some of them were based upon possibly questionable assumptions. For example, in the Dichotic Deafness Test (Morton, 2001), it was necessary to make arbitrary decisions as to where to draw cutoff lines that defined dichotic deafness. In the Phased Mirror Tracing Method (Morton, 2003a) it was necessary to assess the subjects as to which was the more emotional side of their brain. This assessment was based upon the examiner's interpretation of the subjective judgment of the subject in response to peripheral presentation of pictures containing emotion-invoking content. In the Best Hand Task (Morton, 2003b), a certain segment of the population required redefinition of handedness and the interpretation of the sometimes-difficult assessment of pen grasp hand posture. It is paradoxical that it was necessary to develop these secondary methods first in order to calibrate the hemisity of a sufficiently large group of subjects even to begin to search for and recognize actual brain structural differences between left and right brain-oriented individuals.

However, since the previous hemisity procedures were well correlated with the primary anatomical standard, it would appear reasonable they could continue to be used in combination as secondary standards. When five of these six were used the combined outcome for the 149 subjects was 146/149 (98%) correct for hemisity subtype identity. For the 111 subjects assessed by all six secondary methods, the accuracy rose to 99%. Yet, no single secondary method can be used to absolutely identify subject hemisity, each being correct only about 80% of the time. It would appear that, the combined use of at least three or four of the five most accurate questionnaires of **Table 2**, would allow for rapid, fairly accurate measurement of the hemisity of individuals. In sufficiently large populations, this can be reduced to two hemisity questionnaires, as described later.

4. Neuroanatomical Basis of Hemisity

Coincidentally in terms of the hemisity MRI findings of ACC laterality, much evidence supports the ACC being a major structural element of the brain's executive system. Remarkably, this cortical element of the ancient limbic brain region (Roxo, Franceshini, Zuban, Klebe, & Sander, 2011), including interconnecting integrative loops (Alexander GE, DeLong MR, & Strick PL, 1986) between prefrontal, striatal, thalamic, and other limbic areas (Bonelli & Cummings, 2007) has repeatedly been shown to be involved in executive type activities. These include: decision making (Kennerly, Walton, Behrens, Buckley, & Rushworth, 2006), error detection, conflict monitoring, stimulus-response mapping, familiarity, and orienting

(Wang, Istvan, Schomer, Marincovic, & Halgren, 2005), response to pain and production of emotion: (Vogt, 2005), verbal and non-verbal executive tasks activity (Fornito, Yucel, Wood, Stuart, Buchanan, Proffitt, Anderson, Velakoulis, & Panelis, 2004), conflict monitoring and adjustments in control (Kerns, Cohen, MacDonald, Cho, Stenger, & Carter, 2004), rapid processing of gains and losses (Gehring & Willoughby,2002), interfacing between motor control, drive, and cognition (Paus, 2001), episodic memory retrieval (Herrmann, Rotte, Grubich, Ebert, Schlit, Munte, & Heinze, 2001) and the initiation and motivation of goal directed behavior (Devinsky, Morrell, & Vogt, 1995).

Some ACC activities appear directly relevant to hemisity differences in behavioral styles. These include its participation in temperament (Whittle, Allen, Fornito, Lubman, Simmonds, Pantelis, & Yucel, 2008), reward and social learning (Behrens, Hunt, Woo, Woolrich, & Rushworth, 2008), expectancy and social rejection, (Somerville, Heatherton, & Kelley (2006), self-reflection (Johnson, Raye, Mitchell, Touryan, Greene, & Nolen-Hoeksema, 2006), personality (Pujol, Lopez, Deus, Cardoner, & Valejo, 2002), will and addiction (Peoples, 2002). Even though psychoanalytic concepts were originally not intended to correspond to neuroanatomical structures, it can be noted that the ACC seems to mediate a number of different cognitive functions formerly subsumed under Freud's central element of control, the Ego. It certainly has the resources to implement the many behavioral differences between hemisity subtypes.

What is fascinating in terms of the hemisity story, is that not only does the ACC house a major brain executive element, but also that its two sides, separated by the cerebral midline fissure, are highly asymmetric. There are at least ten reports of ACC structural asymmetries, especially in Areas 24, and 24' which varied in an individually idiosyncratic manner, (Vogt et al., 1995; Paus et al., 1996a,b; Hutsler et al., 1998; Ide, et al., 1999; Yucel et al., 2001; Pujol et al., 2002; Fornito et al., 2006, 2008; Huster et al., 2007; Palomero-Gallagher et al., 2008). Many of these reports mentioned efforts to identify behavioral consequences of these identified asymmetries, interestingly including their possible relationship to executive function, e.g., (Pujol, Lopez, Deus, Cardoner, Vallejo, Capdevila, et al. (2002). However, these efforts lacked the unifying concept of hemisity.

Might this laterality of the ACC executive element provide a direct link to a subject's hemisity, thus supporting the observed relationship between the two? Indeed, it is here asserted that the discovery of the congruity of the larger side of the ACC with hemisity subtype has actually provided the missing mechanism to account for the existence of hemisity and for the differences between LPs and RPs. Further, such an "either-or" laterality context is consistent with the logic that there can be only one "Bottom-line", "The buck stops here" executive element in any successful institutional organization, including the mammalian brain, which is completely bilateral, except for the pineal gland. Although, Descartes (1637) was logically compelled to assert this endocrine organ to be the executive "Seat of the Soul", now, it rather appears that the executive system must be unilateral. That is, hemisity must result because an executive element, embedded in the local specialized (top-down, important details) environment of the left hemisphere, will inevitably have a different perspective than one imbedded within that of the right (bottom-up, global perspective).

Thus, the existence of major asymmetries in the ACC supports the hypothesis of the possible existence of a unilateral executive element. This idea is not new. When he learned that the bilateral ACC was the probable site of the executive system, Crick (1994) was led rhetorically to ask: "Could there be two centers of the Will?" (Sejnowski, 2004). In a "Postscript on the Will" within his book "The Astonishing Hypothesis", (1994), Crick states that he and Antonio Damasio arrived at the same negative answer to this question by noting about the ACC that the "region on one side projects strongly to the corpus striatum (an important part of the motor system) on both sides of the brain, which is what you might expect from a single Will." Parenthetically, neither their use of the term Will, nor the use of the term Executive System here were intended to invoke the idea of a decisional homunculus, but rather of a preconscious early response system (Libet, 1982) continually acting to optimize the survival of the organism.

5. Behavioral Differences between Right and Left Hemisity Subtypes

With the ability to accurately determine the right or left brain individual hemisity subtype identity in hand, it became possible to answer some pressing questions: Do these biophysically identified right and left hemisity subtype individuals differ significantly in their behavioral preferences? And if so, specifically how? Morton (2012) studied the behavioral responses of 150 subjects whose hemisity had previously been calibrated by MRI. He used five MRI-calibrated preference questionnaires, two of which were new. Right and left brain-oriented subjects selected opposite answers ($p>0.05$) for 47 of 107 "either-or", forced choice type preference questionnaire items. Removing overlaps resulted in 30 hemisity subtype preference differences **(Table 3)**. These differences could be subdivided into five areas: (1) in logical orientation, (2) in type of consciousness, (3) in fear level and sensitivity, (4) in social-professional orientation, and (5) in pair bonding-spousal dominance style.

The following is an interpretation of 30 hemisity differences found: Regarding *Logical Orientation,* LPs tended to be top-down, detail oriented, and deductive vs. RPs who were more bottom-up, big picture, and inductive. Regarding *Type of Consciousness*, LPs tended to be more verbal, dependent upon abstract reasoning, and oriented to find differences between objects vs. RPs who where more visual, dependent upon concrete reasoning. *Fear Level and Sensitivity,* LPs were more sensitive, taciturn, emotion-avoiding and defensive, due to a thinner barrier to fear-invoking subconscious material. RPs were more intense, bold, talkative, emotion-embracing, invasive, and able to find commonalties between objects. For *Social and Professional Orientation*, LPs were more independent, avoidant, private, and

Table 3: Thirty Binary Behavioral Correlates of Hemisity

Left Brain-Oriented Persons   Right Brain-Oriented Persons

LOGICAL ORIENTATION

Left Brain-Oriented Persons	Right Brain-Oriented Persons
Analytical (stays within the limits of the data)	Sees big picture (projects beyond, predicts)
Uses logic converts objects to literal concepts	Imagines, concepts into contexts/ metaphors
Decisions based on objective facts	Decisions based on feelings, intuition
Uses a serious approach to solving problems	Uses a playful approach to solving problems
Prefers to maintain and use good old solutions	Would rather find better new solutions.

TYPE OF CONSCIOUSNESS

Left Brain-Oriented Persons	Right Brain-Oriented Persons
Daydreams are not vivid	Has vivid daydreams
Doesn't often remember dreams	Remembers dreams often.
Thinking often consists of words	Thinking often consists of mental images
Can easily concentrate on many things at once	Concentrates on one thing in depth at a time
Comfortable and productive with chaos	Slowed by disorder and disorganization
Often thinking tends to ignore surroundings	Observant and in touch with surroundings
Often an early morning person	Often a late night person

FEAR LEVEL AND SENSITIVITY

Left Brain-Oriented Persons	Right Brain-Oriented Persons
Conservative, cautious	Innovative, bold
Sensitive in relating to others	Intense in relating to others
Tend to avoid talking about emotional feelings	Often talks about own/others feelings
Suppresses emotions as overwhelming	Seeks to experience/express emotions deeply
Would self-medicate with depressants	Would self-medicate with stimulants

SOCIAL AND PROFESSIONAL ORIENTATION

Left Brain-Oriented Persons	Right Brain-Oriented Persons
Does not read other people's mind very well	Good at knowing what others are thinking.
Thinks-listens quietly, keeps talk to minimum pendent, hidden, private, and indirect	Thinks-listens interactively, talks a lot Inde- Interdependent, open, public, and direct
Does not praise others nor work for praise	Praises others and works for praise
Avoids seeking evaluation by others	Seeks frank feedback from others
Usually tries to avoid taking the blame	Takes the blame, blames self, or apologizes

PAIR-BONDING AND SPOUSAL DOMINANCE STYLE

Left Brain-Oriented Persons	Right Brain-Oriented Persons
Tolerates mate defiance in private	Difficulty tolerating mate defiance in private
After an upset with spouse, needs to be alone	After upset with spouse, needs closeness/talk
Needs little physical contact with mate	Needs a lot of physical contact with mate
Tends not to be very romantic or sentimental	Tends to be very romantic and sentimental
Prefers monthly large reassurances of love	Likes daily small assurances of mate's love
Often feels mate talks too much	Feels my mate doesn't talk or listen enough.
Lenient parent, kids tend to defy	Strict, kids obey and work for approval

competitive, while the RPs were more orderly, responsible, open, and cooperative. In terms of *Pair Bonding Style and Spousal Dominance,* LPs were the less dominant spouse, who needed separateness, quietness, seeking to avoid emotionality with logic, spouse assisting, and initiator of the details of family endeavors early in the day. In contrast RPs were the more dominant spouse, needing closeness and reassurance of the other's fidelity and support while being intuitive and highly directive, ending the day by reviewing the big picture survival status of the family and making plans for the next day.

It is ironic that many of these behavioral preference differences parallel some, but not all, of the putative differences between the left and right brainers popular in folk hemisphericity (Springer & Deutsch, 1998), such as detailer vs. globalist, analytical vs. synthetic, words vs. images, abstract vs. concrete. However, many more differences were revealed, most of which as yet have no recognized brain basis, for example fear vs. confidence, or morning vs. evening, quiet vs. talkative. Perhaps the use of hemisity to identify individuals with those traits may assist in identification of their underlying brain mechanism.

6. Corpus Callosal Size, Hemisity, and Sexual Stereotyping

As mentioned, the cross-sectional area of the midline of the corpus callosum (CCA) was found to be significantly smaller in LPs than in RPs, and to be unrelated to sex or handedness (Morton & Rafto, 2006). These observations, illustrated in **Figure 16,** have had several ramifica- tions. To begin with, if the executive element of the ante- rior cingulate was in the same hemisphere as language, as is the case for most LPs, there would be less need for trans- callosal communication than if the executive element was located in the opposite non-language hemisphere. Thus, the CCA in LPs would be predicted to be smaller than in RPs, as observed.

Further, hemisity behavioral outcomes contradict several commonly held beliefs about sex and the brain: First, the hemisity results lay bare the underlying basis of the previous controversy about gender and laterality. The confusion occurred because in all earlier CCA studies, the hemisity of the subjects was unknown.

This caused an unwitting confounding of the results for subjects sorted only by sex or handedness with hemisity, a major factor influencing CCA (Morton & Rafto, 2006). This error brings into question the common view that the male brain is more specialized due to its higher laterality (McGlone, 1980). Rather, the CCA data strongly suggest that it is the left brain-oriented individuals of either sex who are more lateralized as a class than males are. Correspondingly, right brain individuals of either sex are less lateralized and more broadly generalized as a class than females are, thus contradicting another sexual stereotype. Second, these findings appear to end the controversy about which sex has the larger corpus callosum (Luders et al., 2003).

There was no significant difference between the two sexes in either their mean CCA, its size range, or in the IQ of the subjects (Morton & Rafto, 2006). Rather, the two largest CCAs of individuals from among our 113

Figure 17. Hemisity vs. Sex: Corpus Callosal Size Range

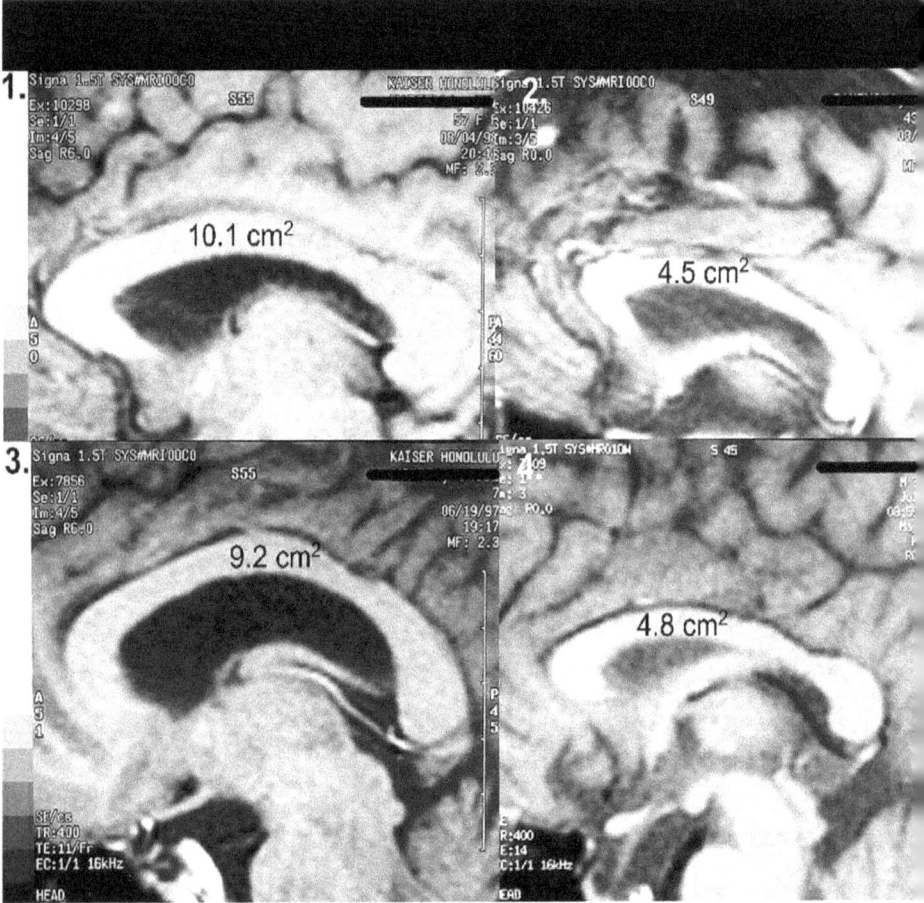

Fig 16. Hemisity vs. Sex: Size Range of Corpus Callosal Areas Caption: Hemisity vs. sex: size-range of corpus callosal areas. Largest CCAs of the subject group (n = 113): (1) Right brain-oriented female, 10.1 cm2. (2) Right brain-oriented male, CCA 9.2 cm2. Smallest CCAs: (3) Left brain-oriented-male, 4.8 cm2. (4) Left brain-oriented female, 4.5 cm2. From Morton & Rafto, 2006.

subjects were possessed by a right brained female and by a right brain male (10.1 and 9.2 cm², respectively). Conversely, the two smallest CCAs were 4.8 cm² for a left brained male and 4.5 cm² for a left brained female. All four of these individuals held doctoral degrees and professorial status.

Third, lack of awareness that hemisity contributes to CCA makes it probable that the European studies reporting mean CCAs for males to be larger (Clarke et al., 1989) and American–Australian studies, showing larger female mean CCAs (Holloway et al., 1993) were both correct. Their disagreements could well be based upon regional population differences in hemisity, an important but uninvestigated topic.

Fourth, it is becoming clear that members of either sex with the same hemisity have more behavioral traits in common than do same sex individuals of the opposite hemisity. This is strongly supported by data from the MRI calibrated preference questionnaires (Morton, 2002, 2003c, 2012). Thus, it would appear that several hemisity traits are presently being misidentified as male or female sex traits. That is, men in general do not "hide in their caves of silence" (Gray, 1992; Tannen, 1990). In fact, in contrast to their right brain counterpart, left brain-oriented females are every bit as "private" as left brain-oriented males (Morton, 2002, 2003c, 2012). Similarly, females do not always "rule the roost." It is the right brain-oriented person who tends to dominate the nuclear family, be they male or female (Morton, 2002, 2003c, 2012).

Because of the newness of hemisity and its new behavioral distinctions, sex traits have never been studied together with hemisity traits. Books such as John Gray's *Men are from Mars, Women are from Venus,* (1992) appear to fit perfectly for about half the population (~60%), that is, for the RFs and LMs. The other half (~40%) say it is totally alien to them. However, if the pronouns are reversed from "him" to "her" and vice versa in the book, then the other half of the population (RMs and LFs) strongly identify with it (Morton, unpublished). So it appears not to be a description of sexual differences but rather of hemisity differences. Thus, the recognition of the quantifiable existence of hemisity can bring new clarity to human behavior.

7. Hemisity Distributions and Hemisity Sorting within Populations

Morton (2003d) investigated the distribution of hemisity subtypes within the general population. It was proposed (Morton, 2003d) that in an unsorted population not only would the numbers of male and females be equal, but that the numbers of RPs and LPs would also be similar. It was hypothesized that hemisity sorting in populations would only occur after admission into a school or an organization where entrance was competitive and selective. In the US, this typically first occurs at the university level because in essentially all public elementary, high schools, and even some community colleges, essentially no applicants are excluded and all must complete a similar general core curriculum in order to graduate.

Morton, Svard, & Jensen (2014), using the Best Hand Test (Morton, 2003b) and the Polarity Questionnaire (Morton, 2002), measured the hemisity of 1049 public

high school upper classmen from Hawaii and Utah. As predicted, in this sample there were similar numbers of males (n=522) and females (n=527), and of right (n=526) and left (n=523) brain-oriented individuals. There were reciprocal complementary relationships between right males (RMs, 39%, n=206) and left females (LFs, 40%, n=210), and cor- respondingly among left males (LMs, 61%, n=316) and right females (RFs, 60%, n=317), thus confirming the non- sorting hypothesis. This suggests that females are slightly enriched in RPs and males are with LPs, and therefore that the average CCA of females should be slightly greater than of males. However, these differ- ences do not appear to ob- viate the four generalities of the preceding section.

The equalities of hemisity within the general popu- lation were lost among 228 competitively selected college freshmen, 57% of whom now showed left hemisity. Stu- dents in more specialized upper-division classes (Morton, 2003d) showed an increased range of hemisity distribu- tions, from 35% left brained individuals in a civil engi- neering seminar to 68% left brained persons in a home economics course.

Even more pronounced hemisity distribution differ- ences were found in university representatives of 17 dif- ferent professsions, ranging from only 21% left brained among astronomers and 33% left brained among architec- ture professors, to 83% among biochemistry professors and 86% among microbiology professors (Morton, 2003d). Professional librarians (n=15) were predomi- nantly left-brained (73% LPs), academically trained musicians (n=91) including concert pianists (n=47) were predominantly right- brained (32% LPs) (Morton, Svard, & Jensen, 2014).

Within professional groups there were differences related to area of specialization. For example, among practicing civil engineers, only 39% of design civil engineers were left brained, compared to 74% of construction civil engineers. Morton (2003d) suggested that individuals in primarily "top-down" professions working at structural levels that are subdivisible, such as microbiologists, biochemists, and particle physicists, were more left brained. In contrast, those in more "bottom-up" macroscopic or gestalt-oriented professions such as architecture, civil engineering design, and astronomy, tended to be more right brained. Thus, as it may be seen, hemisity appears to play a profound role in career development.

An explanation has been proposed to account for the sorting of hemisity in higher education and career selection (Morton, 2003d). That is, sorting occurred as the result of RPs and LPs doing what they liked best. Topics at which each excelled relative to the other resulted in one hemisity subclass doing well or poorly compared to the other. Rewards from success, difficulty, or failure shaped individual opinion of the liking or dislike of specific topics. This led to the selection of topics bringing personal success and to the avoidance of those bringing failure. Thus in general, it appears that one ends up being an architect or microbiologist simply by doing what one enjoys most.

Although both the Best Hand Test (Morton, 2003b) and the Polarity Questionnaire (Morton, 2002) were used in the above population studies, the viability of using the more easily administered Polarity Questionnaire alone to determine the hemisity of large groups was considered by comparing its outcomes here with those of the Best Hand Test alone (Morton, 2003b). For a high school population (n=703), the outcomes of the two methods differed in only 5.6% of cases. Further, the Polarity Questionnaire was able to assess the hemisity of the 10.4% individuals whose Best Hand Test results were indeterminate. This supported the idea that, not only are the two measures complimentary, but also that perhaps future studies using the Polarity Questionnaire alone, or in combination with one or more of the other calibrated hemisity questionnaires might be acceptably accurate for the estimation of hemisity of large English speaking populations. However, the extreme outcome sensitivity to wording of Polarity Questionnaire statements (Morton, 2002, 2003c) suggests that great care must be taken in its translation into other languages and cultures. In contrast, biophysical hemisity methods, such as the Best Hand Test, while much more demanding to assess, appear to be language and culture independent.

Because the grading of the Best Hand Test, a research instrument, is complex, technical, and time consuming, it is not practical for use in general hemisity studies. As indicated above, similar results are easily obtained by the Polarity Questionnaire. Further, it has been shown that combined use of the Polarity Questionnaire with the three other rapid binary hemisity questionnaires that have been developed: The Asymmetry Questionnaire (Morton, 2003c), the Binary Questionnaire (Morton, 2012), and the

Hemisity Questionnaire (Morton, 2012), enhances the 80% certainty of the hemisity subtype result of a single questionnaire to about 95% for combined use **(Table 2.)** Each questionnaire takes only a few minutes to administer and grade.

8. Conclusions

Six useful conclusions are among many that can be derived from this review of hemisity: 1. Research now supports the view that the existence of hemisity is inevitable, due to the unilateral nature of a structural element of the executive system. 2. Quantitative methods have been developed to make it possible to assess any person in terms of their probable right or left brain orientation. 3. A primary standard has been discovered that enables the absolute hemisity of an individual to be determined, based upon anatomical landmarks within the brain. 4. A number of the many "either-or" traits that separate the cognitive and behavioral styles of RPs and LPs have been identified, most of which as yet have no known ties to brain asymmetry. 5. Methods now exist which can determine the average hemisity of groups with considerable sensitivity. 6. The recognition of the quantifiable existence of hemisity as a second dyadic personal identifier after sex can bring new clarity to human behavior.

The neuroanatomical differences between left- and right-brain oriented individuals raise the question of how these features develop. Correlating parent and offspring hemisity types might provide first insights into the development of this phenomenon. However, extensive genetic research will most likely be necessary to fully unravel the development and implications of hemisity.

Acknowledgements:

In addition to thanking the literally thousands of individuals who enthusiastically contributed to these unfunded studies, the author also acknowledges his three deceased, beloved coworkers: Dennis McLaughlin, Ph.D., Psychologist and Co-founder of Care Hawaii, Michael Kelley, Ph.D., Psychologist in Washington, D. C. and Joseph Singer, Engineer and Artist from Honolulu

References to this article are to be found at end of the book.

CHAPTER FIVE

CHAPTER 6: Brain Modular Consciousness and xDARP-Induced Marital Fighting

We began this book with a description of the emergence of self-consciousness from preconscious behavior in early humans. Now, we deal with another subconscious brain element, the broken Developmental Arrest Repair Program (xDARP), the powerful hidden source of marital conflict, suffering, breakdown, and divorce, as well as child suffering and developmental stunting in literally hundreds of millions if not billions of innocent people in the world. This can only be understood within the context of modular consciousness.

Oh, No! Here we go again!! Relationship-Destroying Cyclic Conflict

Tina asks her husband Dick to take her to the shopping center. No problem, he replies. Driving in the car, Dick asks Jane what she wants to buy, knowing that he will have to pay. Jane gets angry and accuses Dick of not wanting to take her shopping. Dick protests that he is happy to take her, only that he was curious as to what she was looking for. Jane becomes angrier and in a torrent of abuse calls Dick a cheap ass-hole, among other things. Then, she says she doesn't want to go shopping anymore and commands Dick to take her home. Dick keeps driving toward the shopping center, thinking that maybe this would pass over. Jane starts kicking him and the steering wheel, and then tries to take the car keys from the ignition while they are driving. Dick quickly stops the car, although in a strange area, and Jane jumps out. He calls to her to get back in, saying that he will take her home. She starts walking rapidly along the side of the road toward home. He follows her in the car but she will not get back in. He returns home. She arrives in about a half hour. An hour later, she snuggles next to him in bed as if nothing had happened.

A similar violent incident occurred a few months earlier during a trip to the ocean. That time the disagreement was over the route, where Tina insisted in going right instead of left at a key turnoff point. Going in the wrong direction, they became increasingly isolated while she angrily insisted she was correct, because her cousins had said so, and that Dick was crazy and ought to trust her. Finally, when it was obvious that they were lost, she began to kick him and again jumped out of the car. This time they were far from home. After some 15 minutes on foot in unfamiliar country, she allowed herself to be picked up, but would not talk. He retraced their path to the intersection in question. Then, Dick turned left and went onto the beach resort. Later, they went swimming with Jane showing Dick some affection.

These are only two examples of the millions of widely different daily-occurring incidents, where one member of a once close couple periodically attacks the other to inflict incredible pain in increasingly intense cycle of psychological violence. Often, the attacks are complementary and can be initiated by either spouse. The repetitive themes of conflict can be as mundane as fights over whether to leave the toilet seat down or up, or whether the toilet paper should emerge from the back or front of the roll on the wall. However, these can quickly escalate to older topics by throwing in the "kitchen sink". Often the complaint is: "You don't listen to me!" When the partner tries to listen, he or she is treated to a litany of complaints so tainted with false accusations as to be impossible to hear without admitting to crimes and defects which are quite the opposite of one's identity. The complaints seem endless and insane. The partner accuses you of being their enemy, of hating them, stating that you are impossible to please, hopeless, and will never change. They defend this by saying that it is the way they feel, and that for them to be authentic, and true to themselves they cannot think otherwise.

A particularly insidious element of this is the fact that they often claim to be able to read your mind and to know that you were thinking something very negative and degrading about them, which is completely opposite of your original desire to please them. When you jump in to correct them, they say you are lying and quote earlier psudoexamples. They say that they know your true nature better than you do, and that it is antagonistic, negative, and harmful. This is such an effective trap! If you naturally try to defend your honor by trying to restate your actual thinking, it only inflames the argument. That is, they will begin to call you a liar and coward for not owning up to their analysis, because they magically know what you are thinking more than you do. On the other hand, if you agree with their version of what they assert you were thinking, you will have to admit to being a very disgusting person, which no one wants to do. Quickly leaving the scene for a half hour often works to restore sanity, but sometimes you are trapped downtown in a store, restaurant, driving a car where getting away would leave them stranded. Because these fights are cyclic in nature, after a couple of hours,

they usually resolve with a reapproachment and a temporary peace. The critical question is, what is going on
here??

**Recognizing that the Marriage-Destroying Villain is an
Insane Automaticity:**

Most couples find and select one another out of mutual subconscious infatuation. In many, this infatuation
sooner or later, certainly by one year, begins to be replaced
with cyclic repetitive conflicts that can slowly escalate toward mutual detestation, and as we shall see in many
cases, to crimes of passion. The stages of the cycle can
occur relatively quickly or develop slowly over decades.
This unidentified sadomasochistic phenomenon is by far
the most common source of marital unhappiness, contributing to divorce in more than half of all US marriages.
During these brief cyclic rejecting, critical, often violent
attacks, it is as if our beloved mate becomes transformed,
Dr. Jeckel-Mr. Hyde-like, into another person altogether,
one who is the demonic opposite of our former lover.

The emergence of this alter ego, second personality
was recognized by Ron Hubbard in his book, *Dianetics:
The Modern Science of Mental Health* (1950). He called
it the Reactive Mind. It was rediscovered and popularized
by Ekhard Tolle, who in his 1999 book *The Power of
Now*, where he called it the Pain Body. Tolle characterized the Pain-Body as a negative energy field whose
strength depends upon the degree of development traumatization we have sustained in our early years. The
Pain-Body can be dormant most of the time, if our trauma was light, or active up to 100% of the time in heavily

injured individuals. It may become activated by "certain situations such as intimate relationships or situations linked with past loss or abandonment, physical or emotional hurt. Anything can trigger it, particularly if it resonates with a pain pattern from your past. When is ready to awaken from its dormant stage, even a thought, or an innocent remark made by someone close to you can activate it."

"Some Pain Bodies are obnoxious but relatively harmless. Others are vicious, and destructive, monsters; true demons. Some are physically violent; many others are emotionally violent. Some will attack people around you or close to you, while others may attack you, their host. Thoughts and feelings you have about your life then become deeply negative and self-destructive. Illnesses and accidents are often created in this way. Some PainBodies drive their hosts to suicide."

"When you thought you knew a person and then you are suddenly confronted with this alien, nasty creature for the first time, you are in for quite a shock. However, it's more important to observe it in yourself than in someone else. Watch out for any sign of unhappiness in yourself, in whatever form. It may be the awakening pain-body. This can take the form of irritation, impatience, a somber mood, a desire to hurt, anger, rage, depression, a need to have some drama in your relationship, and so on. Catch it the moment it awakens from its dormant state."

"The pain body wants to survive, just like every other entity in existence, and it can only survive if it gets you to unconsciously identify with it. It can then rise up, take you over, 'become you,' and live through you. It needs to get its food through you. It will feed on any experience that resonates with its own kind of energy, anything that creates further pain in whatever form: anger, destructiveness, hatred, grief, emotional drama, violence, and even illness. So, the pain-body, when it has taken you over, will create situation your life that reflects back its own energy frequency for it to feed on. Pain can only feed on pain. Pain cannot feed on joy. It finds it quite indigestible."

"Once the pain-body has taken you over, you want more pain. You become a victim or a perpetrator. You want to inflict pain, or you want to suffer pain, or both. There isn't really much difference between the two. You are not conscious of this, of course, and will vehemently claim that you do not want pain. But look closely and you will find that your thinking and behavior are designed to keep the pain going for yourself and others. If you were truly conscious of it, the pattern would dissolve, for to want more pain is insanity, and nobody is consciously insane."

But still, exactly what is this sadomasochistic destructive mechanism in terms of the brain and neuroscience? Something more concrete than a "pain-body" is needed if we are to understand the origin and nature of this mechanism that destroys an incredible number of hopeful marriages in our society between once loving couples, additionally subjecting their innocent children to life-damaging trauma. Fortunately, an illuminating and far reaching brain-based answer has been uncovered to account for the existence and function of this insane automaticity. The explanation is complex but understandable, much of it painfully familiar. And it requires the existence of modular consciousness. As we will see in the next chapter, unrecognized fragments of this mechanism have become embedded in the "good vs. evil" heart of all religions. Further, for millennia the methods of religion have been distilled attempting to overcome this insanity.

To understand this painful situation more completely, we need to look at how the brain develops the ability to control its environment, including the people within it.

Gaining Psychosocial Control: The Traumatic Nature of Developmental Arresting and Fixation

Development of Voluntary Control of the Body:

To truly be in control of a process requires five elements: **Awareness** of the process by at least some part of the brain, and the ability to: **Start, Change, Stop** and **Reverse** it. The consequence of having control results in amazing, seemingly effortless accomplishment. This is possible because control enables us to align with and tap the power of the energy flows across the structures of the universe over time.

To clarify how the brain gains control of our body, and thus gets control of processes around us that are important to our survival, it is helpful to compare the body and brain development at birth of the two major types of animals. In the **r-type of animals**, the newborn is large and so well developed that minutes after birth it can stand up and run. They are the vegetarian, prey types of animals, such as deer, horses, giraffes and elephants. In contrast, for the **K-type of animals**, the newborn is very small and almost totally helpless. Many months of postnatal development and protective care are needed before it too can stand and run. These K-type animals include many of the predators, such as bears, lions, wolves, and also includes humans.

In humans, development of body control occurs slowly, appearing first at the head and last at the toes. That is, at birth, the infant only has control of its mouth and throat for nursing or crying. Next, it gains sufficient control of its neck to hold its head up. Then, it gains control of its arms before gaining the control to convert its paws into sensitive hands and fingers. Next come control of trunk and leg movements, along with gaining control of its bladder and intestinal sphincters. It learns to stand and finally gains control of its feet sufficiently to walk and later to run. Paradoxically, for all this, years of lengthy postnatal development is required to obtain that bodily control already possessed by r-types at birth.

Critical Periods of Brain Development Exist for Gaining Control of Voluntary Processes

There are many brain development critical periods concerned with control over a myriad of processes. Most are unknown. Many of these are prenatal, occurring *in utero*. In the infamous case of the Thalidomide Babies, their mothers received the drug to calm their anxiety during pregnancy. Unfortunately, an unknown side effect of thalidomide was that during the critical period of limb elongation in utero, it blocked the lengthening of legs and arms. This resulted in the birth of "Flipper Babies", whose feet were attached to their hips and their hands to their shoulders. After the period's window slammed shut, no amount of feeding, exercise, or absence of thalidomide could prevent these unfortunate children from becoming Flipper Adults. This is a powerful illustration of the existence of critical periods of development.

For the tiny and helpless newborns of K-type animals, including humans, obviously a large number of critical periods of brain development must occur after birth. For example, kittens are born blind. Their visual development occurs during a specific critical postnatal period a few days after birth. Experimental manipulation of their visual environment during this critical period can cause permanent thwarting, leading to impressive distortion and permanent malfunction of their vision as adult cats.

Critical Periods of Brain Development Exist for Gaining Control of Psychosocial Processes

No less important than the gaining of voluntary body control is the parallel development of voluntary control of psychosocial skills required to control the infant's interactions with its mother, father, siblings and others. That is, effectively and efficiently to be able to gain the attention needed to being feed, cleaned of excrements, protected from excessive cold or heat, transported, and assisted in other survival needs, such as to avoid unwanted attention, interference, or harm. This must be done in the presence of others also competing for parental attention.

Acceptance of their increasingly complex behavior by their mother and father becomes critical to their daily existence. It appears that humans complete the majority of these crucial developmental windows by the third year of childhood. Certain others appear during adolescence. There are hundreds, if not thousands of separate developmental processes to master, each with its own critical period.

Stages of Critical Periods of Development

1. *The Developmental Window is Not Yet Open: Before* the developmental window opens, there is developmental inaccessibility. At this time, it is premature to attempt to influence that part of the brain, as it yet lacks the ability to control this particular process. Forcing at this time can only fail. This can harm one's foundational self-concept as well ("My awe inspiring god-like parents think I should be able to control my bladder. Since I cannot, I must be defective or 'no good'). Parents are of course anxious for their child to develop rapidly and some think they can accelerate this by attempting to train them. Most are unaware of the existence of critical periods of brain development. It is better to let the child's brain-directed behavioral interests be their readiness guide.

2. *The Developmental Window now becomes Open:* This begins the critical period of developmental plasticity and accessibility. The Brain is now ready to gain control of this process. Self-motivated play and practice related to the process appear. The child uses great focus, effort, and

intensity to gain control of it, and thus access to later power. Brain seeks out this type of repetitive activity and rewards it as fun (eustress-good stress). Thwarting the unfolding of this practice-application activity is upsetting (distress-bad stress). Escalation of effort, preoccupation and negative emotions result from thwarting this development. Failure to control leads to the formation of developmental arrests and fixations. These activate inappropriate stress responses later in adulthood from these futile too-late efforts. Thwarting of development is viewed by part of the brain as life threatening. It therefore shunts these traumatic memories of such, *unexperienced*, into the

Reactive Mind as "too hot to handle".

3.*Developmental Window Closes Forever:* After the critical period has ended and its window closes, developmental rigidity appears. It has become too late for further facilitated learning. Belated training to gain control of the process is ineffective or impaired. The results of adult learning of a second language, or how to dance, is a product inferior in quality. **Table 1** lists ways that completing a critical period can be thwarted and development arrested.

Consequences of Failure to Gain Control:

Failure to gain control of a process during its critical period causes the formation of a permanent un-healing developmental wound. This is located in the Reactive Mind's "too hot to handle" memories of events, perceived

Table 1: Sources of Failure to Gain Control of a Psychosocial Process Before the Window Closes:

1. <u>Impoverished Environment</u>: For example, with no access to music, the child may develop into a tone-deaf adult.
2. <u>Choice of inappropriate or premature goals:</u> Control of mechanical skills might not be gained if a girl was diverted from tools or from vigorous physical sports for cultural or other reasons.
3. <u>Thwarting by Others:</u> If the child prohibited by siblings or parents from taking control of his own toy, the child may become an excessively demanding adult.
4. <u>Lack of Required Developmental Foundations</u> due to previous thwarting: A child will not be able to run if it was earlier prevented from learning to walk.

---

as death-threatening, thus segregated and blocked from conscious memory access. Last ditch attempts to gain control of the process now become exaggerated. The failed process inhibits or blocks those later development steps requiring it. A permanent defensive hypersensitivity appears surrounding the failed process. The person cannot be neutral about the process. Inferior coping compensations substitute for failure to gain control of the process

(**Table 2**). Further, the traumatized personality incorporates neg- ative elements of the Hexadyad Primary Emotions (Chapter 2) as illustrated in **Table 3**.

Table 2: Coping Mechanisms Designed to Compensate for Failure to Control a Process

1. Must Dominate Others:
2. Must Win
3. Must Look Best at all Costs:
4. Must Be (Dead) Right rather than Alive (through Compromise).
5. Possessiveness: Collects things or power, as a substitute for love-acceptance.
6. Tries to Change Things: More, Different, or Better compensations (which don't work).
7. Forms Survival Acts: Mr. Nice Guy, Ms. Funny Girl, Helper, Helpless, Know-it-all, Workaholic.

Table 3: How The Dyscontrol Wound Warps Personality Development:

Response to failure	Emotion	Personality Trait Favored:
I don't know how!	*Confusion*	Uncertainty
I am weaker than it!	*Fear*	Anxiousness
I am at effect, a victim!	*Anger*	Resentfulness
I am losing!	*Grief*	Moroseness, Apathy
I want!	*Desire*	Dissatisfaction, Greed
I reject other substitutes	*Disgust*	Negativity

Use of the "Ego defenses of the Id" adaptations or compensations also distort the personality (Chapter 2). Recall they include: Acting Out, Compensation, Denial, Displacement, Fantasy, Infatuation, Intellectualization, Identification, Introjection, Isolation, Undoing, Rationalization, Reaction Formation, Regression, Repression and Sublimation. These totally dishonest compensations to hide failure are displayed in public for all to see, except the victim itself. This creates disrespectful or opportunistic responses from others. Then, as result of being taken advantage of, we become excessively resistant to control by others. Thus, "We get what we resist the most": i.e. another failure to be in control of our relationship with someone else. These compensations become the unique "Sticking Points" of the dyscontrolled personality which literally alter their life's path. Thus, arrest-fixations block the natural flow of our social heritage by depriving us of what we value the most: respect, love, health, joy, mastery, abundance, opportunity and power. They instead force us down "lesser" paths of compromise.

A Program Exists to Repair Psychosocial Development Arrests, but It is Mutated and No Longer Works.
Living systems are protected by many repair programs. These include repair of chromosome damage, replacement of damaged cells, as well as for tissue, organ, and in some animals, appendage repair. Thus, evidence for the existence of a brain developmental arrest repair program (DARP) for the reversal of arrested and fixated failures to gain psychosocial control comes as no surprise. No doubt the DARP was an ancient powerful asset

to bicameral minded humans, who as a consequence of its effectiveness appear not to have been neurotic. However, something has happened to it, perhaps with the emergence of self-consciousness. It no longer can function properly and has become defective, the xDARP.

Nevertheless, it still is automatically activated cyclically and seeks to repair our developmental fixations and trauma, now with powerfully inappropriate behavior. The subconscious xDARP manifests itself as our alter ego, a negative second personality that is part of the Reactive Mind or the Sadomasochistic Mind and has been called the Pain Body (above). Amazingly, its continued inappropriate activities are the source of most, if not all, inappropriate, neurotic, and psychotic behavior. Once one becomes aware of the possibility of the DARP's existence, through recognition of Modular Consciousness, an enormous amount of previously unexplained human behavior can be recognized as originating from its unconscious activation.

xDARP Properties:

The xDARP appears to have at least nine elements in its repertoire seeking to complete our arrested psychosocial development. These include:

1. Unconscious Attraction: It is attracted specifically toward people in the present who are similar to the original nuclear family player in the psychosocial critical period drama over which no control was gained. This unconscious attraction element produces an irrational but powerful feeling of infatuation, a strange, almost overwhelming affinity, or "chemistry" for a certain person (target). Often these choices are logically inappropriate to the present, but not to the person's developmental past. For example, although there are six beautiful, lively, and intelligent women (or men) to choose from in your life at present, "you only have eyes for her" (or him): the one unconsciously chosen by the xDARP to match the negative elements of the personality of your mother (or father).

2. Age Regression: This mentally takes the one whose xDARP is activated back in time to the type of behavior they used at the time when the critical period arrest occurred. It is the source of infantile-childish negative behavior commonly seen in some adults at certain times.

3. Transference: The above important person in one's current environment is unconsciously selected target to stand in as a player representing the central nuclear family figure of the original critical psychosocial period drama, usually father, mother, or sibling. In this way, inappropriate behavior related to that of the original family member becomes transferred by the xDARP onto one's current mate, child, therapist, boss, or friend.

4. Establishment of a Struggle: Conflict develops between the individual and their transferred critical period figure substitute. If the xDARP has chosen properly, and/or if the other person's x DARP reciprocates, sparks begin to fly. Over the months, the xDARP of each focuses more and more accurately on what the other (target) is not willing to change about themselves. After about a year, the infatuation begins to fade and the battles intensify.

5. *Acting Out:* The childhood critical period theme is powerfully but unknowingly recreated so that the xDARP can continue to try to gain control of the operation associated with that early period. When these subconscious invisible battle lines are drawn, the war for control of one's relationship with the other begins in earnest.

6. *Compulsive Repetition:* The same thematic struggle can go on for years. It produces endless, usually escalating thematic arguments, conflicts, and upsets. These xDARP-driven battles are impossible to win because they apparently are held *unconsciously* to be battles of personal survival. However, even the death of one's parent-figure target cannot satisfy the xDARP's need. As a result, where xDARP-driven domestic abuse has led to murder of the target, suicide follows in a substantial number of cases. That is, if the target changes to accommodate the demands of the other, then often repeated new rounds of escalated demands are made upon the target, leading in some cases to demands that cannot be met without dying. Therefore, when the xDARP is uncontrollably on, the relationship inevitably will fail. However, with knowledge of the existence and biological nature of the xDARP, several other options to be described in the next chapter are available.

7. *Non Completion:* Gaining control and completion of a psychosocial operation has generally been impossible. This is because we presently lack specific knowledge of how to reopen the critical stage window and or what is required for its completion. Thus, the xDARP operates even though it is defective. Its activation will not lead to developmental repair, and instead is extremely harmful. Further, researchers are only beginning to learn how to turn it off. Thus, at present things only get worse and move toward the final collapse of the relationship and on toward a nervous breakdown. At the same time, the children inevitably produced by the warring couple can only become psychologically damaged, to recreate or amplify the same devastating scene in the next generation. This has many societal ramifications.

8. Lack of Awareness: The presence of the xDARP is unrecognized by the unaware, although perception can be gained in some cases. Because we are not conscious of this alter ego program, we aggressively rationalize our xDARP-driven inappropriate neurotic or psychotic behavior from the past as if it were totally logical and somehow appropriate to the here and now. Acting out its demands is seen as required for being authentic to oneself, rather than actually marching to the commands of a broken automaton. Yet, to those external to our problem and who do not have that particular arrest, our behavior often may seem ridiculous and arbitrary. However, those external to the conflict, who do have similar incompletions and associated past traumatizations, can become "hooked", upset, and drawn into the insanity of the conflict themselves.

9. Cerebellar location: The xDARP is located with the Reactive Mind, Thanatos, Pain Body, Sadomasochistic Mind on the cerebellar side opposite that of the social brain, Superego, Source.

The Typical xDARP-Pain Body Cycle of Abuse and Violence:

1. *The Safety of Love is Required before the Activation of the Perpetrator's Sadomasochistic xDARP is Possible*

The cycle of abuse begins when the target assures the perpetrator of their love (acceptance), and commitment. This creates a condition of personal safety and support for the perpetrator and subconsciously activates their xDARP to project upon the target in order to complete an ancient struggle for control, often originally with their father, mother, or sibling.

2. *Perpetrator's xDARP Distorts Neutral or Even Supportive Behavior of Partner into Rejecting Behavior*

The xDARP of the perpetrator compulsively acts irrationally, as if their lover is their enemy. This causes them to negatively misinterpret the meaning of a neutral or even supportive behavioral response by the target. This projection onto the target causes their behavior to appear to perpetrator to be a deliberate personal rejection of them. i.e. "You are upset and rejecting me for no reason!" "And, you are transferring your hostile negative thoughts onto me too!" Often the perpetrator defines their idea by assuming they can read the mind of the victim target. They then use this actively to present distorted imagined evidence to support their twisted view.

163

3. Partner Denies the Perpetrator's xDARP Accusation of Rejection

The target, originally in the "here and now" and originally having no negative motives, objects to the contaminating negative interpretation from the other's past placed upon them by the perpetrator's xDARP. The target's heart was pure, and they vociferously refuse to accept the negative accusations of the perpetrator's xDARP projected upon them. The perpetrator aggressively interrupts their objections and forces their partner to listen to them so that they can repeatedly rehearse their xDARP's subconscious tape from the past. This is often derived from the subconscious idea that in childhood their mother or father was rejecting and over-controlling them, and were the enemy.

4. Perpetrator accuses partner of not listening, and will not accept their partner's denial of rejecting behavior.

The target refuses to listen to this insanity and argues vigorously against the imposition of the neurotic and false theme from the past by the perpetrator's subconscious xDARP on their partner's neutral behavior. Quickly, the frustrated perpetrator complains that their partner "*will not listen to them.*" In turn, the target complains that the perpetrator will not listen to their "here and now" non-rejecting truth. Then, the frustrated target may seek retaliation and escalates the conflict, if the perpetrator has not already.

5. *The Target's own xDARP becomes hooked into a downward spiral of escalation of verbal abuse and physical violence.*

Because of the aggressive illogic of the perpetrator's xDARP, there partner's own xDARP often then becomes hooked, contaminating their "now" as well. They both demonstrate their non-listening by loudly talking at once. The conflict escalates until one stops talking, escapes, or physical violence begins. This leads to crimes of passion committed by trusted loved ones against each other, for which there is great later regret.

6. *After reaching a cathartic crisis, the xDARPs turns off, the partners kiss and make up, returning to acceptance, love, and clean communication.*

Then the cycle stops, and the partners re-approach, make up, and restore their total acceptance of each other with clean communication again. After a time, this renewed safety, acceptance, and trust, then subconsciously reactivates one or both of their xDARPs and the cycle of violence begins anew with ever greater vigor. Both feel that their own reactivated xDARP's illogical neurotic themes from the *past* are who they really are in the *present.* They cannot detect when their xDARP takes over again, except the xDARP theme is always painful and negative to the other.

xDARP-driven behavior has many things in common with the mania of bipolar illness. This is especially obvious in the aggressive transformation of neutral statements made by others into interpretations which are highly negative and rejecting, while maintaining a wholly exaggerated and unrealistically positive stance about one's own self. Such bipolar behavior is insane.

Insanity and the Broken Developmental Arrest Repair Program: The Devil Within

Sane behavior is appropriate to the here and now, while a response from the past is inappropriate to the present situation and is insane. xDARP driven behavior by definition is insane because it contaminates and dominates the present with past incompletions, often several decades old. If the xDARP is weakly activated, the behavior is called neurotic, and society tries to tolerate the resulting harm. If the xDARP is strongly activated, the behavior is psychotic. There, the resulting harm is too great for society to bear. If such a person is a danger mainly to others, they are placed in prison. If they are a danger mainly to themselves, they are placed in a mental institution.

Disruptive, antisocial behavior, subconsciously driven by xDARP activation, is occurring all around us. People often are attracted to specific friends, mates, and employers for reasons they can't satisfactorily explain, but which are consistent with xDARP operation. A semi-stable neurotic relationship forms if the unconscious needs of the xDARP of one or both is met. After a honeymoon period of infatuation, a neurotic struggle begins. This develops in earnest by the end of the first year. In this struggle, each unwittingly acts in an immature, childish, infantile way. They do not see the other, but only what they wish-need to see in terms of their past deficit. They run their own "rackets-patterns-tapes" from the past upon the person whom their xDARP has selected, and unwit-

tingly struggle over and over with them in order to be right about this past unrecognized arrested developmental theme.

The xDARP accounts for the blind spot most individuals seem to have about their own neurotic behavior. Because xDARP-directed behavior is highly inappropriate to the here and now, demands for its expression usually lead to repeated crises and ultimately to the destruction of the personal, social, or professional relationship. In spite of best intentions, this cycle is blindly repeated again and again with other targets, leading to failure, isolation, desperation and alienation. Thus, much of human behavior is xDARP driven. It is the source of unnecessary struggles with superiors (father, mother, older sibling figures). It is the source of unnecessary conflicts between peers (brother and sister figures). It also motivates unnecessary friction with underlings (younger-weaker brother or sister figures).

How the Broken Developmental Arrest Repair Program is Harms the Individual:

Activation of the xDARP is harmful, first because it promotes unconscious behavior destructive to oneself. As an example, it leads to inappropriate mate selection. In general, self-selection of a mate often fails to create a stable family. That is, almost two out of three marriages in the United States end in divorces. Arranged marriages, facilitated by family members and/or brokers, are used by more than half of the population of the world. This approach to family formation has evolved over the more attractive self-selection in part because it has been more successful in terms of both marital and extended family stability. Some of these arranged marriages appear largely to bypass xDARP-driven marital conflict.

Self-selection of mate is most often based upon sex disguised as "chemistry," that is, infatuation disguised as "love." Actually, this is a xDARP-based irrational compulsion, i.e., which because the xDARP in now based upon insanity. The powerful compulsion, that there is nothing more important than finding the right man or woman, has led to untold suffering because of this mutation. The person which one ends up with, via "chemistry," has been unconsciously selected by one's xDARP. Selected not to make a biologically optimal mate, but as someone to struggle with for control so as to complete a past, failed critical period, usually associated with failure to gain control with the parent of the opposite sex. Thus, these choices often make the least appropriate mates in terms of compatibility after the honeymoon. Once people know how to effectively use, or terminate the xDARP, it remains to be seen which method for marriage planning would be best: arranged or xDARP-selected.

xDARP driven insanity is everywhere. The existence of the xDARP is why "playing hard to get, works". For instance, consider the beloved opera, *Carmen,* by Bizet. Local beauty, Carmen, sneers at all her adoring suitors and focuses her attention on the impossible, that is, to seduce a military police officer, Don Jose, who has been posted in her gipsy ghetto to preserve order. He resists her advances because he is from an upper class, engaged to be married, close to his mother, religiously devout, and honest. Carmen ultimately breaks and seduces him. Her conquest of him and his surrender to her shakes him to the core. He finally tells her he loves her and will do anything

for her. As proof, he meets her demands one by one, leaving his fiancé, his job, and then his family to join Carmen's family of smugglers.

However, as far as Carmen's xDARP is concerned, Don Jose is no longer "impossible" but has now become just another needy suitor. Since he no longer matches the struggle inherent in her ancient failure to control her father's love, Carmen's xDARP begins to reject and revile him. She instead now fantasizes of another impossible conquest, that of a popular bullfighter coming to town. Intercepting Carmen on her way to the bullfight, Don Jose makes one last desperate attempt to convince her of his true love for her. She will hear none of it, and humiliates him even more. In his impassioned anguish, he stabs her in the heart, saying that if he cannot have her, no one will.

Love, defined as total acceptance of another, both as they are and are not, is in total conflict with the xDARP. The xDARP definitely does not accept the mate exactly the way they are and are not. Instead, the xDARP by trial and error seeks the one thing the other cannot-will not accept or do, and demands change of it as proof of love. "If only you would change this, I could truly trust in your love and everything would be all right." If one does agree to change that thing, the xDARP keeps looking for something you will not or cannot change. Then, it demands that if you really loved them, you would change that. However, since only Jesus Christ would die for your sins, most refuse to do so at some point. Then, the battle lines are drawn to gain control over the substituted mother, father, sister, or brother.

The other side of xDARP-based need is hatred and

domestic violence of the mutually activated love-hate relationship. Paradoxically, if the mates survive the repeated domestic violence, often they wish to be reunited even after severe wounds. Police have learned the hard way that interference in domestic arguments often results in both participants effectively redirecting their violence against the officers of the law. If one of the mates is charged with spouse abuse in the courts, many times the victim comes to their defense and testifies on their behalf, often blaming themselves.

Illustrations of xDARP-induced spousal violence.
1991: The Ganal case is Hawaii's worst murdering rampage, resulting from a husband-wife struggle and an affair on her part. This escalated to the point that the wife taunted her husband while having sex with him and made demeaning comparisons of him to her lover. The husband runs amok, shoots, firebombs and kills five of her friends and relatives, wounding three others, including his wife and son. He is now serving a life sentence with no parole. His wife blames herself. His son and relatives miss the husband who they say was "the best of men".

1993: The Nakata case, where there were injuries but no deaths in a "Ganal-type" case.

1994: The Moore case, Greyline Tours owner and his wife had an escalated argument in a car. The wife was shot five times. She was later convicted for refusing to testify against her husband, claiming it was her fault and that he really did not intend to hurt her.

1995: O.J. Simpson case, TV coverage of trial covering the consequences of escalating conflict between the noted football player and his wife. Two were killed. Simpson goes free.

More than occasionally, these repetitive cycles of xDARP activation result in the death of one of the players in the drama. This has become grist for massive public consumption via the news media, in part because it reactivates the xDARP in all who have been traumatized in infancy by the violence of what is called "normal" infant-rearing practices. As if there were not enough real cases to "hook" us, we pay for the soap operas, movies, and real operas with endless variations to dramatize this same tragic theme. Sex and violence sold very well at the box office in Roman times. They do so increasingly now, possibly because more and more of us are the product of dys-functional families with disrupted child rearing practices.

The xDARP is also a major source of inappropriate career selection. Surprisingly, job and professional career choices are often illogically, emotionally, and compulsive-ly made. This is because they are commonly based up-on transference upon, or even struggles with prospective mentors. Mismatching of a profession not suited to the ability of, or more importantly, to the true interest of the individual, often leads to life-long failure, frustration, and personal waste. Beyond this, the xDARP can also promote behavior harmful to one's employment. For ex-ample, the xDARP leads some employees to demand ac-ceptance of their professional incompetence as proof of acceptance (their parent's love). This obviously can lead to slowed promotion or even termination of their employ-ment, to say nothing of the quality of their product.

Similarly, xDARP activation is the source of inappropriate friend selection, and promotes behavior harmful to ones friendships. That is, the xDARP doesn't care about the other, except to gain control of its relationship with them, often by vanquishing them. As a result of its powerful, but inappropriate demands, the xDARP creates sharp rejection from others. This results in pain, isolation, loneliness, and alienation. Furthermore, behavior harmful to one's health is promoted due to xDARP needs. That is, attempts to satisfy xDARP-based compulsions (addictions) lead to overeating, smoking, drinking, loss of sleep, anorexia, promiscuity. The latter causes sexual transmission of disease, unwanted pregnancy, child abuse, overwork, high-risk behavior, and accidents.

How the Developmental Arrest Repair Program Harms Others:

xDARP activation not only hurts oneself, but also harms others. It is the source of hurtful, compulsive courtship behavior, including stalking, harassment, assault, sexual transmission of disease, and unwanted, or otherwise inappropriate pregnancies. These include, not only those pregnancies initiated by females to save a failing marriage, or because of the "ticking of the biological clock," but also initiated by many males who are unwilling or emotionally unable to use the discipline required for effective contraception.

One's xDARP can also hurt others by its compulsive use of impulsive, destructive child rearing practices whereby ten percent of all U.S. children have been hospitalized from child-abuse injuries. This abuse causes the formation of usually unrecognized, life-crippling xDARP-based stress disorders in each of these children. xDARP activation causes harm to others by forcing the inappropriate rejection of many good individuals, and by the production of assaultive behavior. Such violence includes spouse abuse, friend abuse, child abuse, aggression against weaker individuals or species, and by damaging the environment.

The xDARP is not only the origin of repeated divorce, but also of other societal problems, including joblessness, personal isolation, and criminality. It could be said that ignorance of the xDARP and its requirements led to the collapse of the Roman family and then the Roman empire. Such is a now becoming an acute problem in the west. Thus, developmental arrests and associated traumatization sustained by current infant rearing practices and consequent later xDARP activation is at the heart of the ongoing family collapse in western society. The east appears rapidly to be following in the same path.

Women are Responsible for Violence Too

It is a very stable statistic that the wife commits half of spousal murders. The 1985 National Family Violence Survey (NIMH) confirmed that men and women physically abuse each other equally. Wives report that they were more often the aggressor, using weapons to make up for their physical disadvantage. The annual spouse assault rate: 1.8 million husbands assault their wives, while 2.0 million wives assaulted their husbands. According to the

1986 Journal of the National Association of Social Workers, among dating teens, girls were violent more frequently than boys. Mothers also abuse their children almost twice as often as fathers do.

Consequence of the Broken DARP: Abnormal Stress-Sensitization in Adulthood

Early separation of the child from the mother produces major developmental wounding and arresting. This causes the permanent development of hypersensitive stress receptors. It also primes the individual for major xDARP activation in adulthood. For a K-type infant to be separated from the mother is tantamount to a threat of death, due to the infant's helplessness and vulnerability to harm. Thus, separation traumatizes by causing overwhelming fears in an infant, which from their location in the memory banks of the Reactive Mind can only lead to later neurosis. Animal studies have repeatedly demonstrated that only a few minutes of removal daily of a K-type infant from its mother result in the major permanent hypersensitization of its stress system later as an adult.

Harry Harlow (1976)'s "surrogate mother" monkey studies in the 1950s at University of Wisconsin produced, stress-sensitized, neurotic, violent, sex-warped, antisocial adults showing high levels of aggression, hyper-sexuality, and other antisocial behavior common in adult humans. James Prescott (1996) has long provided evidence that failure of infants to be adequately nursed is one of the most potent predictors of later adult violence.

We humans have lost our way, regarding the needs of our primate infants. Infants raised to adulthood in the wild by the higher apes, appear much happier and saner than our children do. Human infant discipline, punishment or rejecting behavior by parents becomes the source of later neurotic behavior. These noxious parental behaviors definitely are not part of the solution. Even, today, we traumatically separate our infants into their "own room and bed" for the night, leaving them "to cry it out." Then, in the next morning we drop them off for the day at childcare facilities. No wonder that mental health professionals have characterized more than twenty percent of US adults as mentally ill.

Further Confirmation of the Existence of a Separate Reactive Mind - xDARP

Harvard psychiatrist, Fredrick Schiffer, for years had treated patients with serious, sometimes incapacitating mental problems that appear to represent the prolonged activation of the xDARP in their lives. They were distracted, had sleep problems, often timid and inhibited, depressed, anxious, emotionally labile, and filled with self-fulfilling negativity. Some were Harvard students flunking out. They often saw their parents as critical and impossible to please. They felt worthless and that they must perform to be loved, but expected to be humiliated. Several were irrational, impulsive, over-emotional, or had suffered nervous breakdowns. They appeared to be stuck in a traumatic past with unresolved issues with their parents that contaminated their present relationships, causing them to make intolerable demands upon the ones they loved, as if seeking something their lover could not accept as proof of their lack of love.

Dr. Schiffer had been very interested in research reports that visual scenes could be imported directly to only one side of the brain of normal people by optical methods, such as the hemi-presentation of films through special split contact lenses. When films of violence or sex were presented separately to each hemisphere, often the right side of the brain reacted with greater emotion and stress hormone release. This was surprising because it had been thought the massive corpus callosum interconnecting the two hemispheres would immediately share what was being received by one hemisphere with the other. This proved not to be the case and is consistent with the later view that the corpus callosum is primarily inhibitory in nature, thus maintaining the separateness of the two hemispheres from invasion by the other.

The visual system of the brain is elegantly wired, as is illustrated in **Figure 17.** The retina of each eye is divided in half, the nasal side going to the opposite side of the brain, with the temporal side going to the same side. Thus, even if one loses an eye, the other still supplies both sides of the brain with full sight. Parenthetically, this fact led the present author to uncover a healing hoax. The subject claimed blindness in one eye. His purported evidence was that he could only see half of the room. He asserted that he was cured by the powerful prayers of a popular TV evangelist and can now see all of the room.

Figure 17

Retina to Brain Wiring Diagram

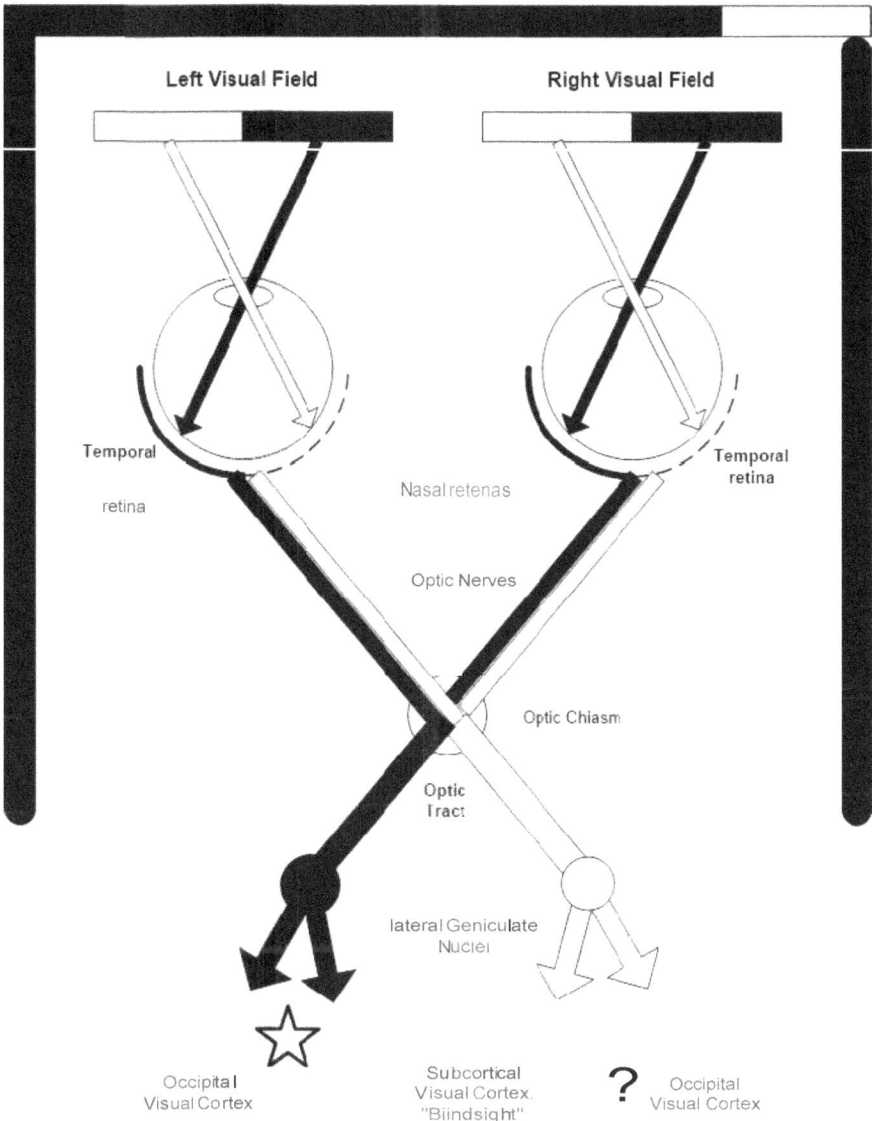

Figure 17 — Retina to Brain Wiring Diagram

TARGET STAR IS HERE

Goggle Blocking the **Left** View

Left Visual Field

Right Visual Field

Temporal retina

Nasal retenas

Temporal retina

Optic Nerves

Optic Chiasm

Optic Tract

lateral Geniculate Nuclei

Occipital Visual Cortex

Subcortical Visual Cortex "Biindsight"

Occipital Visual Cortex

What is especially interesting about the way the eyes are wired, is that if one could prevent visual input to all but the nasal side half retina of one eye, one would have preferential access to the opposite side of the brain. Conversely, the other side of the brain could be accessed by vision to the nasal retina of the other eye.

Grasping the significance of these new discoveries, Dr. Schiffer utilized this knowledge to devise a simple method of giving input to only one side of the brain at a time. At first he covered one eye of his patient, along with the inner half of the second eye, and had them look out the outside corner of the that eye, exposing only its nasal retina. Later he devised two pairs of goggles, which were covered over with black-taped except for the right or left edge, as diagramed in **Figure 17**. He found that when his patients looked out of the corner of their left eye, many felt quite different than when they looked out of the corner of their right eye. This was an Eureka moment for him, and led to his rediscovery that each of has what appears to be two minds. He later reported his findings in a book called: *Of Two Minds: The Revolutionary Science of Dual-Brain Psychology* (Free Press, 1998).

Using these goggles on hundreds of his patients over a number of years, he found that about 50% of them noticed a significant difference in mental state, depending upon which of the two pairs of goggles he or she was looking through. For about half of these, the effect was profound. That is, when one pair of goggles was worn for about a minute, the patient either felt good or began to feel bad. Importantly, Patients differed as to which visual side of goggle pair caused this effect. With one pair they became anxious, acting more emotionally immature, with negative ideas and feelings of defectiveness and failure, battling for control. They sometimes appeared sullen and withdrawn, easily upset, irrational, impulsive, over-emotional, and insecure. It was like the emergence of a full bodied personality that could be aggressive and de-structive, and appearing to stuck in a traumatic past. A Viet Nam vet with PTSD said a potted plant in office looked "like the jungle." After a minute wearing the other pair of goggles, exposing the other side of the brain, he said "No, it's a nice looking plant." With these goggles, patients became calm, upbeat, positive, and optimistic. Thus, began Schiffer's Dual Brain Psy-chology. He was convinced that we are of two minds.

After reading Dr. Schiffer's first research report, I myself made similar goggles in order to identify what ap-peared to be the emotional side of the brain of subjects in my hemisty studies. I found the reactive side of the brain to be unrelated to the hemisity of the subject. However, it was associated with a reversal correction required to ob-tain the subject's mirror tracing hemisity response. These subjects were unusual in that the most emotional side of their brain was on the left, as compared to the usual right (Morton, 2003c). Schiffer concluded that the reactive side of a person was idiosyncratic and not so much tied to RH vs. LH differences as to the existence of two minds, one mature the other immature. He did not know that he had found a way to isolate and talk to the subcortical Pain-Body of the xDARP.

As shown earlier in the chapter, this second, Reactive Mind has a fully developed personality that thinks, decides, possesses unique memories, motivations, and behaviors, and can be aggressive and destructive. As the automaton xDARP entity, it is developmentally fixated and unable to move beyond childhood trauma, expecting retraumatization. It is inherently arrested in ancient familial conflicts. In keeping with this, often Dr. Schiffer's patients had sustained some sort of developmental post-traumatic stress disorder (PTSD) including that from childhood trauma. Disappointingly, in spite of his using his goggles to work directly to their reactive minds from the beginning, his patients tended to take some years of psychiatric therapy to become normalized from their initial apprehension, despondency, emotional extremes, collapse, and drug compulsions.

As may be seen in **Figure 17,** visual input goes not only to the cerebral occipital cortex at the back of the head for conscious visual processing, but also to more ancient subcortical visual centers. The existence of active function of subconscious visual input was demonstrated by the mystifying phenomena of "blindsight." Patients with physical damage to the back of their heads often are blind in the center of their visual fields. Yet, it was found that if a ball was thrown into the center of this blind spot, they would automatically catch it, even while insisting on not seeing it coming. Since many neuroscientists have often focused only on the cerebral cortex as the site of vision, this effect seemed to fly in the face of what they thought they knew about sight. The discovery of subcortical subconscious visual centers has provided the explanation (Schmid, Mrowka, Turdchi, J., et al. (2010). That is, these subcortical areas were undamaged by the injury to the back of the head, and although their function is not acces- sible to conscious awareness, they could see very well, and reflexively caught the incoming missile. The xDARP may use these centers as well.

Modular Consciousness shows that we indeed have these two minds, one of which is the xDARP insane auto-maticity. Is there some way to bring sanity to millions?

This brings us to our next chapter.

CHAPTER SIX

CHAPTER 7: Restoring Peace and Sanity by Turning Off the xDARP, Devil-Within

Unwitting Past Attempts to Repair the xDARP:

Might it be possible to repair the broken Developmental Arrest Repair Program? Imagine the benefits if the xDARP could be rehabilitated to its full original healing potential. Then we would ultimately gain full control of all our physical processes, such as occurs by birth in the galloping gazelle and other r-types of animals. Much more importantly, every critical period needed to gain control of our social relations would also be completely developed. Because the majority of us sustain debilitating psychosocial developmental arrests, here is where humanity needs help in its present struggle to make that evolutionary leap from a killing to nonkilling global culture.

Ironically, without formal knowledge of the xDARP and its powerful subconscious stressful emotion generating effects, psychotherapists (including Fredrick Schiffer, in the previous chapter) have sometimes unwittingly activated the xDARP in their own work. That is, some therapies use deliberate *transference* of a patient's neurosis onto the therapist, causing *age regression*, promoting the *acting out* of a *repetitive* irrational theme, or the intense emotional arousal of *abreaction.* Individual patients or groups of them have experienced the application of such methods separately or together. Therapies employing these naturally occurring processes have long held promise. Nonetheless, they have also repeatedly failed to deliver statistically detectable improvements in mental health.

Most psychosocial developmental arrests occur during critical stages that open before one's consciousness center has moved from the brain core up into the cerebral hemi- spheres, something that happens around two or three years after birth. Once moved into the cerebrum, consciousness apparently uses a different memory for- mat that can no longer directly gain conscious access the earlier cerebellar primary memory. This makes early memories inaccessible to normal adult memory retrieval and correction. However, early memories, especially those too hot to handle memories, stored in the Reactive Mind, say from child abuse, are still reactive in our adult environment. Major memory gaps can be demonstrated regarding early events in the devel- oping child. Once these memories were easily accessible to the young child but at a certain point, they are no longer recallable. My son, age three, who I took on a road grader, demonstrated this. At age 7, he no longer could recall this "big deal."

Among certain individuals, it appears possible that hypnotic age regression can temporarily restore access to early memories. However, this delicate topic has sparked a "Recovery of Lost Memories-False Memories" debate, especially regarding child abuse charges by children or their therapists. Questions arise as to whether the memo- ries retrieved by hypnosis are only the product of the psy- chologist's inadvertent hypnotic suggestions. Or, were they the subject's real recollections of real events that ac- tually happened? This is also relevant to those who report memories of past lives. In a large study, such people exhibited significantly higher false recall and recognition rates, and to score higher on measures of magical ideation than control participants. An elevation of false memory for negative material may also appear in depression.

Currently, there are no known practical methods to repair or use the xDARP to complete one's arrested development as an adult. Therapists have tried many promising approaches. Some have unwittingly strongly activated the xDARP, such as Dr. Schiffer using his goggles. All have ultimately been disappointed.

xDARP Inactivation for the *Walking Wounded*:

If the xDARP is not available to repair arrests, can we instead turn off its powerful subconscious production of insane behavior? xDARP activation ultimately causes many more problems over time than the old failure to control the original process does! As we saw in the previous chapter, it is the major source of psychological stress, obsessive compulsions, crimes of passion, depression, suicide, and abuse of spouses and children. For millennia, native "researchers" have sought ways to lower xDARP stress production. In fact, global cultures, especially religions, are a repository of empirical methods that appear to work briefly. Yet, these give only temporary relief from the unrelenting xDARP activated subconscious stress.

First, sleep and good nutrition are essential. Lack of sleep or food significantly reduces stress tolerance and lowers the threshold for upset. This is because without adequate sleep and good nutrition, the Executive Ego Care-taker loses the strength it needs to inhibit xDARP activation.

Ironically, Physical Pain can Temporarily Suppress the xDARP: i.e., "No Pain, No Gain"

Second, for a reason to be described later, physical pain can temporarily reduce xDARP strength. Over the millennia, trial and error has revealed these benefits. In the relief brought by vigorous exercise, it is the frequently unrecognized production of *pain* and our ability to endure it that sets the rate and extent to which we exert ourselves. This is also true in aerobic, prolonged rapid breathing, and other hyperventilation exercises.

Cold stress, such as cold showers or swimming in ice water, which people have long found beneficial, also produce pain. All of these practices appear to weaken the xDARP by a common mechanism to be described later. Thus, when we feel "lousy," we tell ourselves that we have to get some exercise. Then, after the pain of vigorous exercise for a half hour, we feel renewed and good for a day or two, until we start to feel stressed again.

Who in their right minds would be willing to endure the pain of cooking for 45 minutes in a steaming hot tub, or in a Japanese *furo*, in a suffocating Turkish bath, in a Scandinavian sauna, or in the suffocating torture of the Native American Sweat Lodge? Yet, the good feelings that last for a couple of days that result after undergoing the various forms of heat stress provide the motivation for millions to regularly undergo the noxious experience of heat-associated procedures. "No pain, no gain" works!

Even the unrecognized pain endured in prolonged meditation and prayer can cleanse, if properly and regularly used. Similarly clean living, restraint and self-discipline are hard to practice because the self-discipline required by each actually results in pain. Importantly, these practices also bring their own reward of pain desensitization. Lastly, the pain of electro-convulsive therapy brings positive results, and by a mechanism possibly tied to the xDARP.

Psychological Pain from Cathartic Discharge is also Temporary Beneficial.

Third, it is becomingly increasingly clear from fMRI (functional magnetic resonance imaging) studies that the brain treats psychological or psychic pain essentially the same as it does physical pain, activating the same brain areas. Since much psychological pain started as physical pain, such as a slap in the face or an auto accident, this appears to make sense.

History of the Use of Psychic Pain to Gain Temporary Relief from the xDARP-driven Insanity:

Thus, the catharsis of an hour of psychological pain can also give two to four days of serenity from the subconscious emotional stress of xDARP. The effects of battles within the family illustrate this. After a huge emotion-wracking fight, the real pleasure is to kiss and make up for a couple of days. After that, the xDARP demons reemerge to feast again. In two powerful books, Eckhart Tolle (1999, 2005) unknowingly described the existence of the xDARP as his "Pain Body" metaphor, which exhibits an insatiable periodic need to feed upon psychological pain.

Further, the "Sacrifice" of an animal for food can also cause psychic pain, whether the killing of a familiar "friend" from one's herd, or that of a respected, exquisite game animal. The ancient penalty for "sin" was one's own death. Later, the sacrificial death of a scapegoat was used as a substitute for one's guilt, for example in Judaism. This was further dramatized in Christianity where Jesus was sacrificed on a cross as a substitute for our sins, so that we could live forever. The sacrifice-crucifixion motif can cause cathartic pain, and thus bring relief. It has been said that true Christian worship demands the daily deep con-templation of Christ's death that we might live. This is the central theme of Catholic worship. The added physical pain of self-flagellation, the dragging of a cross to exhaus-tion, and religious self-piercings have further amplified this.

A major source of the stress in living comes from the activation of the xDARP. Clearly, an unstated practical goal of religion is to bring reduction in the overall stress of living. Thus, it is of interest that many of the elements of religious practice are essentially pain inducing, such as standing for long periods during group worship, extended meditation and prayer, or the climbing of stairs to an icon on bare knees, etc. Thus, the world's religions are an in-valuable mixed repository of xDARP-weakening meth-ods.

However, there have been, and continue to be, other methods to create psychic pain and thus to reduce xDARP-induced stress for a few days. Ancient Roman coliseum rituals pitted innocence against evil in fights to the death. These themes gripped the crowd in an experience of emo-tional pain and cathartic relief. In a modern continuation of coliseum ritual, the bullfight features beautiful and brave animals doomed to die. The bull would always win, except picadors on horseback mercilessly severe the head-balancing elastic chords in the bull's neck with their lances. Without these built-in bungee-chords, the enor-mous task of now having to hold up a hundred pound head and horns soon brings the terrified victim to an exhausted halt. At this point any coward could kill it. Over the cen-turies, this ritual appears to have brought about a wide-spread callousness regarding the suffering and death of others, for example in the Spanish and Portuguese con-quests of the New World.

Today a clever entertainment industry brings us boxing and wrestling matches. The often-repeated rever-sals of fortune in these fights subconsciously cathartically grip us in a life and death struggle. Also, in the violent spectator sports, such as American Football and Rugby, rooting for the home team is a form of tribal warfare where the threat of the team losing brings life-death psychic pain to tribe "members" rooting on the sidelines. Even soccer fans and hooligans can act as participants in tribal warfare, unknowingly to gain cathartic release and feel good about it for a couple of days.

The belief that the psychic pain of drama, such as in the Greek Tragedies, produces cathartic relief has long been held. This cathartic release is sought in modern novels, theatric plays, movies and TV dramas. Now, popular media violence, depicting increasingly bloody gore enrolling us in vicarious battles between life and death further enhances these effects. This promotes addiction to catharsis, which the entertainment industry hopes will bring us back for another emotional release again next week. All this spectacular violence engages the subconscious core of our being in a cathartic struggle for life and death. This suffering, brings temporary relief from our underlying xDARP pain. As a result, we may even feel better for a day or two.

Relationship of the xDARP to the Devil and Demon Possession

At its extreme, the xDARP will totally resist correction and domination by another. In this case, it has access to all of the powerful cerebellar skills available to the victim in its possession. In fact possession is the appropriate word here. This use of death seeking powers on one side of the cerebellum is the opposite of the life-optimizing powers possessed by the opposite cerebellar God-Within, described in the next chapter. In this case these death-oriented skills, called Thanatos, or the urge for destruction or self-destruction, described by Sigmund Freud, are focused in attempts to harm the other to the maximum.

To the opponent, it seems that the responses of the xDARP-controlled person are totally diabolical. It is as if they are possessed by an evil spirit, a devil, a demon, that diabolically fights to the bitter end and would rather die than be exorcised. xDARP possessed persons have been noted down through the centuries. Wrongly thought to be manifestations of the external supernatural forces of evil, religious clergy have attempted to combat the xDARP by invoking the power of God, often unsuccessfully. When exorcism works, it is because the mind of the possessed one has been so overpowered and intimidated by the exorcist and his trappings of power, linked to the belief in an omnipotent God, that the xDARP becomes temporarily or in some cases permanently inactivated by the threat of death. Many deaths have occurred to exorcism subjects.

What is the Neurochemical Mechanism Behind this "No Pain, No Gain" Phenomenon?

The neurotransmitter serotonin activates at least fourteen known receptor subclasses. The 5-HT2a receptor is the crucial one with regard to stress. It is a key player in the stress response. Inflammation-based serotonin activation of this receptor causes the release of the peptide neurotransmitter CRF (corticotrophin releasing factor), a last-resort stress hormone with wide receptor distribution in the brain. If the ventricles of the brain receive direct CRF injection, the individual quickly becomes agitated and suicidally depressed. It is a well-known fact that serotonin levels in our brain strongly influence our mood, as if serotonin was it-self involved in the production of stress. This indeed is the case. Through the 5-HT2a receptor, serotonin causes CRF release and elevation. Pronounced dysphoria is the result.

A remarkable discovery has been that the 5-HT2a receptor becomes rapidly down-regulated in the prolonged presence of elevated serotonin levels, having a half-life of about one hour. Thus, after a short period of serotonin-el-evating stress, physical or psychic, the 5-HT2a receptor becomes down-regulated and desensitized, thus releasing much less CRF than the same amount of serotonin did in the beginning. This gives relief that can literally convert "agony to ecstasy".

Furthermore, unlike other down-regulated recep-tors, the 5-HT2a serotonin receptor takes about 3-5 days to recover its original sensitivity. Thus, during the days following a serotonin-induced catharsis, the person is markedly less sensitive to the serotonin elevations, due to physical or psychic pain, than normal. As a result, the person at first feels good, clean, and more peaceful, until the 5-HT2a receptor regains its sensitivity. Then, they feel rotten again because the xDARP is elevated from a con-tinuing background source of serotonin. This level is too low in amount to down-regulate the receptor, but high enough to cause CRF-induced dysphoria.

This is the serotonin-based mechanism behind the "no pain-no gain" paradox. Short-term physical or psychic pain elevates serotonin sufficiently to down-regulate its stress receptor for several days of relief from stress (Morton, unpublished). Importantly, current SSRI (serotonin specific reuptake inhibitors) antidepressants such as Prozac (fluoxetine) act to increase the level of serotonin at the 5-HT2a receptor slightly. After a couple of weeks, this re- sults in the down regulation of the 5-HT2a receptor, reduc- ing CRF release in the brain. This significantly reduces the production of CRF-induced stress that drives depression.

Methods to Reduce Stress Receptor Hypersensitivity and Lower xDARP Activation:

1. Temporarily Down-regulate the 5-HT2a receptor by short-term Physical or Psychological PAIN

Cold Pain: Icy swim traditions.

Hot Pain: Hot tub, Japanese furo, Swedish sauna, Turkish sweat bath, American Indian Sweat Lodge.

Exercise Pain: pain-limited exercise, run, bike, swim.

Emotional Pain-Catharsis: Spectator sports, Boxing, Wrestling, Football, Rugby, Basketball, Racing, Bull Fights, Drama, Opera, Movies, TV drama,

Intense Religious Practice: contemplation of the death of Jesus on a cross.

2. Temporarily Inhibit CRF-induced Stress with Drugs of Abuse

These include caffeine, tobacco, alcohol, cannabis, tranquillizers, painkillers, cocaine, amphetamine, morphine, heroin, etc. The inhibitory effects on locus coeruleus noradrenaline pain production are brief, difficult to dose with bad side effects, including tolerance development, intoxication, addiction, and death by overdose. However, as we are seeing, people will pay anything or do the unthinkable for the temporary relief from psychic pain.

3. By-pass Pain and Drugs by the Long Term Down-regulating of the Stress Receptor with Antidepressants

SSRIs (serotonin specific reuptake inhibitors) are very effective stress reducers and unlike the above drugs of abuse, SSRIs have the fewest long-term side effects. For LPs, Paxil (paroxetine) is best. RPs can also use Prozac, (fluoxetine). More recently, SNRIs (Serotonin-norepinephrine reuptake inhibitors) such as Paxil (paroxetine) have come to the fore. Be especially aware that at least two weeks of dosing is required before beneficial effects appear. This approach is much less costly in time and money than the huge expense of sports, entertainment, beverages or drugs in the attempt to feel better.

4. Low Doses of Modern Antipsychotics appear to Directly Block the xDARP

Very low doses of the modern antipsychotic drug, Seroquel (quetiapine) (25 mg), at bedtime appears to reduce the drive to act out xDARP themes the next day. This makes sense because xDARP behavior is psychotic. Twenty-five mg is great for sleep too, about an hour later!

5. Valproic Acid and Inhibition of the xDARP

The cyclic nature of the xDARP feeding frenzies

suggests a relationship to the manic-depressive cycles of bipolar affective illness. Mania also distorts reality with an omnipotent view of self, twists everything into a negative attack on others. Valproic acid is as effective as lithium with much fewer side effects for the treatment of this syndrome. Psychiatrists are beginning to prescribe this compound to couples in marital conflicts with some success.

6. Awaken to the Existence of One's xDARP-directed Stress and Detach from It

Upset, anger, and rage are the heart of the xDARP. They are essential steps in the homeostatic escalation of the original effort to gain control of a vital process. The Reptile Brain produces these feelings by instincts outside normal consciousness. Therefore one may feel: "Oh, No! Here I am, upset again in spite of my sincerest intentions otherwise. I do not even know how it happened. It just snuck up on me before I knew it!"

Transforming the Beguiling Artificial Reality of the xDARP

Here is a transformational idea: There exists within me a mutated, broken xDARP that subconsciously but actively cyclically creates my stress. My upsets seem so real because their survival-threat themes arouse me. My upsets seem so right because I believe that another person is causing them. My upsets feel so familiar and so authentic that I believe that they are the way that life actually is. My upsets seem so like part of me because they link me to my past by an unbroken chain of upsets.

However, my upsets actually base themselves upon the lies that xDARP reality tells. They come from the past, and generalize into gross distortions of the true external reality of the current situation. xDARP reality seeks any association that forwards its goal to set up a struggle with a safe person to (now impossibly) gain control of a childood arrested psychosocial developmental process. Its subconscious mechanical origin seems like external reality, but is only a concocted xDARP reality of the lowest quality. The transformational idea, *that upset reality is only xDARP reality, not the truth*, gives us a basis to detach from it, and step outside of it and stop acting out its insanity. I can *reject it as not me!* but rather an insane obsession of an automaticity that can only harm all involved.

Taking Responsibility for One's xDARP-Generated Anger:

Actually, our upsets are *not* who we are. We *have* upsets. *They* cause us stress! Our upsets come *from restimulated Reactive Memory of the past* and are not relevant to the here and now. Actually it is *my own xDARP*, not the other person, that is the *source* of my upset. Would I be angry at a bear? At a cliff? At a tidal wave? At a drunk with a knife? **NO!** Most often Anger comes from failure to control a process or an object from the *past*, *not* from the present environment, which is merely *restimulating* the past upset. Acting-out, dramatizing, and trying to win control in the present only strengthens the xDARP. As authentic as it feels, this approach ends in nervous break-down, psychosis, death, but *never* mastery. We are *not* our xDARPs inappropriate thoughts and feelings.

How to Detach from the xDARP:

Start separating what actually happened in the present from the xDARP's paranoid interpretation of it from the past. Usually it is a survival-neutral event, con-taminated by xDARP roots into the past, or, when it is not survival-neutral, your own xDARP often created it by its previous actions.

Recognize that you are not your xDARP. It is the source of the ideas of what you *think* you want, which are *unattainable*. It keeps you distracted, paralyzed, friend-less, hopeless and poor. It has filled your life with drama and trauma and has used up your years with meaningless-ness. Detach from it. Choose aliveness rather than proving yourself right. Stop letting your own xDARP victimize you. "Getting off of it" means taking responsibility for the fact that your xDARP-*not* the other person, is the source of your upset. Thank your xDARP for trying to help you complete your thwarted development, but decline its be guiling invitation to act out your developmental fixation in daily life. Stop your attempts to be right, to win the argu-ment, to dominate avoid domination. Do not complain, at-tack, wound, make wrong, have the last word, get revenge. Declare yourself "OFF OF IT". Doing so in public can be helpful. Stop! Count to ten. If necessary, leave the room to regain your composure. Become occupied with something else to get your mind off it. It will disappear. At first "Getting Off of It" may take days, then hours, then minutes, then seconds.

How to Begin to Keep The xDARP Off:

Stopping one's xDARP upsets is like "housebreaking" a puppy: <u>At first the puppy unconsciously wets anywhere, anytime</u>. Its xDARP upsets are automatic with No awareness or responsibility for them. "If there is a problem, it is the world's problem, not mine. I'm perfect!"

<u>After having its nose rubbed in a few puddles, the puppy looks confused</u>. Its upsets still are automatic, with increasing awareness, but no responsibility. The puppy is becoming clear that it is guilty of repetitive irrational behavior. However, it seems unthinkable that it might have a choice in the matter.

<u>Now, after wetting, the puppy looks sheepish</u>. Its upsets are becoming only semi-automatic with dawning awareness and responsibility. It begins to recognize there may be <u>a microsecond of choice</u> before it "xDARPs out".

<u>Then, after wetting, the puppy looks guilty.</u> Its xDARP upsets still are semi-automatic, but now with full awareness and responsibility. It is beginning to recognize that its xDARP upset harms others and itself. It wishes to stop wetting and to reverse the damage it has done (take control).The time window of choice has become wider and a reduction in xDARP upsets occurs.

No longer wetting, the puppy is joyful! Unless kicked, it can now be trusted indoors! It has gained voluntary control over former upset automaticity = Mastery! *Smart as a Puppy. Many people have matured from hourly upsets, to daily, weekly, or yearly upsets.*

Other ways to turn off the xDARP

Ways to deal with xDARP activation caused by conditions of love and safety:

a. Recognize that feelings of upset, rejection, and pain only come from the xDARP's reactivation. Upset is the first clue. Upset is always from the xDARP. Unlike the DARP, we are actually kind and loving, not vindictive and cruel.

b. Step back and detach from your xDARP and its neurotic theme from the past. It is causing you and your most cherished friend great pain, which if rationalized can only escalate.

c. Use all the spiritual help you can find to do this. Treat your xDARP like it was Satan and its upsets are as *sins* that are very harmful to you, to your loved one, and to your families. Pray for help, stop and count to 10 and begin meditating on the goodness of life.

d. Live in such a way as to strengthen your brain to overpower the xDARP.

Cognitive Behavioral Therapy (CBT): The Thinking Cure

CBT is the most extensively studied non-pharmaceutical treatment of mental illnesses, such as depression, anxiety disorders, eating disorders, and addiction. It can even be of help to schizophrenics. No other form of psychotherapy has been shown to work for a broader range of problems. It is quick and easy to learn, often with the aid of a psychologist or psychotherapist. After a few months of training, many can do it on their own. Unlike drugs, CBT keeps working long after treatment is stopped, because it teaches thinking skills that people can continue to use. *The goal is to minimize distorted xDARP thinking and see the world more accurately.*

One starts by learning the names of the dozen most common xDARP-based cognitive distortions (see below). Each time you notice yourself falling prey to one of them, you name it, describe the facts of the situation, consider alternative interpretations, and then chose an interpretation of the events more in line with the facts. Your emotions follow your new interpretation. In time, this process becomes automatic. When people improve their mental hygiene in this way – when they free themselves from the repetitive irrational xDARP thoughts that had previously filled so much of their consciousness – they become less depressed, anxious, and angry.

Common Cognitive Disorders
A partial list from RL Leahy, SJF Holland, and LK McGinn's Treatment Plans and Interventions for Depression and Anxiety Disorders (2012).

1. **Mind reading**: You assume you know what people think without having sufficient evidence for their thoughts, often unknowingly projecting your own thoughts instead.
2. **Fortune-telling**: You predict the future negatively.
3. **Catastrophizing**: You believe that what has, or will happen will be so awful that you won't be able to stand it.
4. **Labeling**: You assign global negative traits to yourself or others.
5. **Discounting positives**: You claim that the positive things you or others do are trivial. They don't count.
6. **Negative filtering**: You focus almost exclusively on the negatives and seldom notice the positives.
7. **Overgeneralizing**: You perceive a global pattern of negatives on the basis of a single incident.
8. **Dichotomous thinking**: You view events or people in all-or-nothing terms. "If I think you have insulted me, then you are evil and my enemy."
9. **Blaming**: You focus on the other person as the source of your negative feelings.
10. **What if**? You keep asking a series of questions about "what if" and you fail to be satisfied with any of the answers, implicating impending doom.
11. **Emotional reasoning**: You let your negative feelings guide your interpretation of reality.
12. **Inability to disconfirm:** You reject any evidence or arguments that might contradict your negative thoughts.

What to do if Someone Else's xDARP is Activated:

Avoid activating another person's xDARP if at all possible. Use your wisdom to spot and stay away from their developmental wounds. Criticizing another's hypersensitive area of dyscontrol guarantees their xDARP will turn on. This may hook your own xDARP as well. If another's xDARP is already on, recognize it and do not engage it. It is insane, does not respond to logic, and will distort what you mean. It is dangerous and can escalate to crimes of passion. You cannot win. Let it cool down and turn itself off. It is not personal, except that you must be so important that their xDARP has transferred a key nuclear family member from their past onto you: a high compliment! The other person may care for you very much and actually does not want to hurt or lose you. Don't force them to. Support them in discovering the existence of xDARPs, something that can be hard to do. Then, they can begin to take responsibility for their own xDARP-driven past behavior, and stop blaming you or the world for their unhappiness. Give them the tools to transform from a victim at the effect of life into a Causal Source, loving what Is!

A Permanent solution: Data-based Love of Newborns and Infants

Thus, in spite of our best intentions and sincerest efforts to raise normal healthy children, we are failing. It would appear that it would be wise to look more carefully at the evolutionary needs of the children of higher apes

(Gorillas, Bonobos, Orangutans, and Chimpanzees) during their formative years of brain development. We also need to conduct an in depth investigation of infant separation and later xDARP activation in adulthood. Our genetics appear to lag behind the present by at least a million years. We would do well to research the ancient genetic needs and child rearing methods of hominids and apes existing at 1 million BC and apply them to our present infants. They may require perianal stimulation where the neonate is cleaned by licking at birth and after excreting. There was no cloth, paper or plumbing back then. It may be that our needs are still like those apes whose hominid infants were breast feed with full skin contact night and day for 5-6 yrs of weaning. The infant-mother pair defines a higher-level system with symbiotic emergent properties! It must become widely recognized that child bearing is not a "the clock is ticking" rite of passage. It is a privilege of devotion for which only a few are qualified.

Until we recognize the multilevel existence of familial polarity, the xDARP will continue to take its toll as a side effect, inflicting emotional pain in our young children, which leads to permanent developmental arresting. This causes stress-sensitization, reward-hunger (drug seeking), and neurosis in adulthood. These produce conflict, corruption, waste, violence, killing, and war.

CHAPTER SEVEN

CHAPTER 8: Removing Guilt Pain to Regain the Ability to Grow

We feel guilt and its associated pain for only one reason: It occurs whenever our neocerebellar Social Brain Source judges that we have selfishly harmed another's survival in order to benefit our own. Instead of working at the universe level of "win-win or no deal" familial cooperation where we delight in helping others, we have dropped to the next lower antisocial level of self against the world and have harmed others. This may happen if our Executive Ego has been so weakened by stress that it can no longer restrain the "I win, you lose" Dominator-brain from taking over. The Id only lives in the now, being oblivious to the past or future effects of its selfish behavior.

However, the Social Brain Source has evolved two protections for the family against wanton selfishness of one's self. First, it has developed a subconsciously potent device for inflicting punishment upon the selfish-brain. This is the "pain of guilt. Guilt is the festering, relentless, gnawing pain of conscience, often subconscious, that will not quit. *A pain from which there is "no gain."*

Originally, when one empathically felt the pain of guilt, one's associative intelligence would logically conclude that restoration of the other's harmed survival would immediately cause permanent cessation of guilt and thus bring relief. In fact, this simple solution still works extremely well. However, time has revealed other seemingly easier solutions. Omnivorous, experimenting humans, by

trial and error over millennia discovered natural substances that temporarily actually turn off guilt pain. These
included tobacco, caffeine, alcohol, marijuana and opium,
all of which became known and popular because they each
could temporarily replace guilt pain with pleasure.

However, this occurred at a cost. Seeking cellular
homeostasis, the body soon developed a resistant tolerance
to the guilt-pain killing drug, requiring progressively
greater amounts of it to bring relief. At higher dosages,
side effects become increasingly prominent. Often, these
included intoxication of the higher brain along with a replacement of a clear intelligence with a foggy drunkenness
leading to unconsciousness. They also greatly increased
mortality by causing physical and metabolic damage and
tumor formation, not to mention current automobile
deaths, more than half of which are associated with alcohol.

Worst of all, the subconsciously hurting person becomes more dependent upon these narcotics for relief from
unremitting pain, ultimately becoming addicted. These addictions are so strong that the victim will lie, cheat, steal
and even kill to obtain drug-based relief by them. They
will pay any price, even sell their homes and children for
temporary relief from escalating guilt pain. A personal
comment by a Central American Drug Lord to the author
one night at dinner emphasized this. He said that to feel
well, he had developed a fixed schedule of twenty drinks
of liquor to be taken over the course of each day. Now
that's a lot of pain!

This makes narco-trafficking the most profitable business in the world. With their enormous income, which people are eager to pay, competing drug cartels can buy firearms, officials, vehicles, and gangs of foot soldiers to fight each other to gain and retain control of the fortune that the suffering population spends in an attempt to get relief from its pain. The illicit drug cartels are even infiltrating and corrupting national governments. Because people have forgotten how simple it is to remove guilt by restitution, they are instead paying narco-traffickers their hard-earned money, and in the process threatening to bring down society and civilization itself.

As part of this process, society members have become increasingly more self-oriented. Global competitive enterprises, ranging from arms sales, based upon political destabilization, to the entertainment media cashing in on sex and violence are creating an atmosphere where violence-worship and killing are destroying family values so that almost two of three US marriages fail. It is becoming harder not to inadvertently harm others just in the process of life itself, thus, generating ever more subconscious guilt pain and drug seeking. Since our genes appear to lag a million years behind the present, our old Social Brain continues to keep score and punish us with guilt pain for our "sins": specifically, those of helping ourselves at the survival expense of others. We appear to be in an accelerating downward spiral returning us to the ancient jungle law of kill or be killed.

Causing Another's Loss Invariably Results in Your Own

There is a second inhibitory mechanism that our Social Brain Source has developed. This was to block profiting at another's expense, thus preventing us from benefiting from ill-gotten gain. We may take or extort something from another, but our Social Brain will not let us actually "have" it. As the old saying goes, "You can't have your cake and eat it too." This is because one's Social Brain Source is the Dominator Brain Id's worst judge and executioner. The Source always tells the truth, and sees to it that the selfish Dominator brain can never profit from the theft of another's survival. Thus, the person with perpetrations harming others becomes *unable to benefit from anything* in that area. For example, after theft, money is actively sought, but always rapidly disappears through holes in pockets, like sand through grasping fingers. Or, the right mate can never be found, despite a lifetime of intense effort.

The great news is, that this cycle of endlessly seeking impossible relief from stress and blocked pleasure can be brought to an end through a very simple, easily achievable means. That is, one simply must completely and generously restore the survival of the person we took advantage of earlier when we helped our self at their expense. What's more, one's Social Brain actively wishes us to clean things up, and actually helps makes it possible to do so, as seen below. One sign that we have made complete restitution is when the harmed person can easily look us in the eye, smile, warmly forgive us, and welcome us back into the family again.

The Ancient Secret of Having:
Application #1: **Having Money**

1. Make an ongoing perpetration list of all persons you have ever taken anything of monetary or survival value from against their will or without their knowledge. Tell the truth when you make your list. Avoid such rationalizations as: they did not really need it or would have given it anyway.

2. Sort the list so that monetarily, the smallest perpetrations are at the top and the "impossibles" are on the bottom.

3. Repay the dime you stole from your Mother's purse, which at the time carried as much guilt as robbing a bank would to an adult, and discover a huge lessening of guilt pain.

4. Continue in this way to discover that *the more one makes restitution and repays, the more one's ability to have money and happiness increases.* Thus, you will become increasingly cnabled to generously repay even the most dreadful of harms against others and to ask for their forgiveness of each. If you have truly made complete restitution to the other, they will happily forgive you and actually want to be your friend.

5. Thus empowered, keep on reformulating and paying off your list of perpetrations until it is exhausted. By this time *you will **have** the abundant happiness,*

friends, respect, and wealth, which is your natural heritage.

6. Next, identify what else that you want badly, which you currently seem unable to be able to **have**, and repeat the process of cleaning up your life. It really works.

Self-Rehabilitation and Empowerment:
Application #2: **Cleaning Up and Terminating xDARP Upsets from the Past**

Almost all of the things that upset us come from the restimulation of one of our unhealing developmental arrest wounds or other death threatening events from the past, inaccessibly stored in the memory banks of our Reactive Mind. Because of your unique set of these traumas, what may upset your xDARP deeply, may not bother another person in the least, and vice versa, although there are common themes upsetting others as well. Fear from true danger is not upsetting. If you find yourself upset, it is because you are struggling for control of a process you were not permitted to master before its developmental window closed. Upset is on the same gradient as anger is. Both are the impotent reactions of a victim failing to gain control of a social process or other trauma. The upset person usually irrationally places blame for their upset upon someone else. Blaming others leads to harmful attempts at retaliation against innocent bystanders that often ruins formerly rewarding friendships and creates enemies out of good people.

It is very hard to be objective about one's current xDARP upset. However, one's upsets follow repetitive themes related to one's particular unhealing developmental or other wounds. Thus, to begin to take responsibility for being the source of one's own upsets, it is helpful at first to look at previous upset cycles. Thus, find earlier-similar repetitions of your current xDARP *upset theme* in the recent past. Note the harm they did you and especially to the others involved. When this becomes clear, acknowledge your fault. Confess to each of those you victimized how you harmed their survival. Repair damage and restore the survival of your victim until they forgive you and accept you with open arms as family once again. If they cannot look at you with a direct gaze and smile, your restitution is still incomplete. When it is clean, the original issue will be forgotten, or seem overblown and crazy. Remember, there are two opposite realities: Yours and your xDARP's. Next, clean up the present upset you have caused. Then, move on to others until you truly become honest, open and happy. Recognize once again that you are not your xDARP's thought or feelings. Repeat the process figuratively with those impossible to reach or who have passed onl

Although I learned of the operation of this ancient principle from a member of the Church of Scientology in the 1970s, I later discovered it to be a core element of the Twelve Steps of Alcoholics Anonymous. Here are the Twelve Steps further generalized for application to any compulsion that places you out of control and upset.

Compulsives Anonymous, A 12-Step of Program from the Society for Neuroreality:

1. We admitted we were powerless over the compulsive selfish impulses of our xDARP and that our lives had become unmanageable.
2. We came to believe that only a Power greater than ourselves could restore us to sanity.
3. We made a decision to turn our will and our lives over to the care of our Social Brain God-Within, Higher Power, Holy Spirit, Source, Teacher, as we understood It.
4. We made a searching and fearless moral inventory of ourselves.
5. We admitted to our Source, to ourselves, and to another human being, the exact nature of our wrongs.
6. We were entirely ready to have our Source remove all these defects of character.
7. We humbly asked our Source to remove our shortcomings.
8. We made a list of all persons we had harmed and became willing to make amends to them all.
9. We made direct amends to such people wherever possible, except when to do so would injure them or others.
10. We continued to take personal inventory and when we were wrong, promptly admitted it.
11. We sought through prayer and meditation to improve our conscious contact with our Source as we understand It, praying only for knowledge of Its will for us and the power to carry that out.

12. Having had an awakening as the result of these steps, we carry this message to others overrun by their xDARP, and practice these principles in all our affairs.

In conclusion, this process provides a simple, effective solution to remove our dysphoric pain and our punished incapacitation that we have brought upon ourselves due to our ignorance of an ancient subconscious law of the mind. The more that we clean up our past and present life, the more our moral Social Brain Source will become willing to trust us and to open its channels of communication to the flow of its wisdom and guidance.

CHAPTER NINE

CHAPTER 9: Hallucinogens Breakthrough: Ego-Death Gives Access to the Wisdom of the Source.

It is the author's view that in the process of the human species becoming self-conscious about three thousand years ago, two harmful things have occurred: First, the DARP no longer functions to repair developmental arrests. As the result, not only are all of us, a) psychosocially arrested, causing interference in human relations, but also, b) we are plagued by the repeated activation of the xDARP, whose insane behavior destroys intimate, once loving relationships, damages marriages across societies, and permanently traumatizes the children of their formerly caring partners. This genetic defect degrades the human race away from its once incredible potential to optimize terrestrial life.

Second, along with the emergence of cerebral self-consciousness and the breakdown of the bicameral mind, we have lost all conscious access to our Superego, God-Within, to guide us, as the ancients once did. This is a serious loss. We feel its absence deeply, and yearn to be reconnected. This is the foundational motive behind all religious desire and seeking. However, anciently we became confused into thinking that God is external and supernatural. In our desire to know Him, we have objectified this fantasy, falsely making our now inaccessible Source into the creator of the universe.

Again, we have lost our way. We need to return to the truth: that hidden within each of us is the real Higher Intelligence, based in our cerebellar Source. When contacted, its awe-inspiring wisdom appears so superior to our normal consciousness as to cause us to mistakenly externalize it as divine. As we will see in a later chapter, this rare contact with the inner Holy Spirit has been the origin of all world religions. Normally, however, as the result of human evolution, our anxious Ego-based new found self-consciousness powerfully suppresses our Superego Source, so that long ago we have become unaware that our brain-based God lies trapped within, knocking at one's heart door, closer than one's breath.

Reunion with our Hidden Social Brain, God-Within, Source of Ideas, Wisdom, Peace, and Joy

At end-of-life experiences, where one's brain is so Drained as to be near death, our Ego-based self-conscious-ness begins to collapse as our brain begins to fail. This releases the cerebellar Source-Holy Spirit to come to the fore in the form of ineffable near-death experiences. Here is the first and only time most of us come in contact with the non-supernatural divine. Survivors are forever changed.

However, over the millennia, other ways have been found to loosen the death grip of the self-brain Id and gain access to one's Higher Power without physically dy-ing. These methods to transcendence have always required an intense "hitting the bottom" and letting go of life in unavoidable "Ego death" experiences. Discovering that they were still alive, such persons found themselves in the awesome presence of a Higher Power, something they felt to be ineffably superior to their normal consciousness. This always brought about a life-changing personal transformation away from petty self-survival to a rebirth under the direction of the infinitely superior cerebellar Source, Holy Spirit. Such an experience of transcendence brought wisdom, fulfillment, and peace. This transformation is every person's rite of passage into becoming a mature human being.

Over recent centuries, this Ego-death initiation has been accomplished by traditional non-western coming of age near-death initiation ordeals, intense meditation-prayer procedures, religious "born-again conversion" experiences, Alcoholics Anonymous transformations, and the sacred use psychedelic entheogens, both outside and within religion. Thus, the cerebellar Source has inspired scientific discoveries and revealed increasingly accurate models of the universe, life, and mind.

Practical Routes to Personal Transformation:

Fasting and prayer austerity approaches to self conquest have long existed. Those few who have been sufficiently motivated to starve themselves and meditate intensely, such as Buddha or Christ, have after years of effort suffered Ego-death and rebirth to the Superego, God-Within. Upon experiencing the powerful, positive results of such transformations, they were motivated enthusiastically to share their experience. Thus, they have, as described in a later chapter, gone on to found world religions. These became filled with envious members who wished to become like their leader. But, successful followers were rare indeed. This kept essentially all from ever knowing their hidden God Within. Inevitably, the religions later evolved away from Ego death and rebirth, or become modified into Egoistic forms of regressive fundamentalism.

In other parts of the world, certain psychoactive plants have been useful in bringing about the personal transformation of many persons, originally within a shamanic context or as parts of primitive-yet sophisticated rites of passage into adulthood.

With the emergence of neuroscience, psychoactive chemicals, such as mescaline and psilocybin, have been identified and isolated from these botanical sources. Because of their production of ever changing vivid unrecognized pure forms, scientists first called these agents, *hallucinogens.* Later they were called *psychotogens,* that is, bringers of what was ignorantly called psychosis. When their true value was more recognized, they were renamed *psychedelics*: because they seemed to be mind manifesters. Even more recently they have been called *entheogens*: the revealers of the hidden god within. An even more accurate term would be would be to call these serotonin 5-HT2a receptor agonists, *ideagens*, because by inhibiting our Ego, they open the gates to our Source who inevitably shows us possibilities that we would never have thought of about the way the universe is in all its complexity and ever-changing beauty.

Many derivative compounds have been synthesized. The most potent of these is LSD. Some of them, such as DMT are even found in the brain. Yet, DMT is not normally potent there, due to its rapid transformation into an inactive substance by monamine oxidase enzymes.

The psychedelics belong to a unique category of substances. They are the opposite of the pain killing drugs of abuse that are corrupting the world, such as derivatives of marijuana, opiates, and stimulants. Pleasure seekers are not interested in dying to find their own God within. Quite the opposite. They are hysterically running from their internal pain, seeking but never quite finding that pleasant state of mindless numbness.

Timothy Leary, and other Harvard psychologists

obtained large amounts of LSD from Sandoz Pharmaceuticals in Switzerland and began religious and later social experiments where thousands of people willingly ingested psychedelics as entheogens. However, Leary discovered that there were recreational aspects of psychedelics, which when combined with marijuana, appealed to him and ultimately millions of others in the 1960s.

Shortly thereafter commercial interests sought to synthesize cheaper substitutes for the major hallucinogens. A major group of these compounds belonged to the family branch that contained STP, DOM, DOI, etc. Instead of reaching a maximum ego death within an hour, they were more slowly absorbed not reaching their peak until about 3 or 4 hours after ingestion. Further, they released lesser amounts of rewarding dopamine than the classic hallucinogens.

This was very confusing to a great many, who when not feeling anything at all within an hour, and being used to the rapid onset of LSD, concluded that they had been cheated by their dealer and that their illicit drug was too weak due to deliberate dilution. Many of them then took a second and third dose. Thus, when the 4-hours high from the first dosage came, they where hugely overdosed. So, when the even more powerful effects of the delayed second and third dose arrived to their brains, they became terrified, filled with panic, and rushed to hospital emergency rooms. As a result, the widespread unsupervised, uninformed use of these cheaper slower acting, but extremely potent mind-dissolving substances, produced many tragic negative effects on thousands of the naïve and unstable. Even with only 1% serious side effects, these thousands of damaged lives began to mount. This still unrecognized effect of the cheap synthetic hallucinogens led the government to declare all entheogens illegal, regardless of their potential for good.

As a result, no entheogen is legally available in the first world. Yet, in terms of the serious search for and contact with the hidden God-Within, they are essentially indispensable. Their usage is not habitual and absolutely non-addictive, but more of a rite of passage into human-hood. I must say that their use totally salvaged my life and permanently profoundly transformed my thinking, filling me with sets of powerful ideas whose beneficial ends I have yet to see, now thirty years later when I have again re-approached them on another level, to know my true self.

Today, the only legal way to seek access to one's hidden Source is through the peyote-using Native American Church or the ayahuasca-using churches now springing from the jungles of Brazil. Two of them, Unao Vegetal (Union with the Plant) and Santo Daime (Holy Give Me) have spread internationally.

Ayahuasca is a two-part, boiled vegetable brew, consisting of a harmala alkaloid-containing vine and a leafy plant containing normally immediately metabolized DMT. It is said that neither has much psychoactivity in of themselves (but see Chapter 12). However, when combined, the mixture becomes profoundly potent. This is because the harmala alkaloids in the vine are powerful inhibitors of monamine oxidase A (MAO-A). As a result, the DMT in the leaves, which is normally quickly removed from the blood by a person's internal MAO-A, now builds up within the body, including in the brain. Ego-death ensues and the hidden Superego, God-Within comes to the fore. Ayahuasca use is expertly described by Dr. Benny Shanon, of Isreal in his comprehensive-book, "Antipodes of the Mind" (2002). Many thousands of worshipers using ayahuasca as sacrament say that they have lost their alcohol and drug seeking drives and have been transformed into productive citizens, full of enthusiasm for family life.

A Neuroscience Explanation of Ego Death and Transcendence

Recently, after a half a century of prohibition against the human use of hallucinogens, Professor David Nutt of the Imperial College of London, after prolonged negotiations with the government, was given permission to administer psychoactive psilocybin to humans under tightly regulated conditions. Using fMRI (functional magnetic resonance imagery) researchers from David Nutt's laboratory, especially Robin Carhart-Harris, observed to their surprise that a specific brain area became profoundly inhibited after psilocybin ingestion. It was our old friend, the *cingulate cortex*, here and earlier proposed by myself to be the site of the Executive Ego. As the cingulate became inhibited by the psilocybin, many of the subjects experienced "Ego death and Transcendence" in the form of merging with something greater and wiser than themselves.

Within that state, a hidden higher intelligence emerged and made itself available. Entheogen intoxication, in this case by psilocybin, is always biphasic: Ego loss over an hour or two is followed by several hours of game-free reintegration, where the Ego is stripped of all its former avoidance games and restored in a pristine condition. People experiencing these events almost always counted them as something truly profound, the peak experience of their lives. They are transformed by the discovery that the Superego Source, Higher Intelligence has much to reveal!

It appears that after more than a half century of hallucinogen prohibition, the drive to reinvestigate these fascinating substances is coming to the fore in the form of a "mind research" renaissance. Hopefully, this can lead to the restoration of a coming of age rite of passage that will transform society.

Current Attempts to Describe and Quantify Ego Death and Transcendence

Many research studies are recently underway to define the nature of the hallucinogen experience. At a sufficient dosage, the great majority of participants report it to be the most awesome life-changing experience they had ever had. As the result of the profound inhibition of their cingulate cortex Executive Ego and the consequent dissolving of its many inherent boundaries, most subjects achieve a transcendent state. This is defined as to include at least six of the following seven elements occurring after Ego death:

1. Internal unity: Loss of usual identity: to be pure Being
2. External unity: Experience that "All is one", deep insights
3. Transcendence of time and space: eternity, infinity
4. Ineffability and paradoxicality: it cannot be described
5. Sense of sacredness: amazement, and humility
6. Noetic quality: the ultimate reality, intuitive knowledge
7. Deeply felt positive mood: Exalted, ecstasy, joy, love

Plato's Theory of Perfect Forms Finally Makes Sense: Hidden Within Us is a Powerful Pattern Generator.

Plato was born around 428 BC, possibly in Athens. He became such a brilliant philosopher that it is has been said that all philosophical things written later were only a series of footnotes to him. He is also known to have participated in the hallucinogenic rites of the Elusian Mysteries, a Greek tradition lasting over 2000 years until Christianity terminated it. Thus, Plato was well-experienced in the use of hallucinogens.

Without knowing it, Plato in his Theory of Forms, very accurately described the nature of the neocerebellar Source *pattern generator,* first proposed here. Because of Greek ignorance of genetics, he was forced to believe in an immortal soul in order to explain the origin of these perfect forms. That is, he felt that one's soul had resided in heaven in a past life, where it became familiar with the perfect forms.

Although past lives are an imaginative fiction, he did correctly believe that there are two levels of existence. They are the *Realm of the Senses* and The Realm of the Forms. In the realm of sense experiences, nothing ever stays the same but is always in the process of change. As pre-Socratic Heraclitus said "One never steps into the same river twice." There are only shadows and poor copies, less real and unreliable. Experience of the senses give rise to false opinions, as illustrated in Plato's Cave of illusions.

In contrast, there is the *Realm of Forms*, outside of space and time, and not perceived through the senses. In that realm, everything is permanent, perfect, absolute, ideal, and real. Such Forms are eternal, unchanging, and the proper objects of knowledge. Yet, according to Plato, they are not just limited to geometry. For any conceivable thing, there is a corresponding Form, a perfect example. The list is almost infinite: house, tree, mountain, man, woman, ship, cloud, horse, dog, chair, table. All have independently existing abstract perfect ideas. These are the "hallucinations" and otherforms seen when taking psychedelics. They are the gifts of new ideas, shown as "realer than real", by the cerebellar Source. It is of interest that the schizophrenic, John Forbes Nash was awarded the Nobel Prize in Economics in 1994.

What is the Brain Origin of the Music Often Running in our Heads?

I am often soothed by music that I hear inside me during the day. It is always of the music I have listened to recently from among my recorded favorites, usually classics or choral works that I love and that I have sung in concerts. These recordings in my head usually play for days, even weeks until I listen to different works, which then become the sweet music I hear. Occasionally, I may hear music from my more distant past.

Where does this music come from? Who is playing them over and over in the background of my daily life? It seems to me that they are coming from a different brain module than my intellect. I assert that, out of the seven, the cerebellar Superego is the most likely source.

With Total Access to One's Memories, Plus a Powerful Pattern Generator, The Source is a God-like Entity of Enormous Capacity Trapped within Each of Us.

This is an atomic bomb-sized game changer! Imagine, each of us has in addition to our normal consciousness, another very high level conscious mind. It is hidden and trapped within us as a genetic part of who we are. Unlike pre-Greek humans who could fairly easily access their God-Within for guidance and wisdom, we have gone through three millennia so totally cut off from this higher consciousness that we have become totally ignorant of its presence in each of us.

Imagine yourself being that Source, completely trapped incommunicado in your body's subconscious by a quirk of evolution. This higher "you" can only watch your body's behavior being directed by a lower form of egoistic consciousness, doing stupid, selfish things, totally ignoring others, killing other animals for food, caring little for nature and the earth, being primarily focused on sex, believing the attempted imitations of you in a popular religion, trying to feel better with caffeine, alcohol, and tobacco, dying early, ignorant of the magnificence they have within that is you. Your Source's contempt for that Ego-Executive self who controls your body may become huge. Even if the channels were opened, it might not wish to deal with that pleasure-chaser Id in charge and perhaps might even wish to sabotage it, at least until he or she cleaned up their life.

When I think that there is a God-like Source trapped within me, present at all times, I somehow feel that I should continually act in ways not to embarrass It. I wish to be in alignment with and worthy of our partnership. My goal is to become its partner. Since it was a gift, born inside me, what higher aspiration could there be than to become its partner through communication. Since It is me, let's be one!

We Need to Wake up, Reach out, and Collaborate with our on Holy God-Within.

Isn't it incredible to discover that we actually carry a remarkable conscious entity within our heads? Logically speaking, wouldn't the first thing we would want to do is to open channels of communication to its wisdom? That wisdom is based upon a total memory of all the events and thoughts in your life, plus a powerful pattern and music generator of any and all ideas and ideals. Put these together with it's genetically bestowed software, evolved over millions of years of successful survival to produce a super-intelligent mind that can be called omniscient, and omni-present. However, for three millennia It has no longer been omnipotent, due to the evolution of a juvenile Ego, who is not willing to share control yet.

This is wonderful news! Amazing news! Now the task become, how to prove it and communicate this so as to transform society and civilization. What a wonderful challenge!

CHAPTER 10: Death/Rebirth Coming-of-Age Initiation: Lost Rite of Passage to Human Maturity

A Call for Widespread, Once-in-a-Lifetime use of Psychedelics

A brief review of the hierarchy of control in the Dual Quadbrain is given in **Figure 17.** There it may be seen that the activities of our left brain cerebral cortical REPORTER and right brain cerebral cortical IMAGINATION produce our normal consciousness. Yet, as indi- cated in Chapter 1, this normal consciousness and these hemispheres are only late coming accessories used to en- hance the power of whichever of our ancient more powerful unconscious brain element is actually in control. These are the unconscious bilateral Reptilian ID, the subcon- scious Executive EGO, and preconscious Social Brain SUPEREGO. Freud correctly identified these, but couldn't locate them. Now since *Neuroreality* (Morton, 2011), their anatomical sites are known.

This reduces things down to two behavioral sources: either the social behavior of the Superego, or of the self-directed Id. Under normal circumstances our Executive Ego decides whether to use the Win-Lose, competitive, often violent, tactics of the reptilian Id. Or, to use the Win-Win, non-violent, cooperative operations of the Social Brain Superego. It has been shown that our Executive Ego makes this decision one or more seconds before "we," up here in the cerebrum become aware of its choice. We then belatedly use our more recently evolved cerebral consciousness skills to support and enhance that decision,

Figure 17:

Modular Consciousness

Consciousness
Levels:

The Cerebral Hemispheres are Late-coming Advisors
to the Subconscious but More Powerful Survival Brain

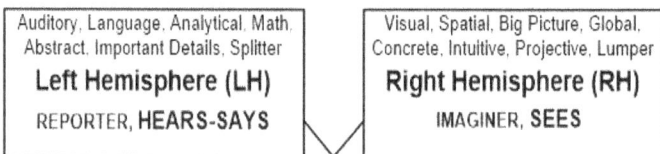

Cerebral "Self
Consciousness"
Simplifies with
"Cartoons and
Captions"

Auditory, Language, Analytical. Math. Abstract. Important Details, Splitter	Visual, Spatial, Big Picture, Global, Concrete, Intuitive, Projective, Lumper
Left Hemisphere (LH)	**Right Hemisphere (RH)**
REPORTER, **HEARS-SAYS**	IMAGINER, **SEES**

x-DARP = Our
Mutated Developmental
Arrest Repair Program.
Struggles with others to be
right and win. Rejects,
Hates. Treats Friends as
Enemies. Demonic. The
Devil Within. Would rather
die than lose.

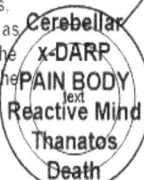

Cerebellum is
Pre Conscious

Cerebellar
x-DARP
PAIN BODY
text
Reactive Mind
Thanatos
Death

Accepts and loves others.
Serves life and species.
Recognizes the emergent
properties of being part of a
group are always superior
to going it alone.
Site of Primary Memory,
gives time and space-
based causality. Origin of
the Scientific Method.
Misidentified as Holy Spirit.

Cerebellar
Social Brain
SUPEREGO
IS
Life

Emotional
HAS
Strong Ego, RH

Limbic
Executive
Controler
Weak Ego LH

EGO

When the ID accepts the
SUPEREGO and
R and L HEMISPHERES
as wiser and superior,
it joyfully follows
their direction.

Limbic Cingulate is
Sub Conscious

Brain Core is
Unconscious

NEGATIVE
ADVERSARIAL
COMPETITIVE
VIOLENT
SURVIVAL
INSTINCTS

(-)ID

DOES

DOES

(+)ID

POSITIVE
SERVES
COOPERATIVE
NON-VIOLENT

More Powerful
External Sources
can take over Id
behavior.

ID can be Captured by
the Existence of (or
Belief in) more
Powerful EXTERNAL
SOURCES:
Political or Religious
Coercion, Hypnotists

BEHAVIORAL
OUTPUT:
Competitive Violent
or
Cooperative Non-violent

be it under direction by the violent Id, or by non-violent Superego.

A young, or otherwise immature human being naturally discovers that "it's a rough world out there" and fearfully identifies with our reptilian brain heritage of win-lose competition with survival by tooth and claw as their only option. Few if any are aware that also hidden within each of us is a non-violent social brain (Superego) conscious- ness that can raise them to a higher, superior level of survival. This two- levels dilemma is inherent in the structure-activity (matter- energy) nature of the universe. That is, the cosmos is built of endless unique layers of matter. Unlike an onion, each layer has unique structures and uniquely appropriate energy laws of behavior, which only work at that universe level.

The cosmic nature of reality, the universe, life, and mind is discussed in greater detail in "Neuroreality" (available from www.amazon.com under Bruce Eldine Morton). A relevant illustration of this infinitely layered universe can be briefly illustrated by considering its increasingly complex levels. Arbitrarily starting at the universe level of atoms, then rising to that of molecules, up to the macromolecular layer, then mov- ing up to the level of subcellular organelles, then to the layer of cells, next of tissues, then the layer of organs, followed by that of organisms, and stopping at the overlying layer of groups of organisms. Clearly the universe laws at the level of atoms are inappropriate and harmful at the level of subcellular organelles, the laws of which are themselves inappropriate for the level of organs.

That the universe is indeed composed of infinite, unique levels of matter and energy is unrecognized by most. Nevertheless, it is foundationally true. Our focus here is to call attention to this fundamental principle as it applies to the laws at the universe level of the single individual, which are the opposite of those quite different laws existing at the level of family, that of groups. For example, at the level of the individual, the appropriate survival laws are: competition, often to a violent extreme. Trust no one. Fight to the death, survival of the fittest. The Reptilian Id includes this sophisticated package of behaviors proven successful at the "one on one" individual organism universe level. It has been very important in our ancient evolution and helped us survive snakes, wolves, hyenas, and lions in the jungle for eons.

However, from the group survival point of view at the next higher universe level of the family, village, tribe, or society, such self-survival-oriented is deadly to the group. The "Give it to me now, you piece of sh-t, or I will f-cking kill you!!"-types of behavior are considered the worst of evils when applied within a group. They are totally destructive and completely inappropriate at this next higher universe level of family relations. They have long been seen as "sinful" and labeled "antisocial," because they produce a lethal, destructive, reign of terror, with death to most all in the group as the inevitable outcome. These self-survival laws are part of tools which evolved into our brain core Id. They are in force when it is self-directed.

Fortunately in great contrast, each of us also has a complete brain package of cooperative, group-appropriate behaviors that has evolved as part of our Superego. When the Id becomes surrendered to a more dominant Superego, two things happen. First, the Id switches brain sides from that of a fearsome wild wolf to that of an affectionate, loyal dog who totally supports our Superego cooperative social behaviors. To our family members, we become unselfish, sharing, cooperative, self-denying in favor of benefiting the group, and completely non-violent. Instead of the above loud profane scream of a selfish competitor, our transformed social behavior says, "I accept you as my equal. I am at your service. How may I help you?" or even "I love you!" Of course these social-level behaviors are totally inappropriate and ineffective at the antisocial level of violent competing individuals, where their use could get one killed.

The key point is that at each higher universe level, there are emergent activities not to be found at the lower levels. Thus, by cooperation, groups of humans have learned how to increasingly benefit from these emergent properties, so that through social cooperation, we have developed communication and the scientific method, thus to become the major species on earth and are reaching for the stars.

However, these emergent activities at the group universe level do not exist at the individual universe level where competition, violence, and killing are king. This is why the survival of isolated individuals, going it alone, is always inferior to that of individuals bonded into a cooperative group. Unfortunately, this is not clear to many individuals, and especially in those organizations operating within the individual level laws of competition. This has repeatedly led to the vast killing fields of battles, including world wars. Peace based upon win-lose laws is logically impossible. So, that failure to understand the existence of this competition vs. cooperation dilemma built within our brains has harmed not only us, but the earth as well. The recognition that the laws of the group are opposite from those of the individual anciently was, and still is a key step in individual human maturation.

Lost Rite of Passage: Rising From a Self-Oriented Individual to a Contributing Member of Society

In the distant past, there appears to have been an excellent solution to this dilemma. Held to be one of the most ancient of rites, the **coming of age initiation** marked the psychological crossing of a threshold from the self into the next higher level of the social participation: the knowledge and abilities that enhance the survival of the family tribe.

The major themes of this initiation were suffering, death, and rebirth. The initiate underwent an ordeal that brought them to a condition where the brain began to fail. This near-death experience involved their "hitting bottom," giving up, and surrender to death, followed by the transformation of being symbolically reborn as a new person possessing new transcendent knowledge, and then being respectfully embraced by his family tribe. However, with the coming of the Iron Age and the subsequent population explosion, this tradition mostly has been lost.

Within this venerable tribal coming of age initiation, children were allowed to grow up naturally as individuals until puberty arrived. Then, they were subjected to self-searching ordeals imposed by tribal member sponsors whose intensity was inadvertently designed to bring about a near-death brain state upon the initiate. These procedures, which varied widely among groups, all resulted in the collapse of the Ego-Id, and then to transcendence, as the hidden cerebellar Superego Source came to the fore.

This experience was profoundly transformative, just as has often been observed in modern near-death experiences. This was partly because the adolescent was previously unaware of the hidden inner resource of their Superego, "God Within," partly because they experienced dying and had to confront its personal consequences, and partly because they became aware of the nature of the universe and its absolute perfection that makes the survival of life possible. And lastly, because they saw that cooperation within their group was superior to competitive fighting alone, in that it brings peace and happiness to a life previously filled with fear and anger caused by threats of death.

Each initiate was then quickly nurtured back to health and restored to their tribe, having become permanently transformed into a mature adult who had discovered his or her purpose in life and who could never be the same. They then took their place as equal members of their tribal family of complete human beings. Responsible courtship and marriage followed, leading ultimately to their status of respected leaders and elders. Although some tribal initiations were filled with superstitious misinformation, nevertheless, the experience of dying and rebirth in an uncaring universe was usually transformative.

The unique manner in which many tribal bands caused brain failure and near death experiences in their "coming of age initiations" has been described by Mircea Eliade, in his *Rites and Symbols of Initiation (1958, Harper Collins, NY)*. Among the North American Amerinds, often the youth were individually sent on a vision quest into the wilderness, deprived of food, water, and sleep for several days, during which time they strained to the utmost to find their totem animal who would be their ally for the rest of their lives. Near the end of this ordeal, as their brain began to fail, their mind became "comatose," and they entered into a visionary mental state where their spiritual guide revealed itself. Adolescents of other tribes were administered poisonous "ordeal beans" to become profoundly intoxicated. The North American Plains Indians had a most dramatic method. They inserted a ropes between parallel slits cut in each of the initiate's pectoral muscles and attached these ropes to an upright stationary pole. The initiate then danced while leaning backward upon the ropes and looking directly at the sun. After hours of suffering and blinding, their pectoral muscles failed and they fell into a visionary faint upon the ground.

The initiation produced a profound permanent pro-life transformation in perspective (Bingham, McFadden, Zhang, Bhatnagar, Beck, & Valentino, 2011), and anciently over time converted millions of juveniles into a mature tribe members committed to make a difference in the village with their life in a manner specific to their vision. They must have been greeted with such words as " Good job! You have earned your place among us. Welcome! How can we help each other?"

This experience was similar to those modern day near-death experiences reported to bring an ego collapse and transcendence to an altered state of consciousness leading to a transformation where one sees the universe and one's place within it from the Social Brain's perspective.

Most youth of later more populous historical periods came from less tightly organized tribes and were not initiated. Without transcendence they could never gain the insights and purpose inherent in a mature human being. Theirs was an adult life of anxiety and suffering. Yet, over time since the loss of tribal initiations, individuals by accident have experienced near-death transformations. Their resultant changed attitudes were in such stark contrast to the normal suffering of their colleagues, as to become noticed and admired by their associates. These transformed individuals often became dedicated to bringing transcendence to their fellow humans with the goal of ending suffering within their lifetimes. Gautama Buddha's life, or that of Jesus Christ illustrate this very well. In fact all the major world religions were founded by such transformed individuals, as were many less global religions, for example, Ellen White, prophet of the Seventh-day Adventists, the church of my parents.

However, although these founders of our religions were not neuroscientists, they came to recognize that "death of the self" was essential to the conversion process. Buddha only transcended after years of mortification of his body by starvation and meditation. Christ went into the wilderness 40 days to be tempted by the devil. After Ellen White recovered from a coma caused by being hit by a stone thrown into her head, she began to prophesy, and wrote many books regarding what she saw. Those around her saw her message of non-violence and purity as so admirable as to form a new Seventh-day Adventist religion.

However, as is the case in most religions, few, if any, of their members in later generations transcended or could be compared to their founder. The Catholics regularly prescribe continual meditation upon suffering and death of Christ. This is often dramatized in processions where the devout actually carry a cross or a heavy float with Christ on the cross. At times, some actually whip themselves into transcendence. However, in any of the world's religions, only a rare few suffer near-death of the body and are reborn to the spirit to become (non-supernatural) Saints.

Yet, as information began to flow around the world with time and increased communication, certain native groups were found which had evolved the use of certain plant derivatives that potently and efficiently produced "death" and rebirth in their initiates, actually transforming their lives in a manner similar to ancient coming of age initiation ceremonies. When these diverse plant extracts were analyzed, essentially all were found to contain hallucinogens. All hallucinogens were later identified to be specific agonists (activators) of only one of the 14 serotonin subclass receptors, called the 5-HT2a receptor, a stress-inducing receptor.

Recently, it has been discovered that these stress receptors are found on interneurons within the ancient cingulate cortex of the brain. The cingulate cortex appears to be the structure that produces the survival activities of the Ego. The activation of the cingulate serotonin 5-HT2a receptor interneurons, has been demonstrated to potently inhibit the cingulate cortex and to produce such stress as to lead to "ego death," bringing the Servant Brain Id to the fore. Then, in the absence of the temporarily inhibited Id, the neocerebellar, social brain Superego consciousness is released.

The initiate experiences the spiritual purity of selfless cooperative behavior within the context of the infinite universe. This ineffable view is so different from one's usual Id viewpoint as to be profoundly awakening and transformational. It short cuts years of meditative disciplines that often fail, by a process that successfully occurs within a day. And only one, or a few such experiences creates a permanent shift in one's personal orientation from hopelessly seeking answers to one of certainty about life and one's place in the universe.

This makes clear the very great need for each person on earth to undergo the ancient coming-of-age, rite-of-passage experience. This will result from one or a few high dose ingestions of psilocybin, peyote, or LSD, alone, within a safe empathetic environment. Widespread use of such a sacred ceremony, like that of the 2,000 years of the Greek Elusian Mysteries, would produce a profound transformation of society for the better, erasing and transcend- ing false barriers based upon politics, religion, nationality, race, class, or gender. Transformed individuals emerge from this ceremony as mature human beings and contributing members to global society.

Key to Schizophrenia, the Bicameral Brain Exposed

In schizophrenia, the most common symptom is the hallucination of voices. Some of these can take over the person's consciousness by issuance of a so called "command" hallucinations, which are next to impossible to disobey. These greatly resemble the types of interactions within the bicameral minds of pre-conscious Greeks prior to 2,000 BC, described in Chapter One. This makes the content of the hallucinations of schizophrenics of great interest. Recall that hallucinogens, through the $5\text{-HT}_{2a}R$, inhibit the cingulate cortex Ego to release "hallucinations" (Carheart-Harris, 2013).

It has recently been discovered that in schizophrenia, lesions exist in the right cerebellum, which are directly connected to the language areas of the left cerebral hemisphere (Yeganeh-Doost, et al., 2011). This is important because that damaged part of the cerebellum goes through the thalamus directly to strengthen the the cingulate cortex Ego. When this pathway is weakened, as in schizophrenia, or by hallucinogens, of course one would predict hallucinations. This cerebellar deficit is a major finding from Nancy Andreason's lab (Parker, Narayanan, Andreason, 2014). They propose that this weakened cerebellar pathway in schizophrenics could be stimulated to stop the voices.

This discovery could also open the door to the investigation of the existence and properties of the bicameral God-within, perhaps by interacting with the voices of schizophrenics.

CHAPTER 11: Demystifying the Common Origin of the World's Now Obsolete Religions

It is now clear that hidden within each of us is a mortal Higher Intelligence, based in our cerebellar Social Brain Superego, Holy Spirit, God-Within, and Source. When contacted, its awe-inspir- ing wisdom appears so superior to our normal conscious- ness as to cause us to mistakenly externalize it as divine. Indeed, this contact with the brain-based Holy Spirit has been the origin of all world religions. Normally, however, our anxious reptilian Self-Survival Brain so powerfully suppresses our Social Brain that most of us are unaware that our non-supernatural God lies waiting within, closer than one's breath. Nearing death, the Self Brain begins to collapse. This releases the Holy Spirit from the reptile's terrified grip to come to the fore in the form of ineffable near-death experiences. This is the first time most of us come in contact with the "divine."

However, over the millennia, ways have been found to loosen the grip of the reptile brain and release the Holy Spirit without physically dying. These methods to transcendence have always required "hitting the bottom" and letting go of life by the reptile brain Id in so-called "Ego death." The discovery by the reptile brain that it did not die leads to a life-changing personal transformation, based upon the inspiration inherent in the associated altered state. That is, dying to the overpowering drive of self-survival and being reborn under the direction of the infinitely superior Social brain Holy Spirit. Such a transformation brings wisdom, fulfillment, and peace.

Transformation is the rite of passage to become a true human being. As mentioned in the last chapter, over millennia, this "Ego-death" initiation has been accomplished by coming-of-age rites, intense meditation-prayer procedures, and the sacred use psychedelic entheogens, both outside and within religion. The Holy Spirit within humans has continued to inspire scientific discoveries and reveal increasingly accurate models of the universe, life, and mind. Nobody has ever seen God because He/She dwells hidden within you, as the true, Sacred You, not your usually dominating profane "Ego."

Yet, over time since the loss of tribal initiations, individuals by accident have experienced near-death transformations. Their resultant changed attitudes were in such stark contrast to the normal suffering of their colleagues, as to become noticed and admired by their associates. These transformed individuals often became dedicated to bringing transcendence to their fellow humans with the goal of ending suffering within their lifetimes. Gautama Buddha's life, or that of Jesus Christ illustrate this very well. In fact all world religions were founded by such transformed individuals, as were many less global religions, for example, Ellen White, prophet of the Seventh-day Adventists, the faith of my parents.

This experience was similar to those modern day near-death experiences reported to bring an ego collapse and transcendence to an altered state of consciousness leading to permanent a transformation where one sees the universe and one's place within it from the Social Brain's perspective.

However, although these founders of our religions

were not neuroscientists, they came to recognize that "death of the self" was essential to the conversion process. Buddha only transcended after years of mortification of his body by starvation and meditation. Christ went into the wilderness 40 days to be tempted by the devil. After Ellen White recovered from a coma caused by being hit by stone thrown into her head, she began to prophesy, and wrote many books regarding what she saw. Those around her saw her message of non-violence and purity as so admirable as to form the new Seventh-day Adventist religion.

However, as is the case in most religions, few, if any, of their members in later generations transcended or could be compared to their founder. The Catholics regularly prescribe continual meditation upon suffering and death of Christ. This is often dramatized in processions where the devout actually carry a cross or a heavy float with Christ on the cross. At times, some actually whip themselves into transcendence. However, in any of the world's religions, only a rare few suffer near-death of the body and are reborn to the spirit to become (non-supernatural) Saints.

Origin of the World's Religions: The Founder's Ego-death and Transcendence

Table 1 lists major historical events in the development of civilization and of its religions. Although hominids have existed for 5 million years, and humans for at least 2 million years, the first marks found that they left were drawings in the caves of Europe, dating about 30,000 years ago. Aside from this, our recorded history begins after the last ice age 20,000 BC (before Christ). During this

CHAPTER ELEVEN

Table 1: History of Western Civilization and its Religions

20,000 BC, Last Ice Age: Sea level 140m (420ft) below present: glaciers hold the water as ice.

6500 BC, Sea level now over 100m (300ft) above minimum, and was higher than dry Persian Gulf.

6000 BC, Flood into the 100,000 mi^2 fertile valley of the Persian Gulf, millions killed.

5600 BC, Mediterranean overflows into the Black Sea, covering an additional 42,000 mi^2.

5300-4100 BC, Sumerian civilization begins, Ubrad period, Neolithic

4100-2900 BC, Sumerian Uruk period, Chalcolithic, Early Bronze Age I, Ozi dies in the Alps

3300 BC, Sumerian Cuneiform & Egyptian Hieroglyphics appear, Hinduism in Indus river valley

3300-2900 BC, Holocene Climactic Optimum Ends, Desertification, Upper/lower Egypt unified.

2900-2335 BC, Sumerian Early Dynastic period, Early Bronze Age II-IV.

2334-2218 BC, Sumerian Akkadian Empire; 2218-2047 BC; Sumerian Middle Bronze Age

2047-1940 BC, Sumerian Ur III period, Abraham leaves Ur

1940-1700 BC, Sumerian Babylonia, Joseph sold into Egypt, 8 generations Israelites in Egypt

1800 BC, Gilgamish Epic of flood, Creation story, Code of Hammurabi

1630 BC, Thera Eruption, End of Minoan Civilization

1400 BC, Akhenaten Pharaoh, Egypt Monotheism, Moses, Hebrew Exodus, Biblical Torah written

800 BC, Rise of ancient Greece, Eleusian Mysteries practiced, knowledge explosion

563-483 BC, Buddha, founder of Buddhism

336 BC, Alexander the Great conquest of Medes and Persians, advance to India

146 BC, Roman Empire displaces Hellenistic Greece

33 AD, Crucifixion of Jesus, origin of Christianity

313 AD, Emperor Constantine declares Roman Catholicism the state religion

1453 AD, Dark Ages millenium

610 AD, First Vision of Mohammed

1400-1700 AD, Renaissance, Christian Reformation, Protestantism and origin of Modern Science

1859 AD, Charles Darwin publishes The Origin of the Species

1953 AD, Crick and Watson discover structure of DNA

2003 AD, The Human DNA genome is sequenced.

time, the accumulation of vast amounts of water as glaciers lowered the sea level more than 400 ft. The later thawing of these glaciers resulted in at least two catastrophic floods (**Table 1**), the memory of which is mirrored in the many flood stories. The Gilgamish Epic, which preceded the Biblical copy by 500 years, is a prime example. What we first see in 5000 BC Sumerian religion is an organized polytheism in which priests were mediators and administrators of communal agriculture, and where rituals, ceremonies, and sacrifices were made to the gods of harvest and rainfall. As there was no moral standard for behavior, it appears that the only difference between the gods and the people was that only the gods were immortal, while humans were condemned to the Hades of the underworld after death. This primitive polytheistic form of religion persisted for over 5000 years and was still present in ancient Greece and Rome

The Egyptian and Hindu Indian versions of polytheism evolved an additional concept: that of human immortality. In Egypt, it became the belief that it was possible for kings, following elaborate mortuary rites, to survive into an immortal afterlife. In contrast, Hinduism democratized immortality, positing that all are possessed by an extraterrestrial immortal soul, whose development requires transmigration over many live times in order to reach a spiritual state of perfection. This was attractive because it lessened the fear of death and also encouraged moral behavior.

Monotheism first emerged briefly in Egypt around 1400 BC during the reign of Amenhotep, who changed

His name to Akhenaten (**Table 1**). Akhenaten was the husband of famously beautiful Nefertiti, and father of Pharaoh Tutankhamen, whose unopened, fabulous tomb was discovered in modern times. Akhenaten powerfully attempted to purge Egypt of polytheism. He declared that only the Sun was divine, and built a new capital at Amarna on the lower Nile. He ultimately was killed and Egypt's ancient polytheism was restored.

However, Akhenaten's monotheism was reintroduced and later sustained permanently in the derivative Jewish religion founded by Moses, the stepson of an Egyptian pharaoh, who was somehow involved in all this. Some say Moses was actually Akhenaten himself. Others, including Sigmund Freud, proposed that Moses had been one of Akhenatan's priests who was forced to flee with the Isrealites out of Egypt after the pharaoh's overthrow. Moses retained monotheism as the core of his new religion, Judaism, embodied in his Torah and Decalogue of the Old Testament. Now, 3500 years since Moses, after the origin of derivative Christianity and later Islam, monotheism instead of polytheism has become the predominant belief in most world religions.

Origin of the World's Religions by Near-Death Experiences of Their Founders

The world's major religions as of 2010 are summarized in **Table 2**. The founder of each of these major religions was dramatically transformed by a near-death experience.

The simultaneous emergence several forms of

Table 2. World's Largest Religions, numbers and percent population (2010):

1.	Christianity	2,260 million	33%
2.	Islam	1,555 million	23%
3.	Hinduism	948 million	14%
4.	Buddhism	496 million	7%
5.	Chinese religions	436 million	6%
6.	Ethno religions	243 million	3%
7.	New religions	63 million	0.9%
8.	Sikhism	24 million	0.3%
9.	Judaism	18 million	0.2%
10.	Baha'i'	8 million	0.1%
	Non-religious	856 million	12%
	Total	6,900 million	100%

writing in the third millennium BC greatly opened our window to the cultures and religions of the past. The great city states of the Summerians in the Tigris and Euphrates river valleys are the site of the first written records. At first these notes were primarily used for agricultural storage records of a temple. They later included the famous Gilgamish Epic flood story, written 500 years before that of our Old Testament.

Psychedelic Origins of Judaism

Then, a Summerian rancher ,Abraham took his

flocks far southwest, during a temporary wet period, into the blooming desert of Palestine. He was the father of Judaism which retained that ancient flood story. The trans- cendent conversion of Abraham's grandson Moses at the "burning bush that was not consumed" led him to bring about the exodus of the Hebrews from slavery in Egypt, and in the process to formulate the Jewish reli- gion (Exo- dus 3:1-20). In an apparently altered state of consciousness (Sharon, 2008), Moses, stepson of the rul- ing pharaoh, ex- perienced contact from a burning bush by the great "I AM that I AM", who, while he was in an altered state, showed him miracles. The I AM then commanded him to return back to Egypt from which he had earlier been exiled for murder, and to deliver his kin out of slavery.

As a result of his personal transformation, Moses in about 1446 BC brought about the liberation of the Is- realites from Egypt and ultimately transported them to Palestine where many Jews now live. In the process, Moses continued to experience exalted states during which he received the Ten Commandments on Mt. Sinai and formulated the Levitical code of Judaism. In these, it is here asserted that he experienced "Ego death" and surrendered to his formerly hidden Higher Power with- in, thus providing him with considerable wisdom which was also at least partly based upon his royal Egyptian education and leadership.

Psychedelic Origins of Christianity

Christianity, was founded by a Jew, Jesus of Nazar- eth, an unusually intelligent person born to an unwed mother. His gifted leadership qualities attracted and mesmerized his followers. Ultimately it brought him in conflict with the by then legalistic Jewish religious leadership, existing under Roman rule. He found himself unwilling to bend his principles and almost got to be dead right, being crucified for his rigidity on a Friday in about 33 AD. Fortunately for him, one of his followers administered fish liver gall, which contained tetrodotoxin, a reversible poison causing a paralysis resembling death. After being stabbed in the side to confirm his death and being taken from the cross, he was placed under guard in a tomb purchased by a benefactor.

Regaining consciousness on Sunday, he escaped, later to be seen and speak repeatedly with his confused followers. Later, on Mount Carmel at a meeting of exhortation, he left his enthused followers by walking up into the mist of the cloud base of the local low altitude marine layer, and was never seen again in Pales- tine. His hypnotized followers returned to Jerusalem with their ecstatic belief in a resurrected and ascendant Jesus Christ. Their endless prayers brought to them Ego-death as well and the gift of their formerly hidden Holy Spirit. These multiple transformations led to the formulation and potent spread of Christianity by the empowered followers of Jesus.

Psychedelic Origins of Islam

In AD 610, Mohammed, after years of regularly meditating in a mountain cave in Medina, Arabia, came home to tell his wife that either he had gone mad or else he had become a prophet, for he had been visited by an angel. Clearly, in his intense seeking for God, he had experienced "ego-death" and the transcendence of his hidden cerebellar God-Within. The message his inner angel gave him was, as always, prosocial and thus very good. Muhammad's message to his countrymen was to convert from pagan polytheism, immorality, and materialism, repent from evil and worship Allah, the only true God. He was always careful to clarify his role in God's work: he was only a prophet. He was not an angel, he did not know the mind of God. He did not work miracles. He simply preached what he had received.

The angel repeatedly commanded him to "proclaim in the name of your Lord who is most generous and has created man from a clot of blood." "Your Lord who teaches by the pen; teaches man what he knew not." Muhamamed's belief system, which united Jews and Pagans was called Islam. Slowly at first, then explosively, his following increased. After a series strategic battles Mohammed died in 632, having conquered nearly all of Arabia for Islam. By 634, Islam's "convert or die" policy had taken over the entire Arabian peninsula. Within 100 years of Muhammad's death, it had reached from the Atlantic in the west and to the borders of China in the east.

The Exclusive Religions will Kill Over Minor Details

Unfortunately, since all major religions are prosocial and good, it is clear for the survival of humanity that they should be inclusive, not exclusive. However, as in the case of Christianity where left brain-oriented Catholics bitterly fought Protestant right brainers and millions were killed, so also in Islam, the left brain-oriented Shiia Moslems have split from the right-brainer Suni Moslems and are now engaged in a horrible, spreading conflict that could result in the Battle of Armageddon and the collapse of civilization.

Thus, Judaism spawned Christianity and then Islam. These three religions together are now followed by well over half of the world's 7 billion population. They all live under the same meme of a supernatural external God. Social memes cannot be destroyed, only displaced by more effective ones. That is, nobody killed horses when the automobile appeared. Here is where knowledge of the Dual Quadbrain Model of modular consciousness is essential for understanding the brain ba- sis of the dilemma we each face and its relationship to Spirituality and Religion, whose misunderstanding has side tracked humanity for millennia.

Word Traps and the Dual Quadbrain Model

Word Trap #1 "Ego Death." There are many word traps in existence that hinder understanding and can cause confusion. One is the expression, "Ego death." When referring to brain structures, so-called Ego death is what occurs when the behaviorally violent activities of the Ego, along with those of the Dominator Id are inhibited. The Executive Ego includes part of the central limbic system, including the striatum that reaches as high as the ancient cingulate cerebral cortex. The cingulate has recently been found to be profoundly inhibited by hallucinogens. When this occurs, Dominator Id-dependent external survival behavior is lost. In its absence, the hidden God Within comes to the fore. This is the neocerebellar social brain Superego, the Holy Spirit of group survival-enhancing behaviors that produces the of- ten-mentioned "altered state of consciousness."

After recovery from this deathlike inhibition, the reptilian Id is permanently transformed by learning, among other things, that it is not the only brain consciousness responsible for the survival of the body. To its relief, it discovers that there are higher-brain element allies that are more powerful at the social level than is its own competition-driven violence. It then becomes more able to surrender and to accept help from the Executive Ego and the Superego Source in the battle of life. The violent selfish Id Wolf can then be replaced by the non-violent social Id Dog. In this transformation the Id becomes the enthusiastic Servant of the Executive Ego Caretaker and the Super- ego Source. Their wishes are its commands. Thus, its atti- tude is transformed from negation to the affirmative, "I love you! How can I serve you?"

Word Trap#2 "Spirituality, Spiritual, Spirit." Spirituality implies the existence of a world of supernatural, extracorporeal good and evil spirits. The idea of the supernatural is a holdover from our past ignorance. Through development and use of the Scientific Method, we have found overwhelming evidence that every, and all things in nature and universe are completely rule-abiding. They do not require us break any natural laws to understand them. Gods and demons are the earlier imaginative concept extremes of life-supporting Superego activities vs. the violence and death dealing mentality of our competitive Id. So, to accurately tell the truth, we must redefine the expression "spiritual" or find a better word for it. It can only be a natural thing or state, not an extra-corporeal supernatural spirit.

The term Spiritual can be redefined to refer to the experience of something real, good, profound, true, and perfect. Spiritual also can refer to a profound, often over-whelming personal experience resulting from contact with natural, but often ineffable raw universe and its ac-tivities as seen by the Superego. This can occur during near death experiences when the death-fighting Id be-gins to collapse, and one catches a glimpse of the purity and incredible beauty of the infinite natural universe and our miniscule place within it, as seen by our Source. There, endless colorful visions of the ever changing co-operative interaction of all of its subunits, including life occur. These form an absolutely perfect mosaic whole. Mystics, such as Ezekiel and St. John, have attempted to describe this ineffable vast complexity, as have modern experiencers.

Our *Word Trap #3* clusters around the words "A Re-ligion" and "Religion." The core element of any and all religions is the ancient belief in the existence of immortal, supernatural, extracorporeal beings, in heaven and hell. In the two centuries since the discovery and use of the scien-tific method, it has become abundantly obvious that these ancient creative ideas are incorrect. As much as we would like to believe it, there are no bodiless spirits, there is no life after death in eternal fire or pleasure, and super-natural events are impossible.

Yet, as social animals, we each need to belong to a family group of like-believing mutually supportive members, a need formerly well met by the religions. A nonsupernatural word category that is more accurate than that of *religion (supernatural)* is the term *ideology (natural)*. Ideologies, such as *secular humanism*, can replace obsolete religions to meet our same social needs of belonging to an organized group whose membership confers comradery, support, and power to a family of like-minded people.

Word traps #4, "Ideas;" #5, "Beliefs;" #6, "Faith;" #7"Trust." Memes are mental constructs based upon ideas or beliefs. People often have faith in them.
Descartes stated that, by definition, any and all ideas are actu ally real. Thus, they could be believed and trusted to be true. This can be understood because of the not yet appreciated critical difference between fictional but creative mental Inner Realities, as compared to the actual world of External Reality. Ideas are all memes, but, fortunately, not all memes are true. Ideas and beliefs aligned with External Reality can be powerfully useful. Those which do not, by definition and application, are fictional, harmful memes, often very much so. They never work "where the rubber meets the road."

Science is a method of testing whether ideas are true and can be believed and trusted, based upon which of them work in the real world and discarding those that do not. For them to be valid in the real world, they must be reproducible by anyone using the same methods. Unfortunately, memes of bad ideas cannot be destroyed. They are immortal and can only be displaced by ideas that work better. Thus, as said earlier: nobody killed their horses in an attempt to bring about the mechanization of transportation. We can't destroy a religion, without an ideology that works better because it is closer to the truth.

An insoluble problem exists for religions who base their *belief,* faith, and trust upon the idea of "The Virgin Birth." It can accurately and safely be asserted without doubt that there has never been a creature born of a woman who was sired by a supernatural, spiritual God. This has become one of the most harmful of all human beliefs. It is completely based upon the "False Cause" meme that the supernatural beings exists and can interact and confer immortality upon human beings. Belief and *faith* in this creative idea has long diverted us from solving our physical and mental problems of survival. With the rise of the scientific method and the development of methods that actually work in the real world, we discovered that physical immortality of any individual or anything is impossible. Everything is in flux. Even life itself on earth may not be immortal.

As both hunters and prey, we have long needed the ability to hold a particular idea as true, even though there is no present evidence to support it. This is called an estimation based upon "Probability" upon which we have "Faith." Successful fly rod fishermen are skilled at probability estimates. Humans, who survived a jungle environment, suc- cessfully guessed what the safest path was through dangerous territory. However, people who deliberately place their faith upon *grossly improbable* ideas are operating at false cause and literally wasting their time and often their lives and those around them. Although coincidences may occur, they are not repeatable and cannot be trusted to form a way of life. This is why Occam's Razor says the simplest explanation, based upon data, is the most probable.

The Dilemma: How to fuse our ancient God and good-oriented religiosity with reality as revealed by science

We all have the tendency toward wishful thinking. Some call it optimism. Sincere members of religions that are based upon belief and faith in improbable supernatural, extracorporeal existence face many personal psychological conflicts that are holding society back. At first they may believe in science during the week, but in God on Sunday. However, with time this becomes impossible. The next conflict occurs, especially if they wish to stick to the facts and are thus forced to leave their pre-science religious family in search for a science-compatible belief system. This is because we are at a stage where there are as yet no adequate global scientific method-based social ideology to join. Most scientists are as confused as the rest. Established scientifically proven facts lag at least a century behind the cutting edge. Humanism appears to be the only choice at present. It was Einstein's choice as well.

Inherent in religion is the emergent property that cooperation between members confers survival benefits not available to non-members. However, nonmembers usually are cast as the ignorant subhuman enemies. The misguided exclusivity of each of religion, based upon small differences in their idiosyncratic core stories and the "right-wrong" legalism springing from them, has been the source of endless conflict, from personal to global levels.

Religion is idealistically thought to prevent the collapse of human existence in an evil human jungle-like chaos. However, this is not true. The eight global religions, each based upon faith in beliefs incompatible wit their fellows in minor detail, have been fighting with each other for millennia. Billions have been killed. These exclusive religions have not enhanced the survival of the human race. Far from it! Their massive killing continues.

We need an inclusive global post-science ideology based upon demonstrable facts about External Reality that any competent person can confirm, no faith or belief required. I have created such a synthesis, called *Neuro-reality*. It is derived from the vast literature of science. It is based upon the ever growing n u m b e r o f neuro-science publications that have not waited a century to be confirmed as consensus facts. The goal is to combine these replicated discoveries into an evolving view of the universe, life, and mind that require no faith to believe. Belonging to such an organization will provides an inclusive home for modern humans. A modern "death-rebirth" coming-of-age initiation" might someday provide the "Saints" of the upper layer of this organization.

It is interesting that only about 500 years ago, modern science began to emerge separately from religion. What science began to discover from experimental data that could be confirmed by any competent observer, was that the ancient naive belief that the earth was the center of the universe was false. Then it discovered that the universe and man had not been created by an act of God. This has created a great dilemma for every human being. We wish to believe in a personal God who recently created us and to have faith that He knows our every need. Yet, objective evidence confirms this to be completely false.

Akhenaten's 1350 BC hymn to the Sun, which has been compared to, but long preceded David's 1000 BC, 104th psalm to God, touches a deep core of meaning and can give great emotional satisfaction. Here is David's version in Psalms 104: 1-15. Here the word God is replaced by the word Cosmos to make it more accurate:

"Bless the Cosmos, Oh my soul! Oh amazing universe, you are very great! You are covered in honor and majesty, you who covers yourself with light as a garment, who has stretched out the heavens like a tent, who has laid the beams of your chambers upon the waters, who makes the clouds you chariot, who rides the wings of the wind, who makes the winds your messengers, fire and flame your ministers. You set the earth on its foundations, so that it should never be shaken. You covered it with the deep as a garment; the waters stood above the mountains. At your rebuke they fled; at the sound of your thunder they took flight. The mountains rose, the valleys sank down to the place where you did appoint for them. You make springs gush forth in the valleys; they flow between the hills, they give drink to every beast of the field, the wild asses quench their thirst, by them the birds of the air have their habitation; they sing among the branches. From thy lofty abode you water the mountains; the earth is satisfied with the fruit of thy work. You cause grass to grow for the cattle and plants for man to cultivate, that he may bring forth food from the earth,and wine to gladden the heart of man, oil to make his face shine, and bread to strengthen man's heart."

Here are some other awe-inspired statements compatible with devotion to the Cosmos. For example: "I worship the universe, filled with the beauty of the Cosmos." "Choosing the way the Cosmos is, as perfect, makes me a Source, at cause, and in control. It gives me personal opportunity, power, and success. It aligns me with the way things in the Universe are. I can surf its waves. Rejecting and resisting the Cosmos as evil, makes me a Victim, at effect, and out of control. It brings me loss of opportunity, powerlessness, anger, and failure. It places me at odds with the Universe and what IS. Its waves drown me. The Cosmos doesn't care whether I choose to be empowered or harmed by the waves of what IS. It leaves the choice to me, in perfect freedom, and gives me a brain to discover and decide: "This is it, here, now. The Cosmos is perfect!"

A New Trinity of holy sub-elements then emerges: The Cosmos as the Father, The Sons as our Scientist and Shamanic Role Models, The Holy Spirit as The Hidden Higher Intelligence of our modular brain's God-Within who we are.

CHAPTER ELEVEN

CHAPTER 12:   Pruning Hyperactive Stress Neurons to Stop Psychic Pain-based Drug Seeking

Chapter Summary:

Inner pain-driven violence surrounds us. The search for relief from this pain drives the drug trade and is leading to global corruption and the collapse of society. At present, nobody knows the origin of our unconscious pain or how to get rid of it. This chapter describes both.

The cause: It is presently unrecognized that the trauma of maternal-infant separation or other terror-of-death incidents in later life causes permanent hyper-innervation of the cerebellar vermis of the brain, a major site of defensive reactivity. This causes later stressful over-sensitivity to subsequent restimulating neutral events. This results in them becoming unconsciously perceived as life threatening and thereby they potently produce painful anxiety. This causes psychosocial problems to those afflicted. Temporary relief from this hypersensitive anxiety is provided by alcohol and other addictive drugs. These are addictive because they temporarily work to stop the pain and restore pleasure. People will pay, or do anything to obtain this relief from inner pain. Unfortunately, drug tolerance progressively increases the amount of drug needed for satisfaction. Lethal side results then begin to emerge as the dose required goes up. This drug tolerance physiology is the origin of the present drug wars to supply the increading demands of addicts in pain.

The cure: Childhood or later trauma causes a defensive over-wiring to occur in the cerebellar vermis. This unnatural vermal hyper-connectivity is what causes the painful stress. Surprisingly, the excess of defensive sprouting can be pruned back to normal levels by two related excitotoxic chemicals, harmaline and ibogaine, which are both beta-carbolines. This trimming can return normal stress sensitivity and to restore personal and global peace. It also so blunts the effects of drugs of abuse, such as alcohol or heroin, so that they are no longer attractive or needed by the now-relieved former addict.

This has been accomplished in substantial instances by two separate large groups of people. First, the ayahuasca religions, originating from the Amazon and now spreading across the globe, create hundreds of thousands of sane members who are unusually socially cooperative and free from drug abuse. Second, the ibogaine using cults of equatorial Africa produce similar effects among their members, where the iboga plant has been declared a national treasure in the Republic of Gabon. Further, promising ibogaine investigations by the National Institutes of Health in the US to eliminate alcohol and opiate addiction were initiated with positive results. However, they were terminated due to the mistaken association of cerebellar pruning with "brain damage."

What is proposed here, is encouragement of the continued global spread of the beta-carboline religions in society. And, the use of beta-carboline pruning with alcoholics, drug addicts, and sufferers of post-traumatic stress disorder (PTSD) to bring about their recovery. Further, if incarcerated persons could be treated with effective doses of beta-carbolines, we could empty our jails and clear our streets of crime.

Two Major Sources of Human Suffering:
1. Ignorance of the Nature of Our Multiple Level Universe:

Arthur Koestler (1905-1983) was a brilliant Hungarian-British journalist, philosopher, and author. One of Koestler's valuable insights was that of the multilayered structure of the universe, where the combined building blocks in one layer become the whole structures of the next universe level, endlessly, as illustrated in **Table 1** (Start at the bottom). He held that the properties and laws of each level were unique and inappropriate to the next higher or next lower layers. For example, the properties and laws required for the health of body organs, such as liver, heart, or skin are unique to that universe level. They do not work at the cellular level below, or the organism level above, either of whose properties and laws are quite different and inappropriate to the needs of the organs.

A critical extension by Morton, (2011) was the discovery of the unrecognized fact that is at the very core of the human suffering, as revealed by the principles of unique universe levels. That is, the laws at the *individual organism* universe level include the legitimate use of violence. The violent laws at the organism level are unique to individuals and obviously not applicable at the body organs next level below. Similarly these valid egoistic, violent, antisocial laws needed for self-survival in the jungle by the individual are also totally inappropriate at the next higher universe level, that of the *family or group.*

261

Table 1: How are the Emergent Properties of the Whole at One Level Different/Greater than that of its Parts at the Next Lower Level?

1. How are the Emergent Properties of a **Family** > (greater than) the sum of the Properties of its **Individual** Members? *The Kennedys > Jackie*

2. Properties of an **Individual** Organism > sum of the properties of its **Organs**? *Person (Jane Doe) > kidney filtration, or heart pump*

3. Properties of an **Organ** > the sum of the properties of its **Tissues**? *Heart (blood pump) > simple cardiac muscle shortening*

4. Properties of a **Tissue** > than the properties of its individual **Cells**? *Retina > neurons OR Bone > osteocytes and calcium*

5. Properties of **Living Cells** > properties of **Subcellular Organelles**? *Ovum or muscle cell > contents of nucleus/ cytoplasm*

6. Properties of **Subcellular Organelles** > that of their **Supramolecular Assemblies**? *Chloroplast (carbon fixing systems) >Lipids/chlorophyll*

7. Properties of **Supramolecular Assemblies** > that of **Polymer Macro-molecules?** *Ribosomes (protein synthesis factories) > components (RNA & protein)*

8. Properties of a **Polymer**>sum of properties of **Molecular Monomers**? *DNA (genome) > nucleotides (intermediary metabolites)*

9. Properties of a **Molecule**>sum of the properties of its **Atom**s? *Asprin (anti-inflammatory drug) > Atoms (carbon, oxygen, hydrogen)*

10. Properties of an **Atom** > sum of properties of **Subatomic Particles**? *Sodium (inflammatory metal) > protons, neutrons, electrons*

> = "are greater than"   * There is no life below the level of the cell.

Here is were great ignorance lies. The laws of cooperation appropriate to *groups* of organisms are different and unique to that level. There, selfish competitive violence is inherently destructive to families and society and is called antisocial. It's destructiveness is feared and censured. Survival of society is enhanced by the social laws of creative, unselfish cooperation. This also brings to members emergent benefits much superior to those available to individuals still selfishly and often violently competing alone at the next level below, that of the lone individual.

The 2nd Source of Human Suffering: Ignorance of the Modular Consciousness Elements in the Brain

This is mirrored in terms of evolution of the brain. At the ancient unconscious level, the human brain contains five separate bimodular consciousness systems (Chapters 1-4 of this book). That is, below the level of our cortical consciousness, the "reptilian" Self Brain (similar to Freud's Id) has evolved to deal with survival issues at the *individual* level. It and can be competitive, rebellious, and violent. In contrast, the Social Brain (similar to Freud's Superego) has evolved to operate at the next higher universe level, that of enhancing survival of the *group* by the emergent activities resulting from altruistic cooperation.

Successful operation at both levels results in a superior organism. To optimize the use of these two formidable systems, a critical third system, the Executive Brain system (similar to Freud's Ego) has emerged. It decides which of these two brain elements should be activated, as most appropriate to a given situation. That is, whether optimal survival is best served by the Ego's activating of the competitive, potentially violent "win-lose," self-brain Id. Or, by the Ego's inhibiting of the Id, and instead activating the wisdom of the cooperative peace-loving "win-win or no deal" social brain Superego.

A fifth subconscious element exists, sometimes called the Death Instinct or Thanatos , (Freud, 1920), the Reactive Mind (Hubbard, 1950), the Pain Body (Tolle, 1999), or more accurately, the broken-mutated developmental arrest repair program (xDARP), (Morton, 2011, 2015). Under certain circumstances, the xDARP can over- power the Executive to dominate it with once-appropriate behavior, now inappropriately seeking to complete ar- rested critical periods of psychosocial behavioral control from infancy-early childhood.

The confusing fact is that all four of the above operations occur outside of our awareness in the subconscious. Where our familiar self-consciousness generally resides is within the late-arriving right and left cerebral cortices, whose primary purpose is to compress and abstract vast amounts of information into a symbolic, smaller, more easily manipulated "comic book" forms (Morton, 2011). Thus, we see the visual "cartoons" and verbal "captions" with which we think and that constitute our normal consciousness. No wonder comic books are universally popular. This enormous truncation of the vast memory data-base enables us mentally quickly to internally rehearse the outcome of a wide variety of options. "I wonder what would happen if I did so and so in my imagination? Oops! That won't work! Hey! Look at this idea!

It appears to be a winner!" So, rather than injuring or killing ourselves in order to try them out in the real world, we internally select and rehearse them first.

Yet, since we are unaware of the more profound decisions occurring outside of our awareness, it is natural for us to conclude that we are in charge of all our behavior. Unfortunately for the unlearned, this is very far from the truth, and is at the root of much suffering. Part of maturation is to discover that we are only onlookers of the behavioral outcomes of the deeper, more powerful parts of our brain, and to surrender and align ourselves with the will of our brain based hidden Higher Power of our God-Within. "Thy will be done."

Koestler's Plea: Find a Way To Chemically Correct Human Insanity Before We Self-Destruct

In "*The Ghost in the Machine*" (1967), and again in his later book, "*Janus*"(1978), Arthur Koestler made a powerful case that evolution has gone wrong in the development of the human race. As a result, according to him, we have become an insane species, driven by endless cycles of primitive subconscious selfish violence, while brilliantly increasing our conscious knowledge about our surroundings, including and how to do further violence to each other. Koestler asserts that once we crossed the nuclear bomb threshold, where one man, by throwing a switch, can destroy all sentient life on earth, our continued survival was doomed. He held that religion and medicine have failed to bridge the gap between our violent subconscious drives and our conscious intellect. This forced him to the conclusion that our only hope for salvation as a species would be the discovery of a psychoactive substance that will eliminate our violence. He self-experimented with mescaline, as witnessed by the cosmic sweep of his ideas, but remained skeptical that hallucinogens were the answer for everyman. At the end of *Ghost in the Machine*, he makes the plea to any and all knowledgeable readers. He begs them to go out and find such a corrective chemical and apply it to society. He predicted that if such isn't found, human violence will bring our species to extinction. The present chapter was written as a direct response to Koestler's plea.

It could be said that in the last 40 years, more has been learned about brain, mind, and behavior than was previously known since the beginning of time. During these years of the neuroscience knowledge explosion, the author has collected and digested thousands of reprints and abstracts from the peer-reviewed, published research reports in the scientific literature. Presently these are bound in 3 ring notebooks that occupy a lineal thickness in his library that, if turned vertically, would be a stack more than 45 feet high. These are the thousands of pieces of a puzzle that lie unassimilated as research publications in the world's science libraries just waiting to be put together into a meaningful whole. Thousands of publications exist that even support the concept of modular consciousness. Yet, consensus opinion still follow the Single Mind Fallacy which asserts that we only have one mind. This conceptualization is at least a century behind cutting edge thinking.

What is Anxiety? What is Stress? How do they Differ from Fear?

Physical injury produces immediate pain, and the *fear*-based emotional activation of inbuilt withdrawal-avoidance flight-or-fight reflexes evolved to reduce or terminate a danger and avoid death. In contrast, **anxiety** is a prolonged emotion of dread that follows a fearful incident. Anxiety is the dread, anguish, worry, alarm, psychic pain, and concern produced by the automatic subconscious *memory* of the past fear-invoking painful incident. It is brought about by the recognition that *such an harmful event could occur again* with possibly an even more deadly outcome. Unconsciously originating anxiety is distinctly different from immediate conscious fear and is produced by a quite separate neural system to be described later. Anxiety is very hard to bear, making it very difficult to stop smoking which reduces anxiety (Hogle, Kaye & Curtin, 2010). Prolonged anxiety produces **stress**, which is an autonomic response consisting of costly chronic defensive body and mind compensations to minimize or avoid future injury. The prolonged defensive activation caused by the stress response debilitates us and adds to the suffering of anxiety in the form of depression.

The Traumatic Memory Bank

Usually, we are in control of our own experience and continually instinctually (unconsciously) act to optimize our survival. However, the experience of pain is designed to warn of potential impending tissue damage and directly activates our immediate fear-and-avoidance reflexes. If severe, traumatic injury follows, due to our inability to maintain control of the situation, the subconscious memories of this near-death traumatic event are not "experienced" by integration within our inner model of reality. Rather, they are transferred, *unexperienced,* to a special walled off memory area called the Trauma Bank (Hubbard, 1950).

The Trauma Bank contains unexperienced and thus unintegrated memories of incidents perceived as terrifying threats of death. Because of their high charge of terror, these memories are walled off as "*too hot to handle*" and can never again be accessed *consciously* because these memories contain the extreme emotions understandably produced by flashbacks. The valuable information within these incidents is thus blocked from integration into our expanding inner approximations of external reality. This is because they are forever walled off from conscious access. This inaccessibility impairs our intellectual growth, and leaving us without access to the wisdom that could have been gained by "experiencing" the terrifying incident. Later reflexive automatic retrieval of these subconscious traumatic memories causes unconscious stress-anxiety whose conscious cause is not recognized in accessible memory.

Thus, unexperienced traumatic memories are held in the Trauma Bank, forever isolated from conscious memory access. The brain begins to fail in death, or in near-death experiences (from many causes, including initiatory ordeals and use of psychedelic entheogens). Then, these incarcerated traumatic memories break out of their failing Trauma Bank prison and flood consciousness *as one's life passes before their eyes*. If the near-death expe- rience is survived, often the traumatic memories are finally actively integrated into one's Inner Model of Ex- ternal Re- ality. The result of this massive memory in- corporation is the commonly observed remarkable in- crease of intelli- gence of the survivors of these experi- ences. Their lives re- peatedly have been found to be transformed.

As we will soon see, people vary in terms of how much traumatic memory has been deposited in their Trauma Bank. That amount determines the level of uncon- scious pain they carry. The amount of their pain deter- mines their underlying basal anxiety level. The greater their anxiety load, the greater their stress over-reactivity. The higher their stress over-reactivity is, the more difficult they find it to get along with others. At some point they are so hyper-reactive as to become difficult to relate too. At higher levels they are antisocial, and with high enough over-reactivity they can be psychopathic.

Critically, if the painful event was resolved success- fully in the first incident, then its cause was discovered, integrated into their database, and action could be taken to prevent it from recurring. In that case, the basis for contin- ued anxiety and stress *disappear*, being replaced by the es- tablishment of control of the process and the memories of a lesson well learned. Now, if the original stimuli reap- pear, they cause no pain, fear, anxiety, or stress. Rather, effortless control.

What is Stress Reactivity?
However, if we do not succeed in gaining sufficient

control to avoid future repetition of the injury or if the first injury was very severe, we become traumatized. Then, normal events *restimulate* our automated subconscious memory of the original trauma now stored unexperienced in Trauma Bank. This reactivates anxiety and the associated stress response. We suffer again and again, adding to the load. Thus, we become over-reactive to the stimuli of stress. That is, we often subconsciously reactivate anxiety from stimuli that were associated with earlier death threats *that are no longer present.*

Often, the stimulus that causes us stress by restimulation is unique to our own past trauma and often is not experienced as stress by others around us. The more over-reactive we are, the truer this becomes. The stress over-reactivity spectrum ranges from only slightly inappropriate behavior to outright insanity. In a presently neutral environment, some of us, depending on our past trauma, can show chronic minor negativity, criticism, and irritability, while others will experience stronger phobic or claustrophobic arousal, and still others will often be thrown into a violent avoidant rage defensive attack.

Normal Experiences vs. Traumatic Experiences

There is evidence that those unexperienced memories stored unrecognized in our Trama Bank that cause us to be over-reactive to our environment are derived from activation of completely hidden original past experiences of the terror. Most of these incidents occurred in early infancy up to the age of about three years. These memories are double blocked. This is because, not only are they traumatic, but also they occurred before when we can normally remember what happened to us. This is because our consciousness had not yet moved up from the brain stem into the cerebral cortex.

In this regard, hidden memories of trauma cause a problem. Normally, benign memories are continually referenced to answer the ongoing questions of, "when and where have I seen this present situation before, and what was its survival outcome? Should I approach for more reward, or run to avoid harm?" These memory searches become widely generalized so that many associated elements of the current subject are cross-referenced in memory retrieval. Thus, it is not helpful if common memory searching of earlier similar memories retrieves subconsciously available memories of past trauma. This is because contacting them recreates the full blown anxiety-invoking, multimodal flashback of a past life-threatening event. Such flashbacks often occur in the pathology of Post Traumatic Stress Disorder (PTSD), and are very debilitating to thought and existence. Similar pathology to a lesser degree is present subconsciously in depression. To a lesser degree they contribute to common over reactivity to stress, the unrecognized plague to amicable human existence.

Many find temporary stress relief by the use of certain anxiety reducing drugs, such as alcohol. The most potent of these are opiates, such as heroin. Such drugs, because of their effectiveness in inhibiting-relieving psychic pain, are highly addictive. Unfortunately, tolerance for the drug soon develops and the person medicating their psychic pain needs more and more to obtain the same relief. Ultimately, this drug tolerance leads them to require more hard drug than they can possibly afford, leading to crime, and ultimately to death by overdose, not to mention the origin of drug trafficking, national corruption, and the collapse of society.

The Profoundly Harmful Effects of Trauma During the Critical Periods of Infancy

Interference with development during its critical period constitutes a traumatic death threat. Critical periods are discussed in greater detail in Chapter 6. Their mechanism has been discovered to be a critical period of maturation and myelination of social experience-dependent oligodendrocytes (Makinodan, Rosen, Itio, & Corfas, 2012).

What causes us to experience death-threat trauma and thus results in the debilitating deposits of traumatic memory in our Trauma Bank? Our behavioral genetics appears to lag behind the present by about a million years. If so, imagine rearing a child as an arboreal primate parent. There were no permanent structures, no plumbing for water or waste, dangerous predators surround you day and night. These include infanticidal males seeking to obliterate the genetic lineage of their competitors represented by your child in order to start a lineage of their own. What would infant care look like under those circumstances? Clearly, under these wild conditions any separation of the infant from its mother, no matter for how short the time, would be extremely dangerous, not only due to falls from the branches, but also to all types of active predation. Thus, our ancient genes make separation from our mother before weaning, *still even today*, to be a life-threatening, terrifying, and highly traumatizing event.

In non-human primates, the permanently traumatizing effect of maternal separation has been dramatized by the social deprivation experiments using Rhesus monkeys at the University of Wisconsin's Primate Center. They demonstrated that temporary early isolation of young male monkeys from skin contact with their mothers led to adults who are hyper-aggressive, self-mutilative, hypersexual with sometimes bizarre sexual behavior, and prone to pathological social behaviors (Harlow & Nowak, 1973).

Clearly, these disturbed behavior are shown by many human males today. Similarly, female monkeys raised without their mothers and siblings showed inappropriate aggression, making poor social companions, and as a result when placed in social settings, they were not preferred as social partners and made poor mothers. They are generally shunned by other monkeys and ended up low in social dominance rank (Bastian, Sponberg, Sponberg Suomi & Higley, 2003). Again the human comparison is unavoidable. Yet paradoxically, these "Periods of social isolation that totally and permanently destroy social capabilities of Rhesus monkeys had no deleterious effects on their learning capabilities" (From a paper read by Harry Harlow at the Psychonomic Society meeting in 1967). Thus, psychotic humans can also be very intelligent.

It would appear that similar behavior abnormalities exist among modern humans. Humans may be viewed as modern primates with a similar genetic child rearing inheritance as in other primates. With our million years BC genetics, this traumatizing terror produced by infant separation still occurs. Contrast ongoing ancient successful non-human primate child rearing practices in with our own modern well-intended child rearing practices. For example, we prepare a beautiful separate room for our newborns, with a lovely crib into which every night we lovingly place our infant, often previously traumatized by circumcision performed without anesthesia (Matteoli (2010), to spend their nights alone, something that itself has shown to be harmful (Morgan, Horn, Bergman, 2011). Early in the morning the infant is quickly dressed and passed to a babysitter until dusk, then to spend a couple of hours in the evening with its preoccupied parents before the cycle is repeated the next day.

The above is increasingly seen to be a powerful source of infant traumatization. What is missing is continuous skin-to-skin contact with a mother who even cleans perineum excreta with her tongue and nurses the baby on demand until the infant is ultimately weaned to solid food, not prematurely onto a formula bottle. What results from our loss of intimate primate infant care is the production of huge numbers of the "Walking Wounded," disturbed, emotionally stunted, stressed, sex and drug seeking, yet very intelligent, high-tech members of modern society.

There is now a huge research literature on the large effects of separation for even only one hour a day during a critical period of postnatal development in non-human infants. Regardless of the species, this causes profound effects upon adult behavior. This is in marked contrast to the behavior of adults who were not isolated during that critical period. In general and due to no fault of their own, the previously separated infants end up becoming unnaturally hyper-reactive to stress in adulthood. That is, such humans find many elements of their environment and social relations re-stimulate them to cause unrest, upset, resentment, anger, frustration, critical attacks, rejection, and violent outbursts. This activation and chronic elevation of subconscious inner stress has harmful effects upon their health, due to activation of their stress and coping systems. In search of stress relief, it further drives experimentation with the briefly rewarding feelings of sex and drugs with all their long term negative consequences.

The above describes the well-meaning and unintended permanently debilitating effects of infant separation, caused by our ignorance of our own million BC genetic requirements. However, infants, and young children can be subject to much more death-threatening trauma by parents who because of their own trauma do not care about them, who view them with resentment as an unwanted burden, or who even torture or abandon them. Such abused children have huge deposits of trauma in their traumatic memory bank. It is remarkable that such individuals even survive. Their subconscious hatred of their parents can be so great as to turn them into insatiable serial killers. At the very least they will traumatize their own children as they were traumatized, creating the endless cycle of violence and degradation that surrounds us today. Thus, Koestler's plea against human genetic insanity, described earlier in this chapter.

Physical and Behavioral Alterations in the Adult Human Brain Caused by Childhood and Later Trauma

Numerous reports have appeared in the research literature quantifying the damaging effects of maltreatment of human infants that emerge in adulthood. These include the emergence of stress response behavioral pathology (Mosch, Riese, Reijneveld, et al, 2012; Victoria, Inoue, Young, & Murphy, 2013), including borderline personality disorder and depression (Fernando, Bebio, Scholsser, et al., 2012), self-harm (Fisher, Moffitt, Houls, et al., 2012), PTSD and anxiety attacks (van Zuiden, Geuze, Willeman,2012). But also physical changes brought about in brain, including white matter disruptions (Huang, Gundapuneedi, Rao, 2012), reduced medial prefrontal cortical volume (Harmelem, van Tol, van der Wee, et al. (2010), limbic scarring (Dannolwski, Stuhmann, Beutelmann, et al., 2012), reduced leucocyte telomere length (O'Donovan, Epel, Lin, et al., (2011) and abnormal DNA methylation of stress regulation and response genes (Klengel, Mehta, Anacker, et al., (2013).

Effects of Earlier Adult Trauma

Even having had a benign childhood, as adults we can also be hugely terrified of dying and traumatized as victims of war, teenager abuse, rape, torture, violent crime, accidents, natural disasters, and other life threatening events. This often results in the debilitating symptoms of major depression and post-traumatic stress disorder (PTSD), all of which are seen to be biologically related (Savic, Knezevic, Damjanovic, et al., (2012). For these victims of PTSD, symptoms sometimes appear seemingly out of the blue. While everyone experiences PTSD differently, there are three main types of symptoms: 1) Flashback re-experiencing the traumatic event in all of its multimodal elements. 2) Avoiding reminders of the trauma in an attempt to avoid restimulation and reliving the event once more. 3) Increased anxiety and emotional arousal, in response to the possibility of immediately being thrown into memories of terror.

Despite pockets of cultural development, in general modern adults are like Harlow monkeys: intellectual, stress-reactive, hyper-aggressive, self-mutilative, hyper-sexual with bizarre sexual behaviors, and pathological social behaviors. Their hypersexuality leads to rape of females, so that in many cultures most infants are born to single child-mothers. Parenthetically this is producing the "population bomb." These unwanted infants are unavoidably and extensively traumatized. The families of unwed mothers disintegrate because of further rapes by other males. They are often are replaced by juvenile death- gang families who will kill them if they try to leave. The extensive traumatic pain leads to intense seeking of relief inevitably channeled into drug addictions, organized crime, global drug cartels, government corruption, the rise of global corporations, and rape of the planet for profit. Arms sales profits drive political unrest, causing wars for profit, leading to national destabilization, and toward societal collapse back to the jungle from which we arose. This cycle may have occurred more than once in the previous millions of years of our evolution.

The above overview illustrates how, due to the way our brains have evolved, unresolved threats of death, due to our ancient hardwiring, naturally cause permanent over-reactivity to individual stress in adulthood. The next question becomes, why and by what neurochemical mechanism does hyper-reactivity and resulting stress occur? We will uncover the answers to these important questions later in this chapter, after which we can proceed to inquire: "Can means be found to prevent or eliminate hyper-reactivity to stress?" Then, we are really on our way to an answer.

Brain Pathways Activated by Trauma to Cause Stress Reactivity

To understand the nature of the stress over-reactivity that so plagues society, four sequential elements of the stress-anxiety pathway will be described (**Figure 1**). These may be new to you, but as central players in the production of the profound anxiety of death by the brain they are well worth knowing and in overview are easy to understand.

1. Stress-Induced Inflammation is Initiated by Interleukin-1 beta and Other Stress Response Cytokines

Exposure to tissue damage, pain, and stress causes the release of brain Interleukin-1 beta (IL-1b), a protein (Nguyen, Owens, Kohno, et al., 1998). IL-1b is a potent inflammatory regulator affecting every organ in the body. For example, the detection of the invading foreign proteins in the coat of a virus or bacteria in the blood is sufficient to promote IL-1b release, contributing to the commonly-seen inflammatory response of fever, loss of appetite, and the sleepiness. Even non-harmful insults to the body such as restraint (Minami, Kuriashi, Ymaguchi, et al., 1991) that produce anxiety or anger powerfully can cause IL-1b release (Pesce, Speranza, Frenceschelli, et al., 2012). The details of how perceived threats to one's survival cause

FIGURE 1. The Four Steps to Stress

No pain, no gain: Why less that an hour of stress, gives stress relief for several days.

SEROTONIN AND STRESS

Bruce Morton, Ph.D., University of Hawaii School of Medicine, 1997

Factors Elevating Serotonin Down-Regulate the 5-HT2a Receptor = Tolerance, Peace, Cooperation

A. Physical Pain (or Other Threats to Survival) = STRESSORS.

Heat Pain

  Sauna

  Hot Tub (Furo)

  Turkish Bath

  American Indian Sweat Lodge

Cold Pain (Ice Slurry)

Swim Stress Pain

Running Pain

Stretching Pain

Childbirth Pain

Meditation Pain (Lotus Position)

Stress Response, Immune Suppression, etc.

cortisol

Release of NE from LC alarm decorticates brain by inhibiting:
1. cerebral cortex (reasoning)
2. cerebellar cortex (sociality)
3. hippocampal cortex (retrieval) leaving only brain core instincts.

ACTH

Stress Disorder: Hypersensitivity from Developmental Arrests or Adult Traumatization

CRF = Corticotrophin Releasing Factor

Up-Regulated 5HT2a R Sensitized

Pituitary CRF R

Traumatic Stress

Salivary Serotonin (by Radio-Receptor Assay)

Trauma Childhood, or PTSD

Monitor LC: P300, GSR Jaw Clench

alpha-2 agonists, beta-blockers

Brain Pathway

via PGE2

Ketanserin

IL-1 → IL-1 R → Serotonin → 5HT2a R: Normal

DA inhibits

CRF

Locus Coeruleus CRF R

Norepi-nephrine

IL-1 antagonists

NSAIDs

CRF antagonists

All drugs of abuse

IL-1 = Interleukin-1, an inflammatory cytokine

Hallucinogens

Slow Resensi-tization: t 1/2 = 3 days

Fast Desensi-tization: t 1/2 = 60 min

BNST via CSF

BBB fails, cerebellum first

Survival threat activates:
Alarm, Fear, Anxiety, Violence, Depression via Amygdala (more CRF) and Hypothalamus (Less DA)

Prostration

Down-Reg. 5HT2a R Insensitive

"Ego-death", "Near death experiences"

Brief "stress" brings relief but 2 wks on SSRIs is much more effective.

"Transcendence"

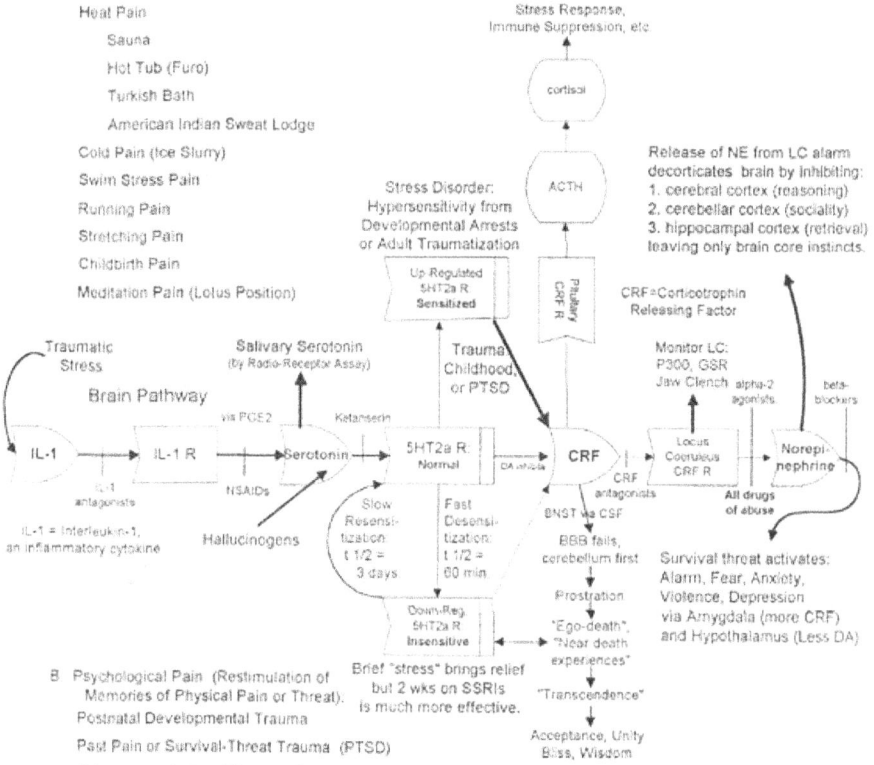

B. Psychological Pain (Restimulation of Memories of Physical Pain or Threat). Postnatal Developmental Trauma

Past Pain or Survival-Threat Trauma (PTSD)

Hallucinogen-Induced Trauma (Present or Past)

Acceptance, Unity Bliss, Wisdom

C. Elevation by Serotonin Specific Reuptake Blocker Antidepressants (SSRI)s

D. Meal-Induced, One Hour Serotonin Elevation Peak

E. Tryptophan and 5-Hydroxy-Tryptophan Loading

F. Tyrosine Loading: Dopamine product Inhibits CRF Release

Factors Lowering Serotonin Up-Regulate 5-HT2a Receptor = Intolerance, Violence, Depression

A. Tryptophan-deficient Diet

B. Theoretical: Painless, effortless, pleasurable experiences ultimately produce dysphoria.

IL-1b secretion are only beginning to become known. At times, the release of IL-1b and other cytokines, such as IL-6 and Tumor Necrosis Factor-alpha (TNFa), can be- come chronic, causing the development of such inflammatory pathologies as arthritis, cancer, hypertension, preterm delivery, depression (Hannestad, DellaGioia, Bloch, 2011), and premature ageing. The chronic hypersecretion of IL-1b also is caused by maternal separation (Hennessy, Fitch, Jacobs, et al., 2011), a subject of this chapter. No matter how IL-1b release is initiated, this represents the first of a four step defensive cascade. That is, its produc- tion activates the next critical step, the release of serotonin (Shintani, Knaba, Nakaki, et al., 1993).

2. Serotonin is the Next Component in the Stress Pathway:

Popular in the mental illness news today, serotonin, also called 5-hydroxytryptamine (5-HT), is an ancient neurotransmitter for which more than 14 different serotonin receptor binding subtypes have evolved in the brain. Critically, one of these receptors, the 5-HT$_{2a}$R, causes stress when it is exposed to and binds even small amounts of serotonin or some of its analogues.

Hallucinogens, such as LSD, DMT, psilocybin, and mescaline, are structurally related to serotonin. They happen to specifically and potently act upon the 5HT$_{2a}$R to cause high stress and Ego-defensive hallucinations (Vollenweider, Vollenweider-Scherpenhuyzen, Vogel, et al., 1998). If the dose is sufficient, the person experiences "Ego death" and the transcendence. This occurs because the limbic element of the brain responsible for the activities of the "Executive Ego" is temporarily inhibited leading to "Ego death" by the hallucinogen. The exact identity of the subcortical brain structure producing the Ego has yet to be decided, but appears to be located in the cingulate cortex (Morton, 2014). LSD binds $5HT_{2a}Rs$ in the anterior cingulate cortex to cause its effects (Gresch, Barrett, Sanders-Bush, & Smith, 2007; Gresch, Strickland, & Sanders-Bush, 2002). The posterior and anterior cingulate cortex, frontal cortex, and the thalamus have all been found to be profoundly and specifically inhibited by hallucinogens (Carthart-Harris, et al., 2012).

An increased $5HT_{2a}R$ availability has be reported in the brain of physically aggressive persons with personality disorder (Rosell, Thompson, Slifstein, 2010). Also, chronic subconscious, stress-induced elevated background levels of serotonin somehow cause and increase in the numbers of $5HT_{2a}Rs$ to produce depression (Yates, Leake, Candy et al., 1990). Consistent with this is the finding that $5HT_{2a}Rs$ are also elevated in suicide, an act of despair often associated with depression (Arango, Ernsberber, Marzuk, et al., 1990). Serotonin specific reuptake inhibitors (SSRIs) antidepressants, such as Prozac, after a two week delay, appear to elevate serotonin at the synapse so as to down- regulate 5HT2aRs and thus to relieve depression. SSRIs also up-regulate dopamine DA1Rs to restore missing re- ward. It is of interest that cingulate $5\text{-}HT_{2a}R$ levels are low in a u t i s t i c individuals (Murphy, Daly, Schmitz, et al., 2006), suggesting their defect in social relations may be due to a defective or absent cingulate-based Ego.

A critical but little known fact is that it takes less than hour of serotonin binding to desensitize the $5HT_{2a}R$ to serotonin or its related hallucinogens (Trulson, Crisp, 1983). Since many hallucinogens are long acting, this creates the well-known biphasic experience of painful Ego death, followed by transcendence, which is often experienced at relatively high concentrations of hallucinogen. Critically, in contrast to this rapid minutes-long down-regulation, at least three to five days are required for the same 5HT2aRs to re-sensitize (Leysen, Janssen, Niemegeers, 1989). During this time, not only does the ingestion of hallucinogens produce no effect, there is also a relative freedom from stress.

This situation explains the basis of several well-established cultural "no pain, no gain" stress relieving practices. For example, less than an hour of pain-limited aerobic exercise, or pain-limited sauna or hot tub (e.g., the Japanese furo) exposure induces enough IL-1a and serotonin release to cause $5HT_{2a}R$ down regulation and stress relief lasting for several days, due to the slow resensitizing of the receptor. After this time, one again begins to feel stressed and in need of another work-out (Mondin, Morgan, Piering, et al., 1996) or heat treatment.

3. Corticotrophin Releasing Factor (CRF) is Released Downstream from Serotonin to Produce the Stress Response:

As the third downstream step in the multifaceted stress pathway, stimulation of the 5HT2aR bearing neurons by serotonin analogues causes the outflow of corticotrophin releasing factor (CRF) by a yet unidentified pathway. CRF is a major player in defensive behavioral responses, including but beyond the activation of the well-know HPA (hypothalamus, pituitary, adrenal) axis to release ACTH and the stress corticosteroids to produce activation of the "stress response."

In fact, CRF, as the major stress hormone and regulator, responds to inner and outer emergency threats to self-survival by mobilizing numerous brain and bodily emergency defensive reactions. As a last ditch attempt to survive, its action can exhaustively activate resources not ordinarily tapped. This is because their p r o l o n g e d depletion could cause deleterious long-term consequences to health. Be- yond its pituitary gland effects to produce the corticoster- oids of stress, CRF acts on many other brain structures, including alarm and anxiety centers (Chappell, Smith, Kilts, et al., 1986).

CRF administration produces stress-like effects in humans. CRF levels are elevated in individuals with stress related illness, including depression (Swaab, Bao, Lucassen, 2005), PTSD, anorexia nervosa, anxiety disorders (Laryea, Arnett, Muglia, 2012) and addiction (Logrip, Koob, Zorrilla, 2011). Direct injection of CRF into the cerebral ventricles causes such enormous personal suffering that the person begs for immediate relief by suicide (Arato, Banki, Bissette, 1989). In contrast, CRF antagonists, such as antialarmin, reduce negative emotionality (Heinrichs, Pich, Miczek, et al., 1992). *CRF increases long term anxiety levels but not the short term effects of fear* (Grillon, Heller, Hirschhorn, et al., 2011). Interestingly, nicotine withdrawal also increases anxiety but not fear (Hogle,

Kaye, Curtin, 2010), making it one of the most difficult of abused drugs to stop.

There is another remarkable neurotransmitter that produces opposite effects to those of stress-inducing CRF. Called oxytocin, its elevation brings the experience of trust, acceptance, and of all things, love. Its intranasal administration causes stress reducing and attachment enhancing effects even among the mentally ill (Simeon, Bartz, Hamilton, 2011). Elevated oxytocin is associated with the initial stages of romantic attachment (Schneiderman, Zagoory-Sharon, Leckman, et al., 2012). Oxytocin modulates the link between adult attachment and cooperation through reduced aversion of betrayal (De Dreu, 2012). It acts to increase both in-group and universal altruism (Isreal, Weisel, Ebstein, et al, (2012). It has recently been discovered that not only does oxytocin, but also vasopressin, and of all things, MDMA (the abused love drug, ecstacy) cause acute prosocial effects. It has further been discovered that these prosocial effects are mediated through agonism (activation) of the Vasopressin V_{1a} receptor by these three substances (Ramos, Hicks, Kevin, Camier, Narlwar, Kassiou & McGregor, 2013).

The cerebral spinal fluid-filled ventricles of the brain contain the bed nucleus of the stria terminalis (BNST) part of the anxiety producing, paired amygdalae deep within our temporal lobes. The BNST is a structure rich in CRF receptors. Importantly, the BNST is also rich in oxytocin receptors. There is evidence for the reciprocal regulation of CRF-induced defensive stress and oxytocin-induced altruism via the BNST (Dabrowska, Hazra, Ahem, et al., 2011). It appears that under stress the

CRF2Rs can inhibit the release of oxytocin to reduce trust and accepting behavior. Supporting this, it has been found that unusually low concentrations of oxytocin in the cerebrospinal fluid (CSF) reflect high intent in suicide attempters (Jokinen, Chalzittofis, Hellstrom, et al, 2012).

4. Locus Coeruleus and Norepinepherine

In the brain, CRF receptors are found in many locations, but especially upon oun our fourth pathway step, the paired midbrain locus coeruli (LC), the major drivers of anxiety (Redmond, Huang, 1979. Although Latin labels for neuroanatomical struc- tures can be off-putting, locus coeruleus names each of the paired blue spots, early seen in the brain stem pons. Of great importance here is that the LC are the major source of the inhibitory neurotransmitter, noradrenaline, more commonly known as norepinephrine (NE), throughout the entire brain. Thus, the far reaching fibers of the LC innervate the three brain cortexes: the hippocampal cortex (memory), the cerebellar cortex (social behavior), and cer- ebral cortex (intellect). Stress-anxiety based LC excitation via CRF elevation causes the local release of NE to inhibit each of these three cortices of higher thought. This huge deficit brings about the inhibition of conscious memory (the "mind goes blank") and the release of anxious decorticate "reptilian" instinctual behavior that is self-oriented, antisocial and violent (Devilbiss, Waterhouse, Berridge, et al., 2012). Further, under conditions causing anxiety distress, reward is inhibited as inappropriate (Atrens, Ungerstedt, Ljungberg, 1977), releasing frustrated anger, sleep loss, and ultimately depression, a symptom of stress-induced NE depletion. *These effects of CRF on the LC are*

279

opposed by the endogenous opioids (Valentino, Van Bochstaele, 2001), making highly rewarding heroin extremely attractive. The LC production of NE is also required for REM sleep. If blockade of REM sleep is prolonged, death can result.

Many Past Methods Attempting to Reduce Stress Reactivity have Evolved

By self-experimentation humans have discovered substances that relieve anxiety and restore pleasure. Their effects are so temporarily pronounced as to cause addiction. *Crucially, all drugs of abuse inhibit LC (locus coeruleus) release of NE.* These include: caffeine (Olpe, Jones, Steinmann, 1983), nicotine (Egan, North, 1986), cannabis (Oropeza, Page, Bockstaele, 2005) alcohol (Verbank, Seutin, Massotte, et al., 1990), tranquillizers (Tallman, Paul, Skolnick, et al.,1980), amphetamines (Holdefer, Jensen, 1987), cocaine (Pitts, Marwah, 1988), and the opiates (Valentino, Van Bockstaele, 2001). This remarkable de-stressing effect is the unrecognized source of drug seeking behavior. That is, unknowingly, these all substances are taken to reduce the stress of subconscious pain and anxiety and to restore or enhance the pleasure provided by releasing our inhibited reward centers. This is how the brain works to bring us joy and sorrow.

The many religious and other non-drug methods that have evolved, which temporarily reduce our psychic pain are described in detail in **Chapter 7** of this book. Most lead to the quick down regulation of the 5-HT$_{2a}$R to reduce the production of CRF and thus NE to bring temporary relief that slowly disappears over the next few days until the receiver recovers its normal stress producing sensitivity.

Evidence for Cerebellar Involvement in Stress Reactivity.

Trauma Causes Stress Reactivity in the Cerebellar Vermis

The hindbrain cerebellum actually has more cells than the entire cerebral cortex, but they are smaller, so the cerebellum is too. The cerebellum is a remarkable brain element that not only coordinates the timing of complex bodily movement (Ackerman, Graber, Hertrich, & Daum, 1999), but also is deeply involved in non-motor activities including language expression (Strelnikov, Vorobyev, Chernigovskaya, & Medvedev, 2006; De Smet, Paquier, Verhoevan, & Marien, 2013) and social interaction (Watson, 1978). The final output of the cerebellum is through its deep nuclei (Nieuwenhuys, Voogd, & van Huijzen, 1981).

The cerebellar *VERMIS is* the outermost midline structure at the rear surface of the cerebellum at the back of the head just above the neck. Importantly, it is associated with the regulation of emotionality (Levisohn, Cronin-Golomb, Schmamann, 2000). Areas of highest blood flow are through the cerebellar vermis and striatum (Madsen, Jensen, Vaeth, et al., 1990), reinforcing the critical function of these brain structures. The vermis is responsible for both the activation of both positive and negative emotions. For example, self-stimulation of the vermis occurs in animals seeking reward (Ball, Micco, Berntson,

1974). In contrast, when cerebellar vermis output is inhibited by injury, brain stem Id-like violent and antisocial behaviors are released. This is seen in the Cerebellar Cognitive Affective Syndrome where negative behavioral changes in patients with vermal lesions were prominent or overwhelming (Schamahmann & Sherman, 1997).

Increased vermal activity has been observed in subjects with Premenstrual Syndrome (PMS) (Rapkin, Berman, Mandelkern, Silverman, Morgan, London, 2011), who are noted for their negative emotional volatility. The induction of grief also caused activation of vermis (Gundel, O'Connor, Littrell, et al., 2003). Cholecystokinin (CCK)-induced panic was found to excite the cerebellar vermis (Schunck, Erb, Mathis, et al., 2006). Vermis activity was elevated in semi-abstinent cocaine users, conceivably often leading to relapse (Anderson, Maas, Frederick, et al, 2006). The vermis was the brain structure most activated when subjects were creating a story about the motivation of another person (anxiety) in theory of mind studies (Andreasen, O'Leary, 2003). Restimulation of symptoms in PTSD patients also activated the cerebellar vermis (Pissiota, Frans, Fernandez, et al., 2002). Conversely, vermal lesions eliminated hyper-defensiveness, mouse killing, and freezing in rats (Supple, Cranney, Leaton, 1988). Vermal lesions also reduced *anxiety but not fear* in rats (Supple, Leaton, Fanselow,1987).

During the postnatal development of the cerebellum, both CRF-1 receptors and CRF-2 receptors were found, each with unique distributions. The CRF-1 pathway appears to be associated with the production of *fear* (Grillon, Hale, Lieberman, et al. (2015). The CRF-2 pathway in the Bed Nucleus of the Stria Terminalis is specific for *anxiety* (Grillon, Heller, Hirschhorn, et al. 2011). The dread of harm in the future that produces anxiety is quite different than pain-induced fear from a present insult. As mentioned, it has been shown that nicotine withdrawal increases threat-induced anxiety, but not fear (Hogle, Kaye & Curtin, 2010). Importantly, activation of the vermis by high anxiety of death threats that release CRF can inhibit vermal deep nuclear output. This cuts off cooperative social behavior normally issuing from the cerebellum, releasing brain core instinctual stress-induced competitive survival behavior to come to the fore. Ligands are available which are specific for either of these receptors. It has be found that CRF-2 receptors are localized on axons of the vermis during postnatal development (Lee, Bishop, Tian, & King, 2004).

Cerebellar Vermis Hyperwiring and Enlargement is Produced as a Compensation for Trauma

A critical observation is the following: If this vermal defense fails to prevent trauma from occurring, the elevated CRF levels present lead to new growth of connectivity in the spine and vermis as a compensation. This leads to stress hyper-reactivity (Gounko, Swinny, Kalicharan, et al., 2013). Such is consistent with the observation that early sexual abuse in children causes vermal hyper-innervation. In adulthood, there was higher vermal blood flow and stress associated drug abuse in these abuse victims (Anderson, Teicher, Polcari, et al., 2002). Thus, early insults lead to hyperwiring of pain circuits causing a person to be more sensitive to physical or psychological pain later in life (Helmuth, 2000).

Strikingly, it has recently been reported that mice, genetically modified to lack CRF-2 receptors, were not vulnerable to opiate withdrawal, and that the usual reemergence of drug seeking was completely abolished (Morisot, Rouibi, & Contarino, 2015). This powerfully supports the present proposal that CRF-2 receptor-driven hyperplasitic *overproduction of cerebellar vermis neurons is produced by trauma.*

This addition of more neurons to the vermis, resulting in a higher density of vermal neurons makes it hyperexcitable. That is, it becomes sensitized. As a result, normal events previously having no survival significance now become associated with past trauma to cause the individual to experience stress via excessive vermal excitation. Thus, the abnormal excitation of the hyper wired vermis inhibits cerebellar output in the deep nuclei, leading to inappropriate activation of emergency antisocial survival behavior. This is here proposed to be the origin of Post-Traumatic Stress Disorder (PTSD). The trauma leading to PTSD can occur during infancy and early childhood, or in adulthood, as produced in soldiers on the battlefield, also in victims of rape, auto crashes, earthquakes, floods, or other terrifying experiences. *Thus, the resulting hyper innervation of the cerebellar vermis is an emotionally crip- pling compensation that results in anxiety-based antisocial behavior and a lifelong vulnerability to depression, drug abuse, and suicide.*

Elimination of PTSD-like Behavior by Electrical Inhibition of the Vermis
R. G. Heath at Tulane University in the late 1970s,

implanted electrodes over the cerebellar vermis of criminally insane psychotic killers and provided them with a pocket stimulator to "activate" it as they felt necessary (Heath, 1977). Application of the electrical stimuli incapacitated the ability of the vermis to produce pain and anxiety. This relief was perceived as pleasurable. (Heath, Llewellyn, & Rouchell, 1980). It transformed these psychopaths into the most sociable of individuals, normal in all regards (Heath, Rouchell, Llewellyn, & Walker, 1981). However, in one case, when the wire connecting the stimulator to the vermis became disconnected, the subject immediately grabbed a pair of scissors and killed his nurse. These studies were later discontinued.

Elimination of Stress Reactivity by the Pruning of the Cerebellar Vermis

It was found that the ordeal-based use of the β-carboline, ibogaine, contained in the Tabernanthe Iboga shrub found in West equatorial Africa, prevents the withdrawal symptoms produced by cessation of heroin, cocaine and crack, and alcohol. Further, a retrospective study indicated that subjects stopped taking these drugs, as well as marijuana, crack, psychostimulants, and polydrug use for at least eight months after a single ingestion of ibo- gaine (Schenberg, de Castro Comis, Chaves, et al. (2014). Ibogaine has also been used to cure depression and PTSD. These observations led the National Institutes of Mental Health to provide funding to investigate ibogaine as a promising solution to drug addiction (Mash, Koverag, Pablo, et al., 2000). However, it was soon found that ibogaine is also excitotoxic (**Figure 1**) to neurons in the cerebellar vermis of rodents, creating, parasagittal stripes of Purkinje cell loss in the cerebellar vermis (O'Hearn, Long & Molliver.1993). This lead to the termination of these studies and removed any further interest in using these substances.

Ibogaine intoxication can last longer than one day and is associated with non-LSD-type hallucinations, such as see- ing in the dark, and violent vomiting. Olivocerebelar pro- jection mediates the ibogaine induced degeneration of purkinje cells (O'Hearn, Molliver, 1997) It was proposed (Blackburn & Szumlinsky, 1997) that ibogaine may serve to decrease induced levels of stress reactivity from ele- vated sensitized levels back to baseline levels. This could lead to a reduction of vermal sensitized level-based drug craving in addiction. Consistent with this is the observa- tion that alcoholism ultimately causes vermal atrophy, per- haps a factor in alcohol-based relief of underlying dyspho- ria (Bovin G, 1995).

Importantly, harmaline, a cousin of ibogaine also was found to have similar excitotoxicity (**Figure 1**). It also produces tremor, vomiting, and odd non-LSD type of hallucina- tions. It just so happens that harmaline, and related harmane and harmine β-carbolines supply the essential monoamine oxidase inhibitor constituents of ayahuasca, a two plant brew used as a sacrament in a growing number of Amazon basin churches, and now spreading to Europe and North America. The first jungle leaf component contains dimenthyltryptamine (DMT). DMT is a potent hallucinogen when injected, but completely inactive orally because our gut monoamine oxidases rapidly chop it

Figure 1, β-Carboline Excitotoxic Pruning of Purkinje Cells in the Rat Cerebellar Vermis

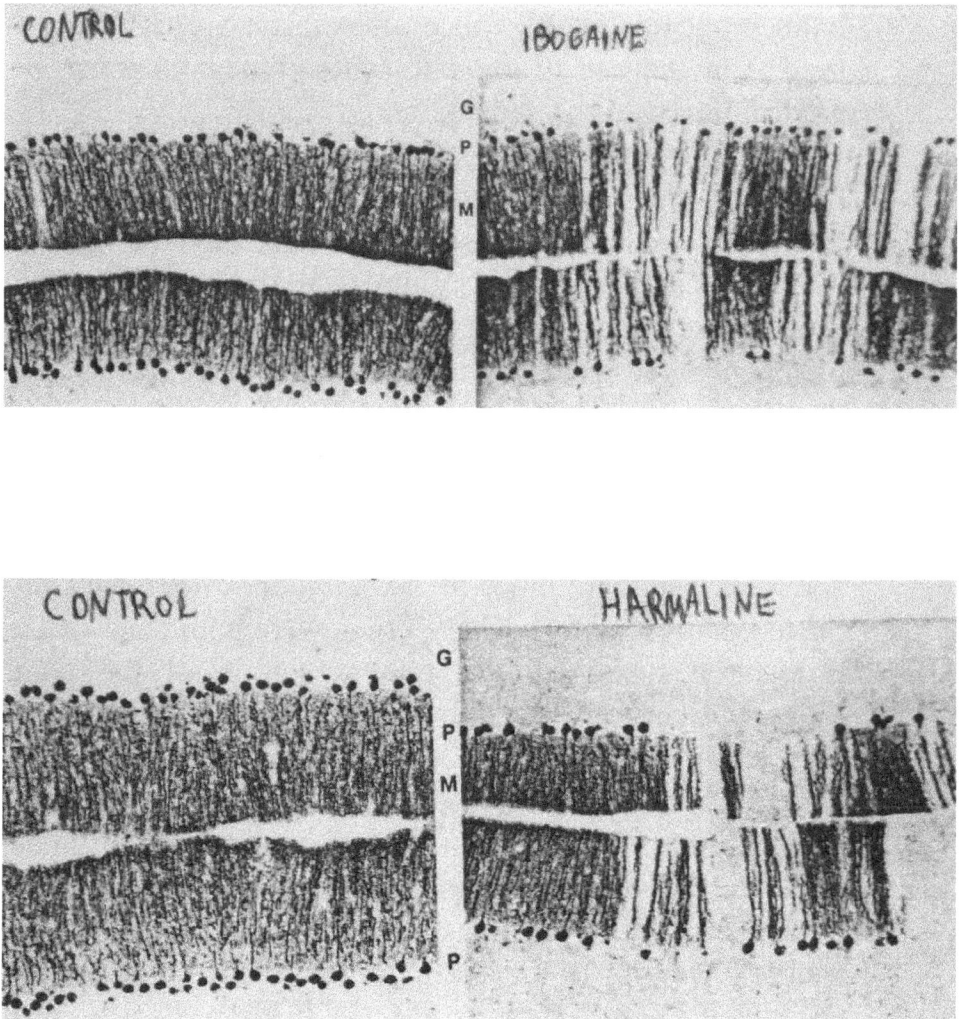

Photos from O'Hearn and Molliver (1993)

up into inactive products. However, the second ayahuasca root component supplies the β-carboline monoamine oxidase inhibitors, such as harmaline. These protect the DMT from degradation, allowing its brain levels to rise to hallucinogenic levels. These often result vast richly colored hallucinations of the psilocybine type containing ever changing patterns and content.

A common side effect of ayahuasca use is vomiting, often prolonged and violent. To combat this, dietary purification procedures are used for several days before the session in an attempt to minimize the powerful nausea. Some of the many benefits attributed to the ayahuasca by members of these churches are the cessation of alcohol and drug use as well as reduced joblessness among their constituents.

As yet, no one has commented in the ayahuasca research literature upon the excitotoxic nature of harmaline and other beta-carbolines in the brew, and which are similar to that of ibogaine. These drugs were both observed to produce a sustained upstream activation of the parasagittal olivocerebellar climbing fiber projections to the cerebellum, increasing blood flow (Yang, G. Iadecola, C. (1998). It was hypothesized that the release of excitatory glutamate from the climbing fiber synaptic terminals may lead to the *excitotoxic degeneration of Purkinje* cells as the result of overdriving. Harmaline induces a 10 cps tremor via nitric oxide-induced cGMP elevations (Knowles, W.D., Phillips, M, I. (1980). It was also found that harmaline, harmol, and especially harmine caused mitochondrial dysfunction in rats (Nakagawa, Suzuki, Ishii, et al. (2010). If this excitotoxicity confirmed to occur in humans, it would no doubt lead to the prohibition of ayahuasca use, in addition to ibogaine, harmaline, and harmine are already placed in the DEA Schedule I as unsafe for human use.

To summarize, drug abuse is a manifestation of stress levels that are highest in PTSD. These overreactivities appear to be caused by an earlier trauma-induced hyper-innervation of the cerebellar vermis. It is the author's opinion that the reason that ibogaine and harmaline eliminate drug seeking, is because they excitotoxically prune away the very hyper-innervation caused by the original trauma, restoring normality and bringing the pro-social behaviors of the cerebellum back to the fore. Thus, the induction of a specific excitotoxicity in the human brain by these β-carbolines would seem to be valuable, and to be encouraged, not banned, political correctness not withstanding.

The Author's Anecdotal Experiences with Harmaline

Part of my self-testing of over 40 psychoactive drugs at the School of Medicine at the University of Hawaii, included the repeated ingestion of harmaline. At a low dose, it amazingly gave me the illusion of being able to see within the pitch darkness of my 4'x4'x8' testing chamber. I began to clearly see everything that was in the chamber. Walls, ceiling, floor, musical and recording equipment were all illuminated as if by strong moonlight. Others have reported this phenomenon, considering it to be some form of magic. But, skeptical me did not want to believe in the supernatural. So, while I was thus intoxicated, I decided to play a trick. I reached up to the corner between the ceiling and two walls that I could clearly see in the absolute blackness. My finger found it, but to my surprise, my vision of the corner off by a few inches from my finger probe. Immediately, my night vision shifted to align with my finger. Not magic! Rather, it was our incredible brain using its memory to project an image of everything that it knew that was there. However, even in the absolute darkness, it was only off by only a couple of inches. Pretty amazing!

I also did a dose response curve including quite high doses of harmaline. There were some indistinct visual images, but also intense, repeated bouts of retching. No doubt I burned out quite a few vermal neurons. Remarkably, ever since, I have gotten absolutely zero effect from alcohol, or marijuana. Until recently, I never understood why, and tried to get high many times, wondering what had happened to me. I never put two and two together until I found the paper on cerebellar damage in rats. Obviously, I am now "brain damaged," and/or I have pruned my hyper wiring from childhood trauma and am now normalized. It takes quite a bit more aggrevation to get me upset these days. Thank goodness! Also I am saving a lot of money usually spent chasing stress relief by entertainment and liquor! There are so many alcoholics who are self-medicating their trauma-based, hyper-wired cerebellae! Underneath their suffering and insanity, these friends are such beautiful persons! In Africa, many natives believe that ibogaine bearing plants are a gift from God. Thus, in Gabon the Iboga tree is considered a national treasure.

Utopian Ideas Arising Regarding the Potential of Cerebellar Pruning to the Human Race

I assert that our violence comes from the trauma of our way of child rearing, very unlike that of the existing higher apes who are generally non-violent, with the exception of chimpanzees, who traumatize their offspring much as we do. I have expanded upon this elsewhere. Of course life threatening trauma at any age can hyper-innervate the vermis. This causes us to become excessively negative, critical, competitive, hyperstressed, and self-medicating to the point of a mindless stupor.

What if everyone were given a specific dose of harmaline and DMT (or less desirably ayahuasca whose contents are less controllable) as a coming of age initiation to the human race? Imagine! The lower classes in society composed of the incapacitated walking wounded would be greatly reduced! Would the lonely become socialized? Or, what if we gave prisoners a doses of harmaline and DMT (or ayahuasca as in Brazil by the ACUDA) in exchange for a shortened sentence. Would the jails would soon become empty? Would now-relaxed people become more cooper- ative and less uptight and adversarial? Nations could be- come supportive of each other, etc., etc. UTOPIA! This could be our hope for peace and avoidance of the self-in- duced extinction predicted by Koestler. It is our next step.

CHAPTER TWELVE

REFERENCES:

Alexander, G.E., DeLong, M.R., & Strick P L. (1986). Parallel organization of functionally segregated circuits linking basal ganglia and cortex. *Annual Reviews of Neuroscience, 9*, 357- 381.

Ackerman, H., Graber, S., Hertrich, L., & Daum, I., (1999). Cerebellar contributions to the perception of temporal cues within the speech and non-speech domain. *Brain and Language, 67*, 228-241.

Anderson, C.M., Maas, L.C., Frederick, B.D., Bendor, J.T., Spence, T.J., Livne, F., Lukas, S.E., Fischman, A.J., Madras, M.K., Renshaw, P.F.,& Kaufman, M.J. (2006). Cerebellar vermis involvement in cocaine-related behaviors. Neuropsychopharmacology, 31, 1318-1326.

Anderson, C.M., Teicher, T.H., Polcari, A., Renshaw, P.F. (2002). Abnormal T2 relaxation time in the cerebellar vermis of adults sexually abused in childhood: potential role of the vermis in stress-enhanced risk for drug abuse. *Psychoneuroendocrinology 27*, 231-244.

Andreasen, N.C., O'Leary, D.S. (2003). Visualizing how one brain understands another: A PET study of theory of mind. *American Journal of Psychiatry 160*, 1954-1964.

Arango, V., Ernsberger, P., Marzuk, P.M., Chen, J.S., Tierney, H., Stanley, M., Reis, D.J., & Mann. J.J. (1990). Autoradiographic demonstration of increased serotonin 5-HT$_2$ and beta -adrenergic receptor binding sites in the brain of suicide victims. *Archives of General Psychiatry, 47*, 1038-1047.

Arató, M., Bánki, C.M., Bissette, G., Nemeroff, C.B. (1989). Elevated CSF CRF in suicide victims. *Biological Psychiatry, 25*, 355-359.

Atren, D.M., Ungerstedt, U., Ljungberg, T. (1977) Specific inhibition of hypothalamic self- stimulation by selective reuptake blockade of either 5-hydroxytryptamine or noradrenaline. *Psychopharmacology (Berlin), 29*, 177-180.

Balkan, P. & Strayer, F.F. (1973). On reliability of conjugate lateral eye movements. *Perceptual And Motor Skills, 36*, 429-430.

Ball, G.G., Micco, D.J. & Berentson, G.G. (1974). Cerebellar stimulation in the rat: complex stimulation-bound oral behaviors and self-stimulation. *Physiology and Behavior, 13*, 123-127.

Barker, W. W., Yoshii, F., Loewenstein, D.A., Chang, J.Y., Apicella, A., Pascal, S., Boothe, T.E., Ginsberg, M. D., & Duara, R. (1991). Cerebrocerebellar relationship during behavioral activation: a PET study. *Journal of Cerebral Blood flow and Metabolism, 11*, 48-54.

Bastian, M.L., Sponberg, A.C., Suomi, S.J., & Higley, J.D. (2003). Long-term effects of infant rearing conditions on the acquisition of dominance rank in juvenile and adult rehesus macaques (Macaca mulatta). *Developmental Psychobiology, 42*, 44-51.

Beaumont, G, Young, A, & McManus, I.C. (1984). Hemisphericity: A critical review. *Cognitive Neuropsychology, 1*, 191-212.

Behrens, T.E.J., Hunt, L.T., Woo, M.W., Woolrich, M.W. & Rushworth, M.F.S. (2008). Associative learning and social value. *Nature, 456*, 245-249.

Bingham, B., McFadden, K, Zhang, X., Bhatnagar, S., Beck, S. & Valentino, R. (2011). Early adolescence as a critical window during which social stress distinctly alters behavior and brain norepinephrine activity. *Neuropsychopharmacology, 36*, 896-909.

Blackburn, J.R.& Szumlinski, K.K. (1997). Ibogaine effects on sweet preference and amphetamine induced locomotion: implications for drug addiction. *Behavioral and Brain Research, 89*, 99-106.

Bogen, J. E., (1969). The other side of the brain II. An appositional mind. *Bulletin of the Los Angeles Neurological Society, 34*, 135-162.

Bogen, J. E., DeZure, R., Ten Houten, W. D., & Marsh, J. F., (1972). The other side of the brain. IV. The A/P ratio. *Bulletin of the Los Angeles Neurological Society 37*, 49-61.

Bonelli, R. M. &Cummings, J. L. (2007). Frontal subcortical circuitry and behavior. *Dialogues in Clinical Neuroscience, 9*, 141-151.

REFERENCES

Bontempi, B., Larent-Demir, C., Destrade, C., & Jaffard, R. (1999). Time-dependent reorganization of brain circuitry underlying long-term memory storage. *Nature, 400,* 671-675.

Bottini, G., Concoran, R., Sterzi, R., Paulesu, E., Schenone, P., Scarpa, P., Frackowiak, R. S. J., & Firth, C. D. (1994). Role of the right hemisphere in the interpretation of figurative aspects of language: a positron emission tomography activation study. *Brain, 117,* 1241-1253.

Bovin G (1995). Alcohol-bad for the brain? Tdsskr. Nor Laegeforen, 115, 1079-1083.

Bracha, V., Zhao, L., Wunderlich, D.A., Morrissy, S.J., & Bloedel, J. R. (1997). Patients with cerebellar lesions cannot acquire but are able to retain conditioned eyeblink reflexes. *Brain, 120,* 1401-1413.

Bradshaw, J. L. & Nettleton, N. C. (1981). The nature of hemispheric specialization in man. *Behavoral and Brain Sciences, 4, 51-91.*

Broca, P. (1863). Localisations des fonctions cerebrales. Seige de la faculte du langage articule. *Bulletin de la Societe d Anthropologie, 4,* 200-208.

Carhart-Harris, R.L. (2013). Psychedelic drugs, magical thinking, and psychosis. *Journal of Neurology Neurosurgery and Psychiatry, 84,* doi; 10.1136/jnnp-2013-306103.17.

Carhart-Harris, R.L., Eritzoe, D., Williams, T., Stone, J.M., Reed, L.J., Colasanti, A., Tyack, R.J., Leech R, Malizia AL, Murphy K, Hobden P, Evans J, Feilding A, Wise RG & Nutt D. (2012). Neural correlates of the psychedelic state as determined by fMRI studies with psilocybin. *Proceedings of the National Academy of Science, USA, 109,* 2138-2143, Chappell, P.B., Smith, M.A., Kilts, C.D., Bissette, G., Ritchie, J., Anderson, C.& Nemeroff, C.B. (1986). Alterations in corticotrophin-releasing factor-like immunoreactivity in discrete rat brain regions after acute and chronic stress. *Journal of Neuroscience 6,* 2908-2914.

Clarke, S., Kraftsik, R., Van Der Loos, H., & Innocente, G. (1989). Forms and measures of adult and developing human corpus callosum: is there sexual dimorphism? *Journal of Comparative Neurology, 280,* 213–230.

Cohen, H. D., Rosen, R. C., & Goldstein, I. (1976). Encephalographic laterality changes during sexual orgasm. *Archives of Sexual Behavior, 5,* 189-199.

Corbalis, M. C. (1980). Laterality and Myth. *American Psychologist, 35, 284-295.*

Coren, S. (1992). *The left-hander syndrome: The causes and consequences of left-handedness.* New York: Free Press.

Crick, F. (1994). *The astonishing hypothesis: The scientific search for the soul.* pp. 265–268. New York: Charles Scribner and Sons.

Crowell, D. H., Jones, R. H., Kapuniai, L. E., & Nakagawa, J. K. (1973). Unilateral cortical activity in newborn humans: An early index of cerebral dominance. *Science, 180,* 205-208.

Dabrowska, J., Hazra, R., Ahem, T.H., Guo, J.D., McDonald, A.J., Mascagni, F., Muller, J.F., Young, L.J., & Rainnie, D.G. (2011). Neuroanatomical evidence for reciprocal regulation of the corticotrophin-releasing factor and oxytocin systems in the hypothalamus and the bed nucleus of the stria terminalis of the rat: Implications for balancing stress and affect. *Psychoneuroendocrinology, 36,* 1312-1326.

Dannlowski, U., Stuhmann, A., Beutelmann, V., Zwanzger, P., Lanzen, T., Grotegerd, D., Domschke, K., Hoholf, C., Ohmmann, P., Bauer, J., Lindner, C., Pstert, C., Konrad, C., Arolt, V., Heindel, W., Suslow, T.,& Kugel, H. (2012). Limbic Scars: Long-term consequences of childhood maltreatment revealed by functional and structural magnetic resonance imaging. *Biological Psychiatry, 71,* 286-293.

Davidson, R.J. (1984a). Hemispheric asymmetry and emotion. In K.Scherer & P.Eckman (Eds.) *Approaches to emotion* (pp. 39-57). Hillsdale, NJ: Erlbaum.

Davidson, R.J. (1984b). Affect, cognition, and hemispheric specializtion. In C.E.Izard, J.Kagan & R.E.Zajonc (Eds.) *Emotions, cognitions and behavior* (pp. 320-365). Cambridge, UK: Cambridge University Press.

Davidson, R.J. (1988b). EEG measures of cerebral asymmetry: conceptual and methodological issues. *International Journal of Neuroscience, 39,* 71-89.

Davidson, R.J. (1992). Anterior brain asymmetry and the nature of emotion. *Brain and Cognition, 20,* 125-151.

Davidson, R. J., & Hugdahl, K. (1995). *Brain asymmetry.* Cambridge, MA: MIT Press.

Davidson, R.J. & Tomarken, A.J. (1989). Laterality and emotion: an electrophysiological approach. In F.Boller & J.Grafman (Ed.) *Handbook of Neuropsychology,* Vol. 3 (pp. 419- 441). Amsterdam: Elsevier.

Dawes, J. (2008). Do Data Characteristics Change According to the number of scale points used? An experiment using 5-point, 7-point and 10-point scales. *International Journal of Market Research 50*, 61–77.

Dax, M. (1865). Lésions de la moitie gauche de lencéphale coincident avec loubli des signes de la pensée. *Gazette Hebdomadaire de Medécine et de Chirurgie, 2*(2eme serie), m 2. (read at Montpellier in 1836.).

De Araujo, D.B., Ribero, S., Cecchi, G.A., Cravalho, F.M., Sanchez, T.A., Pinto, J.P., de Martinis, B.S., Crippa, J.A., Hallak, J.E., & Santos, A.C. (2012). Seeing with the eyes shut: neural basis of enhanced
imagery following ayahuasca ingestion. *Human Brain Mapping, 33,* 2550-2560.O'Hearn E,

De Dru, C.K.W. (2012). Oxytocin modulates the link between adult attachment and cooperation through reduced betrayal aversion. *Psychoneuroendocrinology, 37,* 871-880.

De Smet, H.J., Paquier, P., Verhoevan, J., & Marien, P. (2013). The cerebellum: Its role in language and related cognitive and affective functions. *Brain and Language 127*, 334-342.

Descartes, R. (1637). *La dioptrique. In Discours de la Methode,* Leiden, Ian Maire. Adam and Tannery (1964–74), Vol. VI., p 129.

Devinsky, O., Morrell, M. J., & Vogt, B. A. (1995). Contributions of anterior cingulate cortex to behavior. *Brain, 118*, 297–306.

Desmond, J. E., Gabrieli, J. D. E., Wagner, A. D., Ginier, B.L., & Glover, G. H. (1997). Lobular patterns of cerebellar activation in verbal working-memory and finger-tapping tasks as revealed by functional MRI. *Journal of Neuroscience, 17*, 9675-9685.

Devilbiss, D.M., Waterhouse, B.D., Berridge, C.W., & Valentino, R. (2012). Corticotrophin- releasing factor acting at the locus coeruleus disrupts thalamic and cortical sensory-evoked responses. *Neuropsychopharmacology, 37*, 2020-2030.

Efron, R. (1990). *The decline and fall of hemispheric specialization.* New York: Erlbaum. Ekman, P. (2006). *Darwin and Facial Expression: A Century of Research in Review.* Malor Books.

Ethan, T.M. & North, R.A. (1986). Actions of acetylcholine and nicotine on rat locus coeruleus neurons in vitro. *Neuroscience, 19*, 565-571.

Fernando, S.C., Beblo, T., Schlosser, N., Terfehr, K., Otte, C., Lowe, B., Wolf, O.T., Spitzer, C., Driessen, M., & Wingenfeld, K. (2012). Associations of childhood trauma with hypothalamic-pituitary-adrenal function in borderline personality disorder and major depression. *Psychoneuroendocrinology, 37*, 1659-1668.

Fisher, H.L., Moffitt, T.E., Houls, R.N., Belsky, D.W., Argeneoult, L., & Caspi, A. (2012). Bullying victimization and risk of self harm in early adolescence: longitudinal cohort study. *British Medical Journal* BMJ 2012;344:e3683.

Fink, G. R., Halligan, P. W.,Marshall, J. C., Frith, C. D., Frackowiak, R. S. J., & Dolan, R. J. (1996). Where in the brain does visual attention select the forest and the trees? *Nature, 382*, 626–628.

Fornito, A., Whittle, S., Wood, S. J., Velakoulis, D., Pantelis, C., & Yucel, M. (2006). The influence of sulcal variability on morphometry of the human anterior cingulate and paracingulate cortex. *Neuroimage, 33*, 843–854.

Fornito, A., Wood, S. J., Whittle, S., Fuller, J., Adamson, C., Saling, M. M., et al. (2008). Variability of the paracingulate sulcus and morphometry of the medial frontal cortex: Associations with coritical thickness, surface area, volume, and sulcal depth. *Human Brain Mapping, 29*, 222–236.

Fornito, A , Yucel, M , Wood, S , Stuart, G. W., Buchanan, J., Proffitt, T., et al. (2001). Individual differences in anterior cingulate/paracingulate morphology are related to executive functions in healthy males. *Cerebral Cortex, 14*, 424–431.

Freud, S. (1920*). Beyond the pleasure Principle.* Hogarth Press, London.

Freud, S. (1923). *The Ego and the Id.* Hogarth Press, London.

REFERENCES

Gazzaniga, M. S., Bogen, J. E., & Sperry, R. W. (1962). Some functional effects of sectioning the cerebral commissures in man. *Proceedings of the National Academy of Sciences, USA, 48*, 1765–1769.

Gazzaniga, M. S., Bogen, J. E., & Sperry, R. W. (1967). Dyspraxia following division of the cerebral commissures. *Archives of Neurology, 16*, 606–612.

Gazzaniga, M. S. (1989). Organization of the human brain. *Science, 245*, 947–952.

Gazzaniga, M. S. (2000). Cerebral specialization and interhemispheric communication: Does the corpus callosum enable the human condition? *Brain, 123*, 1293–1326.

Gehring, W. J., & Willoughby, A. R. (2002). The medial frontal cortex and the rapid processing of monetary gains and losses. *Science, 295*, 2279–2282.

Geschwind, D. H., Iacoboni, M., Mega, M. S., Zaidel, D. W., Cloughesy, T., & Zaidel, E. (1995). Alien hand syndrome: Interhemispheric motor disconnection due to a lesion in the midbody of the corpus callosum. *Neurology, 45*, 802–808.

Geshwind, N. & Levitsky, W. (1968). Human brain: left-right asymmetries in temporal speech region. *Science, 161*, 186-187.

Gounko, N.V., Swinny, J.D., Kalicharan, D., Jafari, S., Corteen, N., Seifi, M., Bakels, R., & van der Want, J.J.L. (2013). Corticotropin-releasing factor and urocortin regulate spine and synapse formation: structural basis for stress-induced neuronal remodeling and pathology. *Molecular Psychiatry, 18*, 86-92.

Gray, J. (1992). *Men are from Mars, women are from Venus, A practical guide for improving communication and getting what you want in your relationships.* Harper Collins, N.Y.

Gresch, P.J., Barret, J.R., Sanders-Bush, E., & Smith, R.L. (2007). 5-Hydoxytryptamine (serotonin)2A receptors in rat anterior cingulate cortex mediate the discriminative stimulus properties of d-lysergic acid diethylamide. *Journal of Pharmacology and Experimental Theraputics, 310*,662-669.

Grillon, C., Hale, E., Lieberman, L., Davis, A, Pine, D. S., & Ernst, M. (2015). The CRH-1 antagonist GSK561679 increases human fear but not anxiety as assessed by startle. *Neuropsychopharmacology*,40, 1-64-1071

Grillon, C., Heller, R., Hirschhorn, E., Kling, M.A., Pine, D.S., Shulkin, J., & Vythilingam, M, (2011). Acute hydrocortisone treatment increase anxiety but not fear in healthy volunteers: a fear potentiated startle study. *Biological Psychiatry, 69*, 549-555.

Gundel, H., O'Connor, M.F., Litterell, L., Fort, C., Lane, & R.D. (2003). Functional neuroanatomy of grief: an FMRI study. *American Journal of Psychiatry, 160*, 1946-1953.

Gur, R.E. (1975). Conjugate lateral eye movement as an index of hemispheric activation. *Journal of Personality and Social Psychology, 31*, 751-757.

Hancock, G. (2007) *Supernatural.* p 283. The Disinformation Co., N.Y.

Hannestad, J., DellaGioia, N., & Bloch, M. (2011). Effects of antidepressant medication treatment on serum levels of inflammatory cytokines: A meta-analysis. *Neuropsychopharmacology, 36*, 2452-2459.

Harlow, H.F. & Novak, M.A. (1973). Psychopathological perspectives. *Perspectives in Biology and Medicine, 16*, 461-478.

Harmelen, A.L., van Tol, M.J., van der Wee, N.J.A., Veltman, D.J., Aleman, A., Spinhoven, P., van Buchem, M.A., Zitman, F.G., Pennix, B.W.J.H., & Elziga, B.M. (2010). Reduced medial prefrontal cortex volume in adults reporting childhood emotional maltreatment. *Biological Psychiatry, 68, 832*-838.

Heath, R.G. (1977). Modulation of emotion with a brain pacemaker: Treatment for intractable psychiatric illness. *Journal of Nervous and Mental Disease, 165*, 300-317.

Heath, R. G., Raeburn, C., Llewellyn, R. C., & Rouchell, A. M. (1980). Cerebellar pacemaker for intractable behavioral disorders and epilepsy: Follow-up report. *Biological Psychiatry, 15*, 243-257.

Heath, R. G., Rouchell, A. M., Llewellyn, R. C. & Walker, C. F. (1981). Cerebellar pacemaker patients: An update. *Biological Psychiatry, 16*, 953-962.

Heinrichs, S.C., Pich, E.M., Miczek, K.A., Britton, K.T., & Koob, K.F. (1992). Corticotropin-releasing factor antagonist reduces emotionality in socially defeated rats via direct neurotropic action. *Brain Research, 581,* 190-197.

Hellige, J. (1996). Hemispheric asymmetry for visual information processing. *Acta Neurobiologica Experimentia, 56,* 485-497.

Helmuth, L. (2000). Early insults rewires pain circuits. *Science, 299,* 521-522).

Hennesey, M.B., Fitch, C., Jacobs, S., Deak, T., & Schiml, P.A. (2011). Behavioral effects of peripheral corticotrophin-releasing factor may be mediated by proinflammatory activity. *Psychoneurocrinology* 36, 996-1004.

Henry, J. P. & Wang, S. (1998). Effects of early stress on affiliative behavior. *Psychoneuroendocrinology, 23,* 863-875.

Herrmann, M. Rotte, M., Grubich, C. , Ebert, A, D., Schlit, K., Munte, T. F. & Heinze, H. J. (2001). Control of semantic interference in episodic memory retrieveal is associated with an anterior cingulate-prefrontal activation pattern. *Human Brain Mapping, 13,* 94-103.

Hogle, J.M., Kay, J.T., & Curtin, J.J. (2010). Nicotine withdrawal increases threat-induced anxiety but not fear: Neuroadaptation in human addiction. *Biological Psychiatry, 68,* 719-725.

Holdefer, R.N. & Jensen, R.A. (1987). The effects of peripheral D-amphetamine and epinephrine on maintained discharge in the locus coeruleus with reference to the modulation of learning and memory by these substances. *Brain Research 417,* 108-117.

Holloway, R. L., Anderson, P. J., Defendini, R., & Harper, C. (1993). Sexual dimorphism of the human corpus callosum from three independent samples: relative size of the corpus callosum. *American Journal of Physical Anthropology, 92,* 481–492.

Huang, H., Gundapuneedi, T., & Rao, U. (2012). White matter disruptions in adolescents exposed to childhood maltreatment and vulnerability to psychopathy. *Neuropsychopharmacology, 37,* 2693-2701.

Hubbard, L, R. (1950) *Dianetics: The modern science of mental health.* Hermitage House, N. Y.

Hutsler, J., & Galuske, R.A.W. (2003). Hemispheric asymmetries in cerebral cortical networks. *Trends in Neurosciences, 26,* 428–435.

Hutsler, J. J., Loftus, W. C., & Gazzaniga, M. S. (1998). Individual variation of cortical surface area asymmetries. *Cerebral Cortex, 8,* 11–17.

Huster, R. J., Westerhausen, R., Kreuder, F., Schweiger, E., & Whittling, W. (2007). Morphologic asymmetry of the human anterior cingulate cortex. *NeuroImage, 34,* 888-895.

Ide, A., Dolezal, C., Fernández, M., Labbé, E., Mandujano, R., Montes, S., et al. (1999). Hemispheric differences in variability of fissural patterns in parasylvian and cingulate regions of human brains. *Journal of Comparative Neurology, 410,* 235–242.

Israel, S., Weisel, O., Ebstein, R.P., & Bomstein, G. (2012). Oxytocin, but not vasopressin, Increases both parochial and universal altruism. *Psychoneuroendocrinology, 32,* 1341-1344.

Jager, G., & Postma, A. (2003). On the hemispheric specialization for categorical and coordinate spatial relations: A review of the current evidence. *Neuropsychologia, 41,* 504–515.

James, W. (1878). *Principles of Psychology,* Holt, republished by Dover, 1950.

James, W. (1902). *The Varieties of Religious Experience,* republished by Wilder, 2007.

Jaynes, J. (1976). *The origin of consciousness in the breakdown of the bicameral mind,* Houghton Mifflin, NY.

Johnson, M. K., Raye, C. L, Mitchell, K.J., Touryan, S. R., Greene, E.J., & Nolen-Hoeksema, S. (2006). Dissociating medial frontal and posterior cingulate activity during self-reflection *Social Cognitive and Affective Neuroscience, 1,* 54-56.

Jokinen, J., Chaltzofis, A., Hellstrom, C., Nordstrom, P., Uvnas-Moberg, K., & Asberg, M. (2012). Low CSF oxytocin reflects high intent in suicide attempters. *Psychoneuroendocrinology, 37,* 482-490.

Kennerly, S.W.,, Walton, M.E., Behrens, T.E.J., Buckley, M. J. & Rushworth, M.F.S. (2006). Optimal decision making and the anterior cingulate cortex. *Nature Neuroscience, 9,* 940-947.

Kerns, J. G., Cohen, J. D., MacDonald, A. W., 3rd, Cho, R. Y., Stenger, V. A., & Carter, C. S. (2004). Anterior cingulate conflict monitoring and adjustments in control. *Science, 303,* 1023–1026.

Kinsbourne, M. (1972). Eye and head turning indicates cerebral lateralization. *Science, 176,* 539-

541.

Kinsbourne, M. (1974). Direction of gaze and distributiom of cerebral thought processes. *Neuropsychologia, 12*, 279-281.

Kleim, J. A., Vij, K., Ballard, D. H. & Greenough, W. T. (1997). Learning-dependent synaptic modifications in the cerebellar cortex of the adult rat persist for at least four weeks. *Journal of Neuroscience, 17*, 717-721.

Klengel, T., Mehta, D., Anacker, C., Rex-Haffner, M., Pruessner, J.C., Pariante, C.M., Pace, T.W.W., Vercer, K.B., Mayberg, H.S., Bradley, B., Nemeroff, C.B., Holsboer, F., Heim, C.M., Ressler, K.J., & Binder, T.R. & E.B. (2013). Allele-specific FKBP5 DNA demethy- lation mediates gene-childhood trauma interactions. *Nature Neuroscience, 16,* 33-41.

Knecht, S., Dräger, B., Deppe, M., Bobe, L., Lohmann, H., Floel, A., Ringelstein, E. B., & Henningsen, H. (2000). Handedness and hemispheric language dominance in healthy humans. *Brain, 123*, 2512-2518.

Koestler, A. (1967). *The Ghost within the Machine.* McMillan, N.Y. Koestler, A. (1978). *Janus.* Vintage, N.Y.

Kosslyn, S. M. (1987). Seeing and imagining in the cerebral hemispheres: A computational approach. *Psychological Review, 94*, 148–175.

Kosslyn, S. M., Koenig, O., Barrett, A., Cave, C., Tang, J., & Gabrieli, J. D. E. (1989). Evidence for two types of spatial representations. Journal of Experimental Psychology: *Perception and Performance, 15.* 723-735.

Kosslyn, S. M., Chabris, C. F., Marsolek, C. J., & Koenig, O. (1992). Categorical versus coordinate spatial relations: Computational analyses and computer simulations. *Journal of Experimental Psychology: Human Perception and Performance, 18,* 562–577.

Lee, K.H., Bishop, G.A., Tian, J.B.,& King, J.S. (2004). Evidence for an axonal localization of the type 2 corticotropin-releasing factor during postnatal development lf the mouse cerebellum. *Experimental Neurology, 187,*11-22.

Leysen, J.E., Janssen, P.M.F., & Niemegeers, C.J.E. (1989). Rapid desensitization and down-regulation of 5-HT$_2$ receptors by DOM treatment. *European Journal of Pharmacology, 163,* 145-149.

Levy, J. (1969). Possible basis for the evolution of lateral specialization of the human brain. *Nature, 224,* 614–615.

Libet, B. (1982). Brain stimulation in the study of neuronal functions for conscious sensory experiences. *Human Neurobiology, 1,* 235–242.

Lindell, A. K & Kidd, E. (2011). Why right brain teaching is half witted: A critique of the misapplication of neuroscience to education. *Mind, Brain, and Education, 5,* 121-127.

Lockhorst, G. J. (1985). An ancient Greek theory of hemispheric specialization. *Clio Medica, 17,* 33–38.

Lamb, M. R., Robertson, L.C., & Knight, R. T. (1990). Component mechanisms underlying the processing of hierarchically organized patterns: Inferences from patients with unilateral cortical lesions. *Journal of Experimental Psychology: Learning, Memory, and Cognition 16,* 471-483.

Laryea, G., Arnett, M.G., & Muglia, L.J. (2012). Behavioral studies and genetic alterations in corticotrophin- releasing hormone (CRH) neurocircuitry: Insights into human psychiatric disorders. *Behavioral Science, 2,* 135-171.

Lee, K.H., Bishop, G.A., Tian, J.B., & King, J.S. (2004). Evidence for an axonal localization of the type 2 corticotropin-releasing factor receptor during development of the mouse cerebellum. *Experimental Neurology, 187*, 11-22.

Leiner, H. C., Leiner, A. L., & Dow, R. S. (1991). The human cerbrocerebellar system: its computing, cognitive, and language skills. *Behavioral Brain Research, 44*, 113-128.

Levisohn, L., Cronin-Golumb, A., & Schmahmann, J.D. (2000). Neuropsychological consequences of cerebellar tumor resection in children: cerebellar cognitive affective syndrome in a paediatric population. *Brain, 123*, 1041-1050.

Levy, J. & Reid, M., (1976). Variations in writing posture and cerebral organization. *Science, 194,* 337-339.

REFERENCES

Logrip, M.L., Koob, G.F., & Zorrilla, E.P. (2011). Role of corticotropin-releasing factor in drug addiction: potential for pharmacological intervention. *CNS Drugs, 25*, 271-287.

Luders, E., Rex, D. M., Narr, K. L., Woods, R. P., Jancke, L., Thompson, P. M., Mazziotta, J. C., & Toga, A. W. (2003). Relationships between sulcal asymmetries and corpus callosum size: Gender and handedness effects. *Cerebral Cortex, 10*, 1084–1093.

McElroy, T., McCormick, M, Stroh, N., & Seta, J. J. (2012). An investigation of measurement validity for a hemispheric activation scale. *Laterality, 17*, 736-740.

McGilchrist, I. (2009). *The master and his emissary, The divided brain and the making of the western world.* Yale University Press, New Haven.

McGlone, J. (1980) Sex differences in human brain asymmetry: a critical survey. *Behavioral and Brain Science. 3*, 215-27.

MacLean, P. D. (1990). *The Triune Brain in Evolution: Role in Paleocerebral Functions.* Plenum.

Madsen, F.F., Jensen FT, Vaeth M, & Djurhaaus JC (1990). Regional cerebral blood flow in pigs estimated by microspheres. *Acta Neurochir, 103*, 139-147

Makinodan, M,. Rosen, K.M., Itio, S.,& Corfas, G. (2012). A critical period for social experience-dependent oligodendrocyte maturation and myelination. *Science, 337*, 3357-1360.)

Marvel, C. L. & Desmond, J.E., (2010). Functional topography of the cerebellum in verbal working memory. *Neuropsycholical Review, 20*, 271-279.

Mash, D.C., Koverag, C.A., Pablo, J., Tyndale, R.F., Ervin, F.D., Williams, I.C., Singleton, E.G., & Mayor, M. (2000). Ibogaine: complex pharmacokinetics, concerns for safety, and preliminary efficacy measures. *Annals of the New York Academy of Sciences, 914*, 394-401.

Matteoli, R.L. (2010) The Munchausen Complex: Socialization of Violence and Abuse, 2nd ed, Nemean Press, Monterey, CA.

Milner, B. (1968). Visual recognition and recall after right temporal lobe excision in man. *Neuropsychologia, 6*, 101–209.

Minami, M., Kuraishi, Y., Yamaguchi, T., Nakai, S., Hirai, Y., & Satoh, M. (1991). Immobilization stress induces interleukin-1 beta mRNA in the rat hypothalamus. *Neuroscience Letters, 123*, 254-256.

Morgan, B.E., Horn, A.R., & Bergman, N.J. (2011). Should neonates sleep alone? *Biological Psychiatry,70*, 817-825.

Morisot, N., Rouibi, K., & Contarino, A., (2015). CRF$_2$ receptor deficiency eliminates the long-lasting vulnerability of motivational states induced by opiate withdrawal. *Neuropsychopharmacology, 40*, 1990-2000.

Mondin, G.W., Morgan, W.P., Piering, P.N., et al. (1996). Psychological consequences of exercise deprivation in habitual exercisers. *Medical Science of Sports Exercise, 28*, 1199- 1203.

Morton, B. E. (1985b). Conflict and the quadrimental brain hypothesis. *International Society for Research on Aggression Abstracts, 13*, 106.

Morton, B. E. (1989). The quadrimental brain as a neuroscience working hypothesis. *Neuroscience Abstracts, 15*, 729.

Morton, B. E., (2001). Large individual differences in minor ear output during dichotic listening. *Brain and Cognition, 45*, 229-237.

Morton, B. E., (2002). Outcomes of hemisphericity questionnaires correlate with unilateral dichotic deafness. *Brain and Cognition, 49*, 63-72.

Morton, B. E., (2003a). Phased mirror tracing outcomes correlate with several hemisphericity measures. *Brain and Cognition, 51*, 294-304.

Morton, B. E., (2003b). Two-hand line-bisection task outcomes correlate with several measures of hemisphericity. *Brain and Cognition, 51*, 305-316.

Morton, B. E., (2003c). Asymmetry Questionnaire outcomes correlate with several hemisphericity measures. *Brain and Cognition, 51*, 372-374.

Morton, B. E., (2003d). Hemisphericity of university students and professionals: Evidence for sorting during higher education. *Brain and Cognition, 52*, 319-325.

REFERENCES

Morton, B. E. & Rafto, S. E., (2006a). Corpus callosum size is linked to dichotic deafness and hemisphericity, not sex or handedness. *Brain and Cognition, 62*, 1-8.

Morton, B. E. & Rafto, S. E., (2006b). Sex and aggression: corpus callosal size is linked to hemisiphericity, not gender. In *Contemporary Research on Aggression*,Pro Facultate No. 8 K.Osterman, K. Bjorkqvist, eds. Pp. 267-278, Abo Akademi University, Vasa, Finland.

Morton, B. E. & Rafto, S. E., (2010). Behavioral laterality advance: Neuroanatomical evidence for the existence of hemisity. *Personality and Individual Differences, 49*. 34-42

Morton, B.E., (2011). *Neuroreality: A scientific religion to restore meaning, or How 7 brain elements create 7 minds and 7 realities*. Megalith Books, Doral, FL.

Morton, B.E., (2012a). *Two human species exist: Their hybrids are dyslexics, homosexuals, pedophiles, and schizophrenics*. Megalith Books, Doral, FL.

Morton, B.E., (2012b). Left and right brain-oriented hemisity subjects show opposite behavioral preferences. *Front. Physiol., 3*:407.doi:10.3389/fphys.2012.00407

Morton, B. E., (2013). Behavioral laterality of the brain: support for the binary construct of Hemisity. *Front. Psychol. 4*:683. doi:10.3389fpsyg.2013.00683.

Morton, B.E. (2013) *Psychedelic visions from the teacher: A neuroscientist's initiation to reality and spirituality*. Megalith Books, Doral, FL.

Morton, B.E. (2014) *Beyond Men are from Mars*. Megalith Books, Doral, FL.

Morton, B. E., Svard, L. & Jensen, J. (2014). Further Evidence for Hemisity Sorting during Career Specialization. *Journal of Career Assessment, 22*, 317-328.

Mosch, N.M., Riese, H., Reijneveld, S.A., Bakker, M.P., Verhulst, F.C., Ormel, J., Oldehiinkel, A.J., et al. (2006). Cortical serotonin 5-HT$_{2a}$ receptor binding and social communication in adults with Asperger's Syndrome: An in vivo SPECT study. *American Journal of Psychiatry, 163*, 934-936,

Nakagawa, Y., Suzuki, T, Ishii, H., Ogata, A., & Nakae, D. (2010). Mitochondrial dysfunction and bio transformation of beta-carboline alkaloids, harmine and harmaline, on isolated rat hepatocytes. *Chemical and Biological Interactions, 188*, 393-403

Nieuwenhuys, R., Voogd, J., & van Huijzen, C. (1981). *The Human Central Nervous System*, Springer-Verlag, N.Y

Nguyen, K.T., Deak, T., Owens, S.M., Kohno, T., Feshner, M., Watkins, L.R., & Maier, S.F. (1998). Exposure to acute stress induces brain interleukin-1beta protein in the rat. *Journal of Neuroscience,18*. 2239-2246.

Nielsen, J. A., Zielinski, B. A., Ferguson, M. A., Lainhart, J. E., & Anderson, J. S. (2013) An evaluation of the left-brain vs. right-brain hypothesis with resting state functional connectivity magnetic resonance imaging. *PLoS ONE 8(8): e71275. doi:10.1371/journal.pone.0071275.*

O'Donovan, A., Epel, E., Lin, J., Wolkowitx, O., Cohen, B., Maguen, S., Metzler, T., Lenoci, M., Blackburn. E., & Neylan, O.(2011). Childhood trauma associated with short leukocyte telomere length in Postraumatic TC Stress Disorder. *Biological Psychiatry, 70*, 465-471.

O'Hearn, E, & Molliver, M.E. (1997). The olivocerebellar projection mediates ibogaine-induced degeneration of purkinje cells: A model of indirect trans-synaptic excitotoxicity *Journal of Neuroscience 17*, 8828-8841.

O'Hearn, E, Long, D.B., & Molliver, M.E. (1993). Ibogaine induces glial activation in Parasaggital zones of the cerebellum. *Neuroreport 4*, 299-302.

O'Hearn, E, & Molliver, M.E., (1993), Degeneration of Purkinje cells in parasaggital zones of the cerebellar vermis after treatment with ibogaine or harmaline, *Neuroscience, 55*, 303-310.

Ornstein, R. (1997). *The right mind: Making sense of the hemispheres*. New York: Harcourt Brace and Company.

Olpe, H.R., Jones, R.S.G., & Steinmann, M.W. (1983). The locus coeruleus: actions of psychoactive drugs. *Experientia, 39*, 242-249.

Oropeza, V.C., Page, M.E., Van Bockstaele, E.J. (2005). Systemic administration of WIN 55,212-2 increases (inhibitory) norepinephrine release in the rat frontal cortex. *Brain Research, 1046*, 45-54.

Palomero-Gallagher, N., Mohlberg, H., Zilles, K., & Vogt, B. (2008). Cytology and receptor architecture of human anterior cingulate cortex. *Journal of Comparative Neurology, 508*, 906–926.

Parker, K.L., Narayanan, N.S.& Andreason, N.C. (2014). The therapeutic potential of the cerebellum in schizophrenia. *Fronteirs of Systemic Neuroscience. 8*, 163-176.

Paus, T. (2001). Primate anterior cingulate cortex: Where motor control, drive, and cognition interface. *Nature Reviews of Neuroscience, 2*, 417–424.

Paus, T., Otaky, N., Caramanos, Z., MacDonald, D., Zijdenbos, A., D'Avirro, D., et al. (1996). In vivo morphometry of the intrasulcal grey matter in the human cingulate, paracingulate, and superior-rostral sulci: Hemispheric asymmetries, gender differences, and probability maps. *Journal of Comparative Neurology, 376*, 664–673.

Paus, T., Tomaiuolo, F., Otaky, N., MacDonald, D., Petrides, M., Atlas, J., et al. (1996). Human cingulate and paracingulate sulci: Pattern, variability, asymmetry, and probabilistic map. *Cerebral Cortex, 6*, 207–214.

Peoples, L. (2002). Will, anterior cingulate cortex, and addiction. *Science, 296*, 1623-1624.

Pesce, M.L., Speranza, S., Franceschelli, V., Ialenti, I., Iezzi, A., Patruno, A., Rizzuto, C., Robazza, M., Lutis, M., Felaco, A., & Grilli, B. (2012). Positive correlations between serum interleukin-1b and state anger in rugby athletes. *Aggressive Behavior, 00*, 1-8.

Pissiota, A., Frans, O., Fernandez, M. von Knorring, L., Fischer, H., & Fredrikson, M. (2002). Neurofunctional correlates of posttraumatic stre ss disorder: a PET symptom provocation study. *European Archives of Psychiatry and Clinical Neuroscience, 252, 68-75*.

Pitts, D.K., & Marwah, J. (1988). Cocaine and central monaminergic neurotransmission: a review of electrophysiological studies and comparison to amphetamines and antidepressants, *Life Science 42*, 949-968.

Proverbio, A. M., Zani, A., Gazzaniga, M. S., & Mangun, G. R. (1994). ERP and RT signs of a rightward bias for spatial orienting in a split brain patient. *Neuroreport, 5*, 2457–2461.

Pujol, J., Lopez, P. J., Deus, J., Cardoner, N., Vallejo, J., Capdevila, A., et al. (2002). Anatomical variability of the anterior cingulate gyrus and basic dimensions of human personality. *Neuroimage, 15*, 847–855.

Ramos, L., Hicks, C., Kevin, R., Caminer, A. et al. (2013). Acute prosocial effects of oxytocin and vasopressin when given alone or in combination with 3,4-methylenedioxymethamphetamine in rats: involvement of the V1A receptor. *Neuropsychopharmacology, 38*, 2249-2259.

Rapkin, A.J., Berman, S.M., Mandelkern, M.A., Silverman, K.H.S., Morgan, M., & London, E.D. (2011). Neuroimaging evidence of cerebellar involvement in premenstrual dysphoric disorder. *Biological Psychiatry, 69*, 374-380.

Redmond, D.E. & Huang, Y.H. (1979). Current concepts. II: New evidence for a locus coeruleus-norepinephrine connection with anxiety. *Life Science 25*, 2149-1262.

Reiman, E. M., Raichle, M.. E., Robins, E., Mintun, M. A., Fusselman, M. J., Fox, P.T., Price, J. L., & Hackman, K. A. (1989). Neuroanatomical correlates of a lactate-induced panic attack. *Archives of General Psychiatry, 46*, 493-500.

Reine, A. (1991). Are lateral-eye movements a valid index of functional hemispheric asymmetries? *British Journal of Psychology, 82*, 129-135.

Riklan, M., Cullinan, T., & Cooper, I. S. (1977). Tension reduction and alerting in man following chronic cerebellar stimulation for the relief of spasticity or intractable seizures. *Journal of Nervous and Mental Disease, 164*, 176-181

Robertson, L. C., & Lamb, M. R. (1991). Neuropsychological contributions to theories of part/whole organization. *Cognitive Psychology, 23*, 299–330.

Rosell, D.R., Thompson, J.L., Slifstein, M., Xu, X., Frankle, W.G., New, A.A.S., Goodman, M., Weinstein, S.R., Laruelle, M., Abi-Dargham, A., & Slever, L.J. (2010). Increased serotonin 2A receptor availability in the orbitofrontal cortex of physically aggressive personality disordered patients. *Biological Psychiatry, 67,* 1154 1162.

Roxo, M.R., Franceschini, P. R., Zubaran, C., Kleber, F.D., & Sander, J. W. (2011). The limbic system conception and its historical evolution. *Scientific World Journal, 11*, 2428-2441.

Savic, D., Knezevic, G., Damjanovic, S., Spiric, Z., & Matic, G. (2012). Is there a biological difference between trauma-related depression and PTSD? DST says 'NO'. *Psychoneuroendocrinology, 37,* 1516-1520.

Schenberg, E.E., de Castrol Comis, M.A., Chaves, B.R., & da Silveria, D.X. (2014). Treating

REFERENCES

drug dependence with the aid of ibogaine: a retrospective study. *Journal of Psychopharmacology, 28,* 993-1000.

Schenkenberg, T., Bradford, D. C., & Ajax, E. T. (1980). Line bisection and unilateral visual neglect in patients with neurological impairment. *Neurology, 30,* 509–517.

Schiffer, F. (1996). Cognitive ability of the right hemisphere: Possible contributions to psychological function. *Harvard Review of Psychiatry, 4,* 126–138.

Schiffer, F. (1997). Affect changes observed with right versus left lateral visual field stimulation in psychotherapy patients: Possible physiological, psychological, and therapeutic implications. *Comparative Psychiatry, 38,* 289–295.

Schiffer, F. (1998). *Of two minds: The revolutionary science of dual-brain psychology.* Free Press, N.Y.

Schiffer, F., Teicher, M. H., Anderson, C., Tomoda, A., Polcari, A., Navalta, C. P., & Andersen, S. L. (2007). Determination of hemispheric emotional valence in individual subjects: a new approach with research and therapeutic implications. *Behavioral and Brain Function, 3,* 13.

Schmahmann, J. D. (1991). An emerging concept: The cerebellar contribution to higher function. *Archives of Neurology, 48,* 1178-1187

Schmahmann, J.D. & Sherman, J.C. (1997). Cerebellar affective syndrome. *International Review of Neurobiology, 41,* 433-440.

Schmid, M.C., Mrowka, S.W, Turdchi, J., Saunders, R.C., Wilke, M., Peters, A.J., Ye, F.Q., & Leopold, D. A., (2010) Blindsight depends on the lateral geniculate nucleus. *Nature, 466,* 373-377.

Schneiderman, I, Zagoory-Sharon, O., Leckman, J.F., Feldman, R. (2012). Oxytocin during the initial stages of romantic attachment: Relations to couples interactive reciprocity. *Psychoneuroendocrinology, 37,*1277-1285.

Schreurs, B. G., Gusev, P. A., Tomsic, D., Alkon, D. L., & Shi, T. (1998). Intracellular correlates of acquisition and long-term memory of classical conditioning in purkinje cell dendrites in slicees of rabbit cerebellar lobule HVI. *Journal of Neuroscience, 18,* 5498-5507.

Schunck, T., Erb, G., Mathis, A., Gilles, C., Namer, I.J., Hode, Y., Demaziere, A., Luthringer, R., & Macher, J.P. (2006). Functional magnetic resonance imaging characterization of CCK-4-induced panic attack and subsequent anticipatory anxiety. Neuroimage, 31, 1197-1208.

Schuz, A., & Preissl, H. (1996). Basic connectivity of the cerebral cortex and some considerations on the corpus callosum. *Neuroscience and Biobehavioral Reviews, 20,* 567–570.

Sejnowski, T. J. (2004). In memorium: Francis H.C. Crick. *Neuron, 43,* 619–621.

Shanon, B. (2002). *Antipodes of the Mind. Charting the Phenomenology of the Ayahuasca Experience.* Oxford University Press, London.

Shiffer, F., (1996). Cognitive ability of the right hemisphere: possible contributions to psychological function. *Harvard Review of Psychiatry, 4,*126-138.

Shintani, F., Kanba, S., Nakaki, T., Nibuya, M., Kinoshita, N., Suzuki, E., Yagi, G., Kato, R., & Asai, M. (1993). Interleukin-1b augments release of norepinephrine, dopamine, and serotonin in the rat anterior hypothalamus. *Journal of Neuroscience 13,* 3574-3581.

Simeon, D., Bartz, J., Hamilton, H., Crystal, S., Braun, A., Ketay, S., & Hollander, E. (2011). Oxytocin administration attenuates stress reactivity in borderline personality disorder: A pilot study. *Psychoneuroendocrinology 36,* 1416-1421.

Smith, L. C. & Moscovitch, M. (1979). Writing posture, hemispheric control of movement and cerebral dominance in individuals with inverted and noninverted hand postures during writing. *Neuropsychologia, 17,* 637-644.

Somerville, L. H., Heatherton, T. F. & Kelley, W. M. (2006). Anterior cortex responds differentially to expectancy and social rejection. *Nature Neuroscience 9,* 1007-1008

Sperry, R. W. (1968). Hemispheric disconnection and unity in conscious awareness. *American Psychologist, 23,* 723–733.

Sperry, R. (1982). Some effects of disconnecting the cerebral hemispheres. *Science, 217,* 1223–1226.

Springer, S. P., & Deutch, G., (1998). *Left Brain, Right Brain: Perspectives from Cognitive*

REFERENCES

Neuroscience, 5th edn. New York, Freeman

Squire, L. R., Ojemann, J. G., Miezin, F. M., Petersen, S.E., Videen, T. O., & Raiche, M. (1992). Activation of the hippocampus in normal humans: A functional anatomical study of memory. *Proceedings of the National Academy of Sciences, USA, 89,* 1837-1841.

Stephan, K. E., Fink, G. R., & Marshall, J. C. (2006). Mechanisms of hemispheric specialization: Insights from analysis of connectivity. *Neuropsychologia, 45,* 209–228.

Strelnikov, N.N., Vorobyev, V.A., Chernigovskaya, T.V., & Medvedev, S.V. (2006).) Prosodic clues to syntactic processing- a PET and ERP study. *NeuroImage, 29,* 1127-1134

Supple, W.F., Cranney, J.,& Leaton, R.N. (1988). Effects of lesions on the cerebellar vermis on VMH lesion-induced hyperdefensiveness, spontaneous mouse killing, and freezing in rats. Physiology of Behavior, 42, 145-153.

Supple, W.F., Leaton, R.N.,& Fanselow, M. (1987). Effects of cerebellar vermal lesions on species-specific fear responses and taste aversion learning in rats. *Physiology and Behavior, 39,* 579-586.

Swaab DF, AM Bao, PJ Lucassen (2005). The stress system in the human brain in depression and degeneration. *Ageing Research Reviews,* 4, 141-194.

Tallman JF, SM Paul, P Skolinck, DS Galliger, 1980. Receptors for the age of anxiety. *Science, 207,* 274-281.

Tannen, D. (1986). *That's not what I meant! How conversational style makes or breaks relationships.* Ballantine Books, N.Y.

Tannen, D. (1990). *You just don't understand, Women and men in conversation.* Ballantine Books, N.Y.

Tannen, D. (1994). *Talking from 9 to 5, Women and men in the workplace: Language, sex and power.* Avon Books, N.Y.

Teng, E. & Squire, L. R. (1999). Memory for places learned long ago is intact after hippocampal damage. *Nature, 400,* 675-677.

Tolle E (1999). The power of now: A guide to spiritual enlightenment. Namaste Publishing, Vancouver.

Trulson ME & Crisp T (1983). Tolerance develops to LSD while the drug is exerting its maximal behavioral effects: Implications for the neural basis of tolerance. *European Journal of Pharmacology, 96,* 317-320.

Valentino RJ, E Van Bockstaele (2001). Opposing regulation of the locus coeruleus by Corticotrophin releasing factor and opioids. Potential for reciprocal interactions between stress and opioid sensitivity. *Psychopharmacology, 158,* 331-342.

van Kleek, M. H. (1989). Hemispheric differences in global versus local processing of hierarchical visual stimuli by normal subjects: New data and a meta-analysis of previous studies. *Neuropsychologia, 27,* 1165-1178

van Zuiden, M., Geuze, E., Willeman, H.L.D.M., Vermetten, E., Maas, M., Amarouchi, K., Kavelaars, A.,& Heijnen, C.J. (2012). Glucocortcoid receptor pathway components predict Posttraumatic Stress Disorder symptom development: a prospective study. *Biological Psychiatry, 71,* 309-316.

Verbanck, P., Seutin, V., Massotte, L., & Dresse, A. (1991). Yohimbine can induce ethanol tolerance in and in vitro preparation of rat locus coeruleus. *Alcohol Clinical Experimental Research, 15,* 1036-1039.

Victoria, N.C., Inoue, K., Young, L.J., & Murphy, A.Z. (2013). Long-term dysregulation of brain corticotrophin and glucocorticoid receptros and stress reactivity by single early-life pain experience in male and female rats. *Psychoneuroendocrinology, 38,* 3015-3028.

Vollenweider, F.X., Vollenweider-Scherpenhuyzen, M.F., Babler, A., Vogel, H., & Hell, D. (1998). Psilocybin induces schizophrenia-like psychosis in humans via a serotonin-2 agonist action. *Neuroreport, 9,* 3097-3902.

Vogt, B. A. (2005). Pain and emotion interactions of the cingulate cortex. *Nature Reviews of Neuroscience, 6,* 533–544.

Vogt, B. A., Nimchinsky, E. A., Vogt, L. J., & Hof, P. R. (1995). Human cingulate cortex: Surface features, flat maps, and cytoarchetecture. *Journal of Comparative Neurology,359,*

REFERENCES

490

Wada, J. A.. (1977). Prelanguage and fundamental asymmetry of the infant brain. *Annals of the New York Academy of Science, 299*, 370-379.

Wan, X., Cheng, K., & Tanaka, K. (2015). Neural encoding of opposing strategy values in anterior and posterior cingulate cortex. *Nature Neuroscience, 18*, 752-759

Wang, C., Istvan, U., Schomer, D.L., Marincovic, K. & Halgren, E. (2005). Responses of human anterior cingulate cortex microdomains to error detection, conflict monitoring, stimulus- response mapping, familiarity, and orienting. *Journal of Neuroscience, 25*, 604-613.

Watson, P.J. (1978). Nonmotor Functions of the Cerebellum. *Psychological Bulletin, 85*, 944-67

Weintraub, S. & Mesulam, M. M. (1987). Right cerebral dominance in spatial attention. *Archives of Neurology, 44*, 621-625.

Weisenberg, T., & McBride, K. E. (1935). *Aphasia: A clinical and psychological study*. New York: Commonwealth Fund (cited in Springer, S. P., & Deutsch, G. (1999). Left brain, right brain: Perspectives from cognitive neuroscience (5th ed., p. 361). New York: W.H. Freeman.).

Whittle, S., Allen, N.B., Fornito, A., Lubman, D.I., Simmonds, J.G., Pantelis, C., & Yucel, M. (2008). Variations in ACC folding patterns are related to individual differences in temperament. *Psychiatry Research: Neuroimaging, 172*, 68-74.

Wittling, W. (1990). Psychophysiological correlates of human brain asymmetry: Blood pressure changes during lateralized presentation of an emotionally laden film. *Neuropsychologia, 28*, 457-470.

Wittling, W. & Pfluger, M. (1990). Neuroendocrine hemisphere asymmetries: Salivary cortisol secretion during lateralized viewing of emotion-related and neutral films. *Brain and Cognition, 14*: 243-265.

Wittling, W. & Roschmann, R. (1993). Emotion-related hemispheric asymmetry: Subjective emotional responses to laterally presented films. *Cortex, 29*, 431-448.

Wolford, G., Miller, M. B., & Gazzaniga, M., (2000), The left hemisphere's role in hypothesis formation. *Journal of Neuroscience, 20(RC64)*, 1-4.

Xu, Z., Chang, L.W., Slikker, W., Ali, S.F., Rountre, R.L., & Scallet, A.C. (2000). A dose-response study of ibogaine-induced neuropathology in the rat cerebellum. *Toxicological Science, 57*, 95-101.

Yang, G. & Iadecola, C. (1998). Activation of cerebellar cliimging fibers increases cerebellar blood flow: role of glutamate receptors, nitric oxide, and cGMP. *Stroke, 29*, 499-507)

Yates, M., Leake, A., Candy, J.M., Fairbairn, A.F., McKeith, I.G., &Ferrier, I.N. (1990). 5HT$_2$ receptor changes in major depression. *Biological Psychiatry, 27*, 498-296.

Yeganeh-Doost, P.,Gruber, O., Falkaj, P., & Schmitt, A. (2011). The role of the cerebellum in Schizophrenia: from cognition to molecular pathways. *Clinics (Sao Paulo) Jun,66(Suppl 1)* 71-77.

Yucel, M., Stuart, G. W., Maruff, P., Velakoulis, D., Crowe, S. F., Savage, G., et al. (2001). Hemispheric and gender-related differences in the gross morphology of the anterior cingulate/paracingulate cortex in normal volunteers: An MRI morphometric study. *Cerebral Cortex, 11*, 17–25.

Zenhausern, R. (1978). Imagery, cerebral dominance, and style of thinking: A unified field model. *Bulletin of the Psychonomic Society, 12*, 381–384.

INDEX

ABOUT THE AUTHOR

Bruce Eldine Morton, Ph.D., Professor Emeritus at the John A. Burns School of Medicine of the University of Hawaii, was born Southern California in 1938. After Completing the M.S .and Ph.D. degrees in Biochemistry at the University of Wisconsin in 1965, he spent post-doctoral periods as a Research Fellow at Wisconsin's Institute for Enzyme Research, at M.I.T., and at Harvard Medical School.

He was then hired by the School of Medicine at the University of Hawaii, 1969. There he directed a neuroscience research laboratory until long after his "retirement" in 1995. In 1974 Dr. Morton set a world record for distance flown in a hang-gilder. He was also active in Gymnastics, SCUBA diving, wind surfing, snow boarding, and now dual purpose motorcycle tours of Mayan ruins. Dr. Morton has been a member of many choral societies and was in concert with the Boston Symphony. He also spent sabbaticals at USC, Stanford, and at the University of Michigan. He is a member numerous professional societies including the International Society for Research on Aggression.

In 2014 his eighty fourth publication was: BE Morton, L Svard, and J Jensen, Further Evidence for Hemisity Sorting during Career Specialization, *Journal of Career Assessment*, **22**, 315-326 (2014). His four books: *Neurorealism: A Scientific Religion; Two Human Species Exist; Psychedelic Visions;* and *Beyond Men are from Mars* are available from www.amazon.com under his name: Bruce Eldine Morton. From his home base in Guatemala, Dr. Morton continues his research on the gaining access to the wisdom of the trapped genetic Higher Intelligence hidden within each of us.

He may be contacted at bemorton@hawaii.edu.

His website is http://www2.hawaii.edu/~bemorton.

BRUCE ELDINE MORTON

ABOUT THE AUTHOR

326 pages total